Urban Life and Urban Landscape Series

Getting Around *Brown*

Desegregation, Development,
and the Columbus Public Schools

Gregory S. Jacobs

Ohio State University Press
Columbus

Maps on pp. xiv and 73 were drawn by William Nelson.

Library of Congress Cataloging-in-Publication Data
Jacobs, Gregory S., 1969–
    Getting around Brown : desegregation, development, and the Columbus public schools / Gregory S. Jacobs.
        p.   cm. — (Urban life and urban landscape series)
    Includes bibliographical references and index.
    ISBN 0-8142-0720-0 (alk. paper). — ISBN 0-8142-0721-9 (pbk. : alk. paper)
    1. School integration—Ohio—Columbus—History—20th century. 2. Public schools—Ohio—Columbus—History—20th century. I. Title. II. Series.
LC214.23.C65J33   1997
379.2′63′0977157—dc21   97–17202
                                                                                              CIP

Type set in Adobe Trump Mediaeval by G&S Typesetters, Inc.
Printed by Thomson-Shore, Inc.

The paper used in this publication meets the minimum requirements of the American National Standard for Information Sciences—Permanence of Paper for Printed Library Materials.
ANSI Z39.48–1992.

9   8   7   6   5   4   3   2   1

For Dee Dee

Contents

Acknowledgments

Having written these acknowledgments in my head many times over the last six years, I suddenly find myself paralyzed by the prospect of singling out a few among the many who have been so helpful since this accidental journey began. So I'll start by thanking those responsible for the accident in the first place: the Yale history department, for receiving the earliest form of this book well enough to give it an award (and late enough to give it a "B"); and Professors Doron Ben-Atar and Steve Gillon, for telling me I should develop my research into a book (and not telling me just how long that would take).

At Ohio State, Marshall Stevenson, Warren Van Tine, Martha Garland, Dale Bertsch, and Marcia Caton Campbell provided timely doses of encouragement. Thanks also to staff members at the Ohio State and Columbus Public Libraries, the Columbus Development Department, and the Columbus Public Schools' Communications Department, especially Nancy Bachman, whose kindness and cooperation were invaluable; to Bill Nelson, maker of maps; and to all the interviewees, for their time and candor.

I am enormously grateful to everyone at The Ohio State University Press for their commitment to this book. Special thanks to Charlotte Dihoff, Ruth Melville, and Urban Life and Urban Landscape Series editors Zane Miller and Harry Shapiro for their always on-target (and occasionally very funny) comments and questions.

Finally, I would like to thank my family and friends for their inspiration, exhortation, conversation, and confidence, especially Andrew McLaughlin, Deborah Jo Miller, and David Franklin, without whose critical eyes and crucial suggestions I would still be working on the conclusion; Geoff Shandler, Erin Hogan, and David Thompson, who helped me navigate the foreign waters of the publishing world; Jamie Gilmore, who always asked the right question; and, most of all, my "in-house editors" Julie and Ian Jacobs, Liz, whose patience, faith, and smile are part of every page of this book, and my parents—had their love and support been anything less than unwavering, this whole project would have been unthinkable.

Introduction

It is both an axiom of American history and a staple of American mythology that, like a midcentury big bang, the enduring glory of *Brown v. Board of Education* rests in the moment of its inception. Some may challenge the 1954 ruling's established status as the opening salvo of the "Second Reconstruction," finding instead the first shot fired to be the desegregation of the armed forces or the murder of Emmett Till, or even maintaining that there was in fact no break in the struggle for civil rights. Others might argue that *Brown*'s blend of questionable legal and social science reasoning made it from the beginning a poor foundation on which to build a movement. Few, however, dispute the real and symbolic moral force of the event itself, the moment that a unanimous Supreme Court doomed the doctrine of "separate but equal" by declaring segregated public schools unconstitutional. It was, as J. Harvie Wilkinson observed, "among the most humane moments in all our history."[1]

As I began writing this book in the spring of 1994, America's newsmagazines and editorial pages were filled with fortieth-anniversary reflections on *Brown*'s legacy. Reading them, I was struck less by their inevitable reverence—the strength of Thurgood Marshall, the savvy of Earl Warren, the bravery of the children—than by their inescapable melancholy. Unlike many such observances, the commemoration of *Brown* marked the birthday of a living process, not the memorial of a finite event. Instead of conveying the frozen beauty of youthful martyrdom, as too many felled giants of the Civil Rights movement do, *Brown* bears the baggage and blemishes of middle age.

Indeed, the midlife uncertainty that characterized the occasion seemed appropriate for a fortieth birthday. A product of the progressive optimism of baby boom America, *Brown* spent much of its adolescence in search of an identity. The massive resistance of an intransigent South left it largely powerless, and little school desegregation had taken place as late as the mid-1960s. It was not until the end of that decade that *Brown* truly came of age, exhibiting the impatient idealism of a generation convinced it could change the world. From 1968 to 1973, racial isolation in America's public schools faced its most concentrated assault, with a series of Supreme Court rulings that spread school desegregation nationwide. As *Brown* grew older, however, its ambitions grew more limited, diminished by the inevitable compromises and disappointments of adulthood. Demographic trends, the bitter backlash against busing, the persistence of residential segregation, and other unforeseen forces undermined *Brown*'s arguably outsized confidence; by 1994, racial isolation in the public schools was actually increasing.[2] As a result, the ruling that had embodied such promise at its inception found itself at forty confronting a problematic past and an uncertain future.

Desegregation as it was carried out in large, urban school districts proved a too unwieldy tool with which to reshape a fluid, flexible, and unpredictable set of circumstances. Unequal educational opportunity initially seemed an edifice to be smashed. But the line between public schools and private markets turned out to be not so bright, and it gradually became apparent that education is not the primary *cause* of racial inequality but one of its many interconnected contributors. Because scholars have too often isolated school desegregation from such significant sociopolitical forces as business community influence on education, metropolitan jurisdictional fragmentation, and the rise of the black middle class, the flaws of the current literature have come to mirror the failings of *Brown* itself. With desegregation now largely anathema to politicians and judges, as well as increasingly disdained by African Americans and liberal whites, new approaches are needed to address new problems. As the first historical case study to explore the interplay of business, metropolitan development, and school desegregation, this book, I hope, will contribute to the development of a "postdesegregation" literature of desegregation.

I will argue that the desegregation of the Columbus, Ohio, public school system failed to ensure equal educational opportunity not because it was inherently detrimental to learning, but because it was intrinsically incompatible with the city's steady geographic and economic growth. Even before the first buses rolled in 1979, the threat of desegregation had redefined the parameters of single-family home building in the city, essentially turning the boundaries of the Columbus school district into a residential development redline. The myriad resources that typically follow new housing were both exiting and avoiding the city schools by desegregation's implementation; busing simply solidified and intensified this already extant process.

Moreover, because the borders of the city school district and the borders of the city had been diverging since 1965, suburban school systems had come to serve a major portion of Columbus by 1979. For the powerful, business-led "growth consensus" that had long shaped political and economic activity in the city, the existence of these "common areas"—the sections of Columbus served by suburban school systems—provided a development safety valve, disengaging Columbus's growth from the growth of the Columbus schools. In essence, the health of the city school district was sacrificed to preserve the expansion of the city itself. The gradual abandonment of urban education in Columbus has resulted in both the concentration of poor and African American students within the central city school district and the emergence of a politically powerful form of defensive activism within the area's overwhelmingly white suburban systems—a phenomenon I call "educational NIMBY."[3] This potent combination makes *Brown*'s promise of equal educational opportunity appear increasingly remote in Columbus.

Desegregation in Columbus provides an untapped case study that is both narratively rich and nationally resonant.[4] The goal of this book is to combine both elements into a single story, to present not just a small slice of the Civil Rights movement but a vivid urban

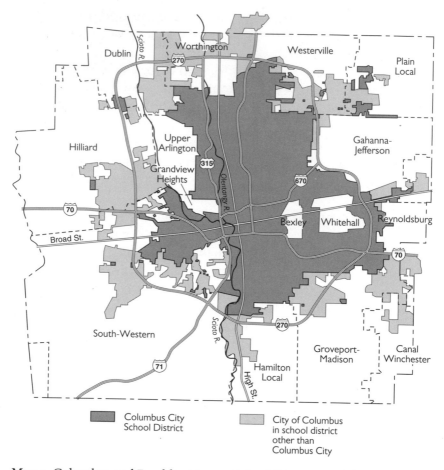

Map 1. Columbus and Franklin County School Districts and the "Common Areas," as of 1995
Source: Columbus Development Department

portrait as well. Still, the question remains, why a history of Columbus school desegregation? For scholars, such a chronicle offers a much-needed look at the desegregation of a large, northern urban district. Case studies of school desegregation above the Mason-Dixon line have focused almost exclusively on Boston, the still-searing symbol of busing's racial volatility, while generally ignoring the far less dramatic—but no less important—desegregation plans implemented in hundreds of school systems across the North.[5] As Columbus was one of the last districts to begin a sweeping, system-wide busing remedy, its history affords a unique summation of *Brown*'s turbulent first quarter century. Moreover, the Columbus desegregation case, *Columbus Board of Education v. Penick*, proved the coda to a decade of controversial litigation, the Supreme Court's final declaration of its commitment to public school desegregation.

Perhaps even more intriguing to scholars than what Columbus reveals about the nation's recent educational past is what it suggests about America's urban future. Columbus's experience with school desegregation is at once unique and typical, a singular story with policy implications that reverberate far beyond the Buckeye State. The issues this book raises—the uneasy relationship between business and education, the incompatibility of urban schools and residential development, and the troubling educational ramifications of jurisdictional fragmentation, to name a few—are applicable to urban areas around the country. Columbus is just one of many American cities seeking politically and legally viable ways to maintain urban growth while improving urban education. Yet the vitriolic and occasionally violent history of school desegregation has chilled debate over the complex connections that race, class, and living patterns have to educational opportunity. Not until we honestly begin to reassess the politics of place can we adequately begin to address the problems of America's public schools.

I was a fifth grader in the Columbus schools when desegregation began in 1979, and I can still recall being ordered to evacuate Olde Orchard Elementary one gray October morning. At the time, I did not fully understand that what appeared to be an unexpected recess was actually something far more serious: a bomb threat directed at Tracey Duncan, my classmate and the daughter of the district court judge who had ordered the schools desegregated. A generation of students later, school desegregation remains a contentious and unresolved issue both in Columbus and around the country. Unfortunately, all too often the debate is reduced to simplistic diagnoses and misguided prescriptions. By conveying the maddening complexity of the issues involved, I hope to illustrate the creativity required to address them. For if it is easy and accurate to assert that desegregation failed us, it is far more troubling—and no less accurate—to admit that we failed desegregation.

1

"A Problem for Our Community": Segregation, Litigation, and the Path to *Penick*

In January 1977, Columbus, Ohio, was hit with its worst winter weather in one hundred years. Storms that caused dozens of deaths nationwide dumped a foot of snow on the city, bringing frigid weather that halted garbage collection for a week and, for the first time since the legendary "Snow Bowl" blizzard of 1950, closed the massive Ohio State University. High demand due to record low temperatures and biting winds worsened an already serious natural gas shortage, forcing Republican Governor James Rhodes to declare a statewide natural gas crisis on January 26.[1]

The cold snap kept the Columbus Public School District's 96,571 students home for several days in January, but the fuel shortage posed an even more vexing problem. The local gas company had already sliced the district's allocation 40 percent, and when regional shortfalls prevented the purchase of emergency reserves, the utility announced that another 85 percent would be cut in February.[2] With 149 of its 172 buildings heated entirely by gas, the financially strapped school district faced the expensive prospect of having to "mothball" its buildings for most of the month.[3] Although about

1

70 percent of Ohio's schools would be closed for at least some time that winter, the *New York Times* found "no other city as hard-hit" as Columbus.[4]

The morning of Rhodes's announcement, the seven-member Columbus Board of Education met with Superintendent John Ellis to ponder the district's dismal options. In the middle of the meeting, Ellis received a phone call from Gene D'Angelo, general manager of WBNS, the electronic media arm of the city's most powerful family, the Wolfes. "I was busy," Ellis recalled, "and I was going to tell my secretary, 'No, we don't have time. Don't they know we have a gas crisis here?' And she said what they said they were going to do, and I said, 'I'll be there. I'll be right over.'"[5]

D'Angelo, assuming the inevitability of some form of system-wide shutdown, had offered the district four free hours of educational radio and television time daily for the duration of the crisis, insisting only on mandatory student participation. By 2:30 that afternoon, Ellis, WBNS representatives, and a dozen school administrators had begun round-the-clock planning; within ten days, they had developed a comprehensive electronic curriculum, backed by what Ellis called Columbus's "greatest outpouring of community spirit since World War II." Administrators and teachers cooperated closely to create daily televised "classrooms" just two years after a bitter, weeklong teacher walkout. All three local television channels and several radio stations opened their studios to the schools; both daily newspapers printed course schedules, lesson plans, even baby-sitting announcements; and public and private institutions from city hall to Schmidt's Sausage Haus offered assistance. "What followed," said one education journal, was "a model of how the human and physical resources of business, industry and government can be used for educational value."[6]

On the first day of February, the notoriously fractious school board unanimously approved "School without Schools." From February 7 to 25, students were required to watch televised lessons, read newspaper supplements, attend specially scheduled field trips, and meet once a week—somewhere—with their teachers to turn in homework and take tests. While acknowledging that "some of what is going to happen . . . will just be rubbish," Ellis framed the situation not as a crisis, but as "the most unusual opportunity any city has ever seen," predicting that "an unbelievable array of activities and creative use of time, talent, and community resources will keep learning alive in Columbus." Indeed, classes were held in bank boardrooms and bars, motels and movie theaters, even Ohio State president Harold Enarson's kitchen. "We swam in a couple of the hotel swimming pools and we went everywhere to have school where business functioned," said Ellis. "Even little Pizza Huts have training rooms where they train their employees that we met in."[7]

The beginning of March marked the end of School without Schools. While nobody hailed the improvisational three-week effort as an educational panacea, at least classroom continuity had been preserved. Commented Assistant Superintendent Howard Merriman, "The main thing is that we were able to keep the momentum of learning going. It is a good feeling." For an embattled urban school district still reeling from a devastating levy loss and awaiting an inevitably controversial desegregation decision, School without Schools provided both a much-needed morale boost and a valuable public relations boon. The emergency demanded the dismantling of barriers among teachers, administrators, school board members, the media, and the business community; and the solution that emerged received national attention as a model of creative, bureaucracy-busting educational innovation. "We discovered a great deal of talent we didn't know we had," Ellis said.[8]

School without Schools also served as an unintentional dress rehearsal for the implementation of desegregation, demonstrating that the school system could mobilize itself and the community effectively when forced to institute systemwide changes. Among these changes was a complete overhaul of the district's transportation system, including the busing—or, as the district officially chose to call it, "bus riding"—of over one-third of its students. This irony was not lost on desegregation backers in Columbus's African American community. Black school board member Watson Walker, noting the praise heaped on School without Schools, observed that "no one complains about busing unless it is for racial integration." A reporter for the *Call and Post*, Columbus's weekly black newspaper, wrote, "The most massive school busing effort the city of Columbus has seen . . . went into motion with the full support of the city's staunchest busing opponents." The paper's editorial postmortem was even more caustic, predicting that "when the results of [Ellis's] 'School Without Schools' substitute for 'real education' is assessed for what it is, the shine on his publicly related star will reveal only that Columbus learned without a court order how to bus kids around town. Education, it ain't."[9]

Despite such criticisms, the positive publicity that School without Schools generated earned Ellis a national reputation as a dynamic educational innovator. In mid-February, President Jimmy Carter appointed Ellis deputy executive commissioner of the U.S. Office of Education, second in command to Education Commissioner-designate Ernest Boyer. As both School without Schools and his superintendency came to an end, Ellis gushed in a valedictory letter to the community, "America has never seen the equal of what you have just done. . . . If we were in the Olympics, Columbus and its marvelous people would be on the victory stand receiving gold medals."[10]

The momentum captured by Ellis's metaphorical medal ceremony proved sadly short-lived, however. Mounting financial woes, declining public support, a hopelessly divided school board—these problems had only been obscured temporarily by the glow of School without Schools, and all were exacerbated by the news the district received the first morning back from spring break. At 10:00 A.M. on Monday, March 8, 1977, Sixth District Court judge Robert Duncan released his long-awaited ruling on *Penick v. Columbus Board of Education*, the Columbus Public Schools' desegregation case.[11] Duncan's opinion was thorough, cautious, even sympathetic, but his conclusion was unmistakable: The defendants were guilty of intentionally creating and maintaining an illegally segregated school system.

Penick v. Columbus Board of Education culminated years of intensifying African American disenchantment with the Columbus

Public School District. Following World War II, a convergence of economic, social, political, legal, and demographic forces allowed Columbus blacks to seek for the first time a socioeconomic status that combined both access to and control of civic resources. By the end of the 1960s, fully desegregated public schools came to be seen as a necessary component of this vision, a permanent, progressive guarantor of equal opportunity that drew upon blacks' historically powerful faith in education as the gateway to economic and social advance. However, while integration was proceeding in Columbus from community demand to judicial mandate, the issue also was being transformed from a peculiarly southern problem to a divisive national dispute. By the time of Judge Duncan's decision, the moral luster of *Brown v. Board of Education* had dulled, and the debate over desegregation had given way to a battle over busing.

Black Columbus and the Solidification of Segregation

For much of the nineteenth century, blacks in Columbus lived in a kind of limbo between slavery and freedom. Though both the Northwest Ordinance of 1787 and the first Ohio Constitution prohibited slavery, "black laws" passed by the state legislature beginning in January 1804 stripped "Black and Mulattoe Persons" of most citizenship rights. Barred from residing in Ohio without a $500 bond guaranteeing their good behavior, blacks who did settle could not vote, hold political office, fight in the militia, serve on juries, or testify against whites.[12]

Despite the restrictions, free blacks and manumitted slaves looking to farm Ohio's fields and find work in its emerging river towns slowly streamed into the new state. Many were from neighboring Virginia and Kentucky, migrants escaping slavery's omnipresent shadow. Columbus, planned and designated Ohio's capital in 1812, became a common stopping point for black newcomers. The same attribute that made Columbus an attractive site for the state's capital—its central location—also made it a well-traveled station on the Underground Railroad; fugitive slaves found the city something of a safe haven from the stricter security of the regions near Ohio's border state and northern boundaries. Black settlers teamed with white abolitionists to safeguard runaways in haylofts, church basements, and private homes. A crossroads for both free blacks and fugitive slaves, Columbus by 1840 had a far higher proportion of black residents than the state as a whole.[13]

The Civil War and the ensuing debate over black citizenship generated bitter political conflict in Ohio. Although the state produced some of Washington's leading antislavery voices—Joshua Giddings, Salmon Chase, Benjamin Wade—Democrats controlled the state legislature and dominated Columbus and Franklin County. Warning of an impending flood of low-wage, job-stealing former slaves, Democrats responded to emancipation and the movement for black suffrage by playing on white fears of "a total eclipse of the Caucasian race in the United States." Still, they could not stave off passage of the Fifteenth Amendment, which the legislature narrowly ratified in early 1870.[14]

The bestowing of black male suffrage ushered in what one historian called a "golden age" of African American politics in Columbus. Between 1881 and 1912, ward-based elections placed five blacks on the city council and two on the board of education. But the death in 1907 of the Reverend James Poindexter, Columbus's first black city councilman and school board member, marked the waning of this era of unprecedented black political voice. Progressive reforms solidified de facto black disenfranchisement, neutralizing the impact of the black ballot and eliminating African American machine influence; the shift in the 1912 city charter from ward-based to at-large elections kept blacks out of public office for the next half century.[15]

By 1910, there were 12,739 blacks in a city of 181,511. They lived in pockets throughout Columbus, generally near the jobs available as factory laborers, railroad workers, domestics, waiters, bartenders, and draymen.[16] Preachers and teachers made up most of the city's small black middle class, and few service organizations existed to address problems of substandard housing and limited employment opportunity. As southern migrants fleeing Jim Crow trickled into the city, the racism of Columbus's primarily native-born white population intensified. "Columbus," wrote one contemporary observer, "has a feeling all its own. . . . It is not so much a rabid feeling of prejudice against the Negroes simply because their skin is black as it is a bitter hatred of them because they are what they are in character and habit. The Negroes are almost completely outside the pale of the white people's sympathy."[17] In the absence of legally sanctioned segregation, a caste-conscious code of custom began to take its place. Though Columbus blacks by 1910 possessed the full rights of citizenship, theirs was decidedly second class, as well as increasingly separate.[18]

It was in the years surrounding World War I that the city's modern black community began to take shape. Though Ohio experienced less of an influx than did neighboring Michigan and Pennsylvania, the state's black population increased 67 percent from 1910 to 1920, with most of the growth concentrated in the state's eight largest cities.[19] There were nearly 9,500 more blacks in Columbus in 1920 than there had been in 1910, a demographic surge that one researcher at the time observed "was very noticeable on the streets and in public places and gave rise to wild estimates at the close of the war, some citizens asserting that one of every four inhabitants of the city was colored."[20] While the actual ratio was closer to one in ten, the perception that a black tide was sweeping up from the South panicked many whites and spurred the solidification of geographic and social segregation. Despite state laws banning discrimination in public accommodations and segregation in public education, black access to white hospitals, movie houses, schools, hotels, and restaurants was uniformly restricted by the 1920s.[21]

During the postwar real estate boom, white developers began using restrictive covenants and deeds and exclusionary zoning to preserve the racial homogeneity of the new suburbs and subdivisions sprouting around the city's periphery. "Negroes" were considered nuisances, as detrimental to property values as saloons, slaughterhouses, and chicken coops.[22] Realtors took advantage of this by "blockbusting": secretly selling a home on an all-white street to a black family, then subdividing the houses abandoned by fleeing whites and renting them at exorbitant rates to needy blacks, leaving overcrowded neighborhoods to fall into disrepair. "It was fun to see the white people run after a Negro family moved onto the street," commented one African American East Sider in the 1920s. During this time, according to Patricia Burgess's history of housing development in Columbus, "Real estate developers, particularly professional developers, determined the spatial and social structure of the city. . . . They in effect decided who would live where in the growing metropolis."[23]

Migration and segregation combined to create for the first time in Columbus a self-contained black community, the East Long Street District. Located east of downtown, north of exclusive Broad Street, and proximate to the city's central railroad station, this area in the 1920s became the economic and social hub of black Columbus.[24] Migrants, assisted in their resettlement by Nimrod Allen, head of the newly formed Columbus Urban League, crowded into the district, often finding work in the nearby factories and earning wages unheard of in the South. Although many employers still refused to hire blacks, from 1910 to 1920 the percentage of Columbus African Americans employed in manufacturing and industrial jobs grew from 26.5 percent to 41.9 percent.[25]

Constrained by discrimination and forced to meet the social and economic needs of a burgeoning and increasingly concentrated population, Columbus blacks in the 1920s developed a vibrant economy within an economy. Black entrepreneurs established insurance, mortgage, lending, and real estate companies; doctors, dentists, lawyers, printers, caterers, and other professionals opened offices on the Near East Side; black businesses, social clubs, and service organizations multiplied; and the theaters and music halls lining Long Street lit up at night.[26]

The emergence of an African American business and professional elite gave rise to class divisions within the community itself. Long-settled black "Buckeyes" often viewed the newly arrived "North Carolina Negroes" with disdain for their southern mores, blaming the rise in racism during the 1920s in part on the "embarrassing" behavior of the migrants.[27] The relative success of this black middle class, along with Columbus's general economic stability, produced a comparatively more complacent and conservative black leadership than those that arose in more industrialized northern cities. Problems tended to be addressed incrementally, ameliorative social service solutions rather than redistributive political and economic policies pursued. Consequently, organizations made conservative by their dependence on white political and philanthropic largesse prevailed in Columbus, the best example being the Urban League, the city's preeminent black institution. The result was a racial milieu in which confrontation was kept quiet, civic order maintained, and African Americans received more than the crumbs but less than the loaf.

In the face of escalating political, geographic, and economic segregation, Columbus blacks during the 1920s fashioned an energetic community culture and a vigorous middle class. Though discrimination isolated blacks from the larger market of the white majority, it also allowed them to establish a certain degree of institutional independence and economic self-reliance. The onset of the Great Depression, however, swiftly demonstrated the fragility of this superficially separate economy. Black-owned businesses were closed or sold, black laborers were the first fired and last rehired, and impoverished whites occupied domestic and menial jobs previously left to African Americans.[28] By 1931, black unemployment had reached 37.6 percent, and as the depression ground on, as few as 30 percent of black wage earners held full-time jobs in the private sector.[29] Although it remained the hub of black commercial activity in Columbus through the 1960s, the East Long Street area never quite recovered its predepression vibrancy.

The 1940s and 1950s saw the focus of black advancement swing back slowly toward integration. In Columbus, the first target was the denial of equal access to employment opportunities and public accommodations. During the years immediately following World

War II, the Vanguard League, a comparatively radical spin-off of the city's historically ineffectual NAACP, held a series of sit-ins and demonstrations demanding an end to the segregative customs that had emerged over the previous half century. Slowly, throughout the 1940s, 1950s and early 1960s, long-established barriers began to fall. Restaurants, hotels, and movie theaters were integrated. Downtown office buildings for the first time began renting space to African Americans. The city hired its first black bus driver, fire chief, and police inspector, and blacks began to get face-to-face service jobs as secretaries, salespeople, and bank tellers.[30] Still, while symbolically significant, these advances were primarily cosmetic and were accomplished with little pressure and minimal resistance. At the same time, just as the city was taking its first tentative steps toward integration, federal and local policies were reshaping it in ways that would both cluster blacks closer together and drive the races farther apart.

Unlike many large, northern cities, Columbus was not at the time of the depression encircled by suburbs. Consequently, after World War II, when low housing construction costs, pent-up demand, and federally underwritten long-term loans sparked an explosion in single-family home building, Columbus was able to use an aggressive annexation policy and water and sewer service monopoly to capture much of the new development that in other metropolitan areas occurred in the suburbs. Yet keeping this growth within Columbus's boundaries did not prevent the abandonment of the central city by a burgeoning white middle class. Federal lending policies funneled funds away from older areas to the new subdivisions, from which blacks were almost solidly excluded by an ingenious array of discriminatory strategies. The beginning of the interstate highway system accelerated the white exodus, pulling jobs, services, and shopping toward the city's booming periphery.[31]

While the city rapidly sprawled outward, surrounding several older suburbs in the process, its African American population became increasingly concentrated in the deteriorating areas spreading in an arc east of downtown. Urban renewal and freeway construction exacerbated this process, bulldozing some of the city's cheapest (albeit often most dilapidated) housing and plowing through established black neighborhoods. The Near East Side, bisected by Interstates 70 and 71, saw a quarter of its residents displaced by "Negro removal" during the 1960s.[32] Residential population in the area around downtown dropped 50 percent between 1950 and 1964, due largely to the demolition of the "Flytown" neighborhood and the construction of the "Innerbelt," a downtown bypass freeway. And the extension of I-70 east necessitated the razing of more than half the homes in Hanford Village, where dozens of black servicemen and their families had settled after the war.[33]

Between 1950 and 1970, Columbus's black population increased 112 percent, from 47,000 (12.5 percent of the city's total) to 99,627 (18.5 percent); yet in 1970, only 15 percent of the city's blacks lived outside of the 1950 boundaries.[34] Though some public housing was built to warehouse the displaced, Columbus's rapidly growing African American population could not be entirely compacted within the previously established borders of the black community. As in the 1920s, when overcrowded African Americans began moving into older white neighborhoods, blockbusting and panic selling ensued, followed inexorably by capital flight and physical decay. South Linden, for example, a once prosperous area along Cleveland Avenue northeast of downtown, turned from 6.8 percent minority in 1950 to 84.6 percent by 1970.[35] By the mid-1960s, these transitional areas had become the front lines in the fight for racial equality in Columbus, as the battle returned to one of its oldest arenas: public education.

The Columbus Public Schools, 1845–1945: The Rise, Fall, and Rise of Separate and Unequal

African American efforts to secure educational resources in Columbus date back before the 1845 establishment of the Columbus Board of Education. Because an 1829 state law barred them from attending property tax–funded common schools, Columbus blacks in 1840 bought a plot of land at the corner of Long and Third streets and built their own school. Eight years later, the Ohio Legislature authorized the creation of segregated public schools for African American children, and in 1853, the first black public school opened in Columbus; by 1855, four black schools dotted the East Side, serving virtually all of the city's black schoolchildren.[36]

The buildings provided, however, were small, overcrowded, and dangerously dilapidated, conditions blacks began protesting during the politically volatile post–Civil War years. The Reverend James Poindexter, in an 1870 letter to a local newspaper, described one of these buildings as "a PEN at the north end of the city—an old shanty, bounded by two alleys, devoid of playground, closely girded about with outhouses, the privy and well being in such proximity as makes it quite certain that the seepings from the privy find their way into the water our children are forced to drink." In another letter, Poindexter emphasized the importance of the issue to the city's blacks: "No people ever attached greater value to education than do the colored people. They are more worried about their ignorance than about their poverty. They feel slavery, in depriving them of the means of education, inflicted upon them greater wrong than it did in working them 200 years without pay."[37]

In 1871, the school board decided to shut down the smaller black schools and concentrate black students in a single centrally located building, named after school board member Dr. Starling Loving.[38] Located in the middle of the "Badlands," an area known for "three institutions: the saloon, the gambling hall, and the house of prostitution," Loving School occupied a run-down and eventually condemned building too far away for many black children to attend conveniently.[39] Armed with the vote and scattered throughout the city, blacks began for the first time calling for the creation of "mixed" schools. Finally, in 1881, the school board agreed to demolish Loving and assign black children to schools around the district. Seven years before the Ohio Supreme Court declared that local boards of education could not maintain separate schools for black and white children, the Columbus Public Schools were officially integrated. Wrote a hopeful newspaper editor, "A little time will be necessary to wipe out prejudices on both sides, when it is believed, by wise and delicate management, harmony and just feelings will be brought about."[40]

Even at the time of this inaugural integration effort, however, some blacks doubted that mixed schools meant better education. The racism of unwelcoming white students and unsympathetic white teachers would hamper the education of black children, they believed. Wrote a group of South Side blacks to the *Ohio State Journal* in 1881, "Colored children will never make the same amount of progress in a mixed school that they would if not troubled about the opinion of their fellow white pupils, and vice versa." Moreover, because white parents vociferously opposed having black teachers assigned to their children, segregated schools translated into more jobs within the system for black educators. Thus, as early as the 1880s, Columbus blacks were of two minds: some supported limited control over greater educational resources, while others backed greater control over limited resources. Richard Minor's 1936 encapsulation was appropriate a half century before it was written and would still be appropriate a half century later: "The Negroes of Columbus are divided between a desire for a segregated school system and a mixed school system. There are numbers of Negroes in Columbus who believe that Negro teachers are best for their children in that they would be more sympathetic. Some fear, however, that it would not be as well equipped as the present school system."[41]

Still, it is safe to say that the bulk of the African American community in Columbus has always favored integration as the best way to ensure access to both the tangible and intangible advantages afforded the white majority. Thus, in 1907, when school board member and Ohio State University president William Oxley Thompson declared, "It is in the best interests of both [races] that they be educated in separate schools," eight hundred blacks gathered at a Mt. Vernon Avenue skating rink to "condemn" school board plans to gerrymander attendance boundaries and open an all-black school. At the meeting, they approved a resolution that read, "We feel that the white citizens of our city owe it to us to give us that benefit which accrues as a result of education by contact and association in the public schools as they now are." A second resolution, a year later, stated, "Such separation of the races, even if the laws of the State did not forbid it, always results ultimately in inferior school equipment for colored children, and, moreover, tends to set the races father and farther apart, and so to hinder that mutual sympathy and understanding which close personal contact in the plastic years of childhood helps to cultivate." At this time in Columbus, however, white racial antipathy was growing while black political access was disappearing. African Americans were thus powerless to prevent the 1909 opening of all-black Champion Avenue Elementary School.[42]

The creation of Champion began the solidification of an unofficially separate school district in Columbus, a process that both followed and accelerated the city's increasing residential segregation. In 1922, again over black protests, the board of education added junior high grades to Champion in order to funnel more black children and all of the district's black teachers to the school.[43] During the next two decades, the board carefully manipulated attendance boundaries to reinforce the racial transition of neighborhoods, leaving five all-black schools by 1943—Champion, Garfield, Mt. Vernon, Pilgrim, and Felton—and concentrating black students at East and Central High Schools.[44] A booklet published in 1943 by the Vanguard League described attendance zones "skipping about as capriciously as a young child at play" and decried the district's race-based faculty assignment policy.[45] Despite black objections, however, by the end of World War II, the board had forged a de facto dual district, with the bulk of Columbus's African American students restricted to a handful of central-city schools.

Black, White, and Brown: Postwar Columbus and the Revival of Integration

By 1946, years of depression-era and wartime neglect had left the district's physical plant in disrepair, inadequate for the 40,000 students already served by the system and unprepared for the swarm on the way.[46] Enrollment grew 87 percent during the 1950s alone, not peaking until it reached 110,725 in 1971. The district built furiously during this period to keep up with the city's booming growth and skyrocketing birth rate: from 1951 to 1964, five bond issues, approved by an average of 71 percent of the electorate, funded the construction of 100 schools and 158 additions. Still, much of the school district's growth remained off-limits to African Americans; by 1964, more than 50 schools were 100 percent black or white.[47] The board of education built dozens of schools to serve the all-white subdivisions springing up within Columbus's northern perimeter, establishing and altering boundaries to accelerate or fortify racial identifiability. The board opened other schools in already all-black areas or in transitional neighborhoods where rapid racial turnover made predominantly one-race enrollment inevitable. Meanwhile, optional and discontiguous attendance zones enabled some white students to evade black "neighborhood schools," and escape hatches were provided for teachers who resented the gradual integration of all-white staffs. Don Pierce, a teacher at Roosevelt Junior High in the late 1950s and early 1960s, recalled a new black teacher visiting the school where she had just been assigned: "She looked in the teachers' boxes and there was a letter to all of the teachers. And it said words to this effect, 'We are hiring a black teacher in your school and if any of you are upset about this, you have the right to transfer to another school.'" In short, white preference for a segregated educational environment was not just sanctioned by the school district, it was often assumed.[48]

Despite this persistent segregation, Columbus blacks remained largely silent about the city school district throughout the 1950s.

The decade was a time of transition for the community: the retirement of Nimrod Allen in 1954 after thirty-three years at the Urban League's helm left a significant leadership void, and the anticommunist conformity of the cold war, an especially potent force in conservative Columbus, dulled African American activism and led to the dissolution of the Vanguard League. Employment barriers and urban renewal were the dominant issues, as blacks assumed a wait-and-see attitude toward the board of education's response to *Brown*. A decade of bricks and mortar failed to eliminate the "separate" that still existed within the system, however, leaving instead a larger core of mostly black central-city schools. Said civil rights activist Anna Mae Durham, "There wasn't any effort by the school board to follow *Brown*. The black community got started because the board didn't do anything."[49]

Though other legal and political decisions contributed more to the dismantling of state-sanctioned segregation, it was the moral clarity that *Brown* seemed to embody that made integration both gospel and grail to a generation of civil rights pioneers. In addressing America's darkest hypocrisy, *Brown* captured its most brilliant promise, resonating with all of the possibility, hope, and mystery of exploration. "Integration," observed Robert Duncan, "to me meant I could go where I had not been able to go before." Ed Willis, a teacher at all-black Champion Junior High at the time of *Brown*, said, "If you isolate me, then I'm always wondering what's going on the other side of the mountain. I never can go to the other side."[50]

Brown also enshrined the progressive basis of the NAACP's long-pursued legal strategy: Segregated public education was the foundation of racial inequality, so once this foundation was removed, the whole structure gradually would collapse, giving way to better schools, improved race relations, and a more harmonious, open society. While the reality of segregation marginalized blacks from the broader marketplace, the ideal of integration meant the opportunity to compete on equal terms with whites for the same pool of resources. If the grass were always greener on the white side of the fence, it was not because blacks were inferior growers, but because whites had more and better land, superior tools, and more advanced training. In an era of unprecedented affluence, the cultural richness of the black institutions that segregation produced could not compensate for the sense of deprivation that inevitably accompanied them. Recollected Willis, "You know what my mother said to me? I'll never forget it, even if I get to be 200. She said, 'There's one set of rules for white people, and there's another set of rules for colored people.' . . . There was always a resentment in the black community, even though nothing was said. If there're two sets of rules for the game, and you're involved with the game, you might not say anything, but obviously you know that the rules are not fair. And so underneath, it was always there."[51]

Thus, a school like Champion, with its deep tradition and strong staff, could be simultaneously a source of pride and a symbol of inadequacy to the black community. Because black teachers in Columbus were restricted for so long to the five predominantly black elementary and junior high schools, competition was fierce for the few positions that occasionally would open. Champion, the system's only black secondary school through the 1950s, became the repository for the district's most qualified African American teachers. A 1959 school district fact sheet noted that fourteen of the school's thirty teachers had master's degrees, "giving the Champion School a high rating in the city for the educational training of its staff." "Champion," said Willis, a teacher and administrator at the school from 1952 to 1971, "was an all-black school, black staff, all black students and one of the best experiences I've ever had in my life. Of all of the teachers I've seen since then, as a group—none could compare." Recalled Amos Lynch, general manager of the Columbus *Call and Post*, "Probably the best teaching staff that was ever assembled [in Columbus] was that team of people who were at Champion Junior High during the late fifties through the mid-sixties." As the school into which all of the Near East Side elementaries fed, Champion educated students from every stratum of black society, creating a sense of racial identification and ownership inseparable from the restrictions that shaped black life in Columbus. "We had students whose parents were doctors, lawyers, ministers," said Will Anderson, a teacher at Champion from 1955 to 1966. "That's the only place they could go."[52]

By removing the barriers obstructing access to the resources and opportunities of full citizenship, blacks believed that public school integration could disperse this sense of ownership without diffusing it, to the ultimate benefit of society as a whole. "We saw [integration] as a way to improve the quality of education for all children," said former Columbus Urban League executive director Frank Lomax. "In the minority schools in Columbus, we saw an unevenness in terms of achievement as well as resources. We felt an integrated system would begin to even that out, because if people were making decisions on the basis of race, then they couldn't very well discriminate if white kids and black kids were in the same environment."[53]

Consequently, Columbus blacks, inspired and emboldened by civil rights victories in the South, began in the early 1960s to voice intensifying disenchantment with their second-class status within the school district. Proportionate population growth had yielded more political muscle for the black community. In 1961, Dr. Watson Walker became the first African American in the twentieth century to be elected to the board of education. Until Walker's election, board members routinely neglected the particular problems of predominantly black schools. "I sat at board of education meetings," said black administrator Ted Turner. "Those people were not thinking about Main Street and Pilgrim [two mostly black elementaries]. . . . There were 'black schools' and 'Columbus schools.'" Walker, a surgeon at the Ohio Penitentiary who had been denied employment at segregated hospitals when he arrived in Columbus in 1948, cautiously began to challenge the discriminatory assumptions that permeated the school system, using the subtle survival stratagems of a Georgia native long accustomed to pervasive public racism.[54] To illustrate this approach, Walker often told the story of how he finagled lights for all-black East High School's football field during a closed-door board meeting early in his tenure:

> I knew this was one of the things the black community was incensed about. They had been working on it for years and had been rebuffed at every turn. The only reason [white board members] didn't want lights for East was the white schools would prefer to play East at daytime because they figured if they came out in the East end at nighttime they were going to get beat up. These were prevalent racial attitudes that had to be erased.
>
> . . . I asked the question, "How many schools with football fields do you have that are not lighted?" Everything got quiet. Of course, I was playing the part of not knowing that I was asking a racially loaded question. They finally said, "One," and I said, "Which one?" And everybody got quiet again. The attitude they had was, "Is he crazy? Does he know the answer to this or is he pulling our leg?" And I had this angelic face and they couldn't tell what was going on. They finally said, "East High."[55]

As the decade progressed, however, such incremental victories became increasingly unsatisfactory. The Supreme Court had yet to address the question of whether or not *Brown* applied to the de facto segregation of northern school systems, and lower court guidance remained murky.[56] Without tangible legal barriers to tear down, the ideal of "non-discrimination" that *Brown* expressed, the Reverend Martin Luther King Jr. embodied, and the Civil Rights and Voting Rights Acts affirmed proved inadequate to deal with the social, physical, and economic complexities of racial inequity in northern cities. In a society fissured by racial segregation and economic inequality, the idea of a "race-neutral remedy" seemed to many blacks and liberal whites an oxymoron; active steps, conscious of the correlation between race and class, had to be taken to allow blacks to compete on equal terms with whites. "You do not take a person," declared President Lyndon Johnson, "who, for years, has been hobbled by chains and liberate him, bring him to the starting line of a race and then say, 'you are free to compete with all the others,' and still justly believe that you have been completely fair."[57] And so even as the Civil Rights movement was achieving its greatest triumphs, its tactics were being superseded by more fragmented strategies that sought to achieve what Lyndon Johnson called "not equality as a right and a theory, but equality as a fact and result" and Stokely Carmichael labeled "Black Power."[58]

From Rights to Remedies: The Blurring of Brown Locally, 1964–1971

During the mid-1960s, the idea that equality of condition could be achieved by blacks being granted both access to and control over a greater portion of the nation's resources was shaped by Washington into policy buzzwords such as "compensatory education," "maximum feasible participation," and, eventually, "affirmative action." In Columbus, the shift from rights to remedies was signaled by an escalating series of grassroots protests and civil rights reports condemning continued school segregation and demanding remedial action.

In 1964, after the Columbus Board of Education had issued a statement opposing segregation, supporting "neighborhood schools," and rejecting transportation to solve "social problems," four hundred people protested the opening of nearly all-black Monroe Junior High, claiming it reinforced de facto segregation within the district.[59] Two years later, the Columbus chapter of the NAACP issued a report accusing the school board of supporting "separate educational standards for Negroes and Caucasians." The report charged the district with "systematically" segregating staff; providing fewer teachers, less space, and less money to black schools; inadequately administering compensatory programs; and "hid[ing] behind the so-called 'neighborhood school concept,' especially when the board invokes this concept only when necessary to confine Negro children to substandard schools." The NAACP recommended a combination of integrative steps (altered attendance zones and white-black school pairings to desegregate the district) and targeted resource allocation (a "massive 'saturation' program to bring quality instruction to the inner-city schools") to overcome inequalities within the district.[60]

The Columbus Urban League echoed these recommendations the following year, offering a specific desegregation plan of its own.[61] And in 1968, an Ohio State University Advisory Commission, appointed at the request of the school board and headed by the dean of the College of Education, Luvern Cunningham, issued a report and series of recommendations after a comprehensive three-month study of the district. In an elaborate examination of reading and math achievement test scores, the Cunningham Report revealed the educational disparities between the district's poorest ("priority I to V") schools, most of which were between 75 and 100 percent black, and its most affluent ("non-priority") schools, most of which were between 95 and 100 percent white: "At every grade level on each of the tests the priority I and II school average scores fall far below expectation. The non-priority school average scores fall at or above expectation. . . . Priority I, II, and III schools start out in the first grade at three, two, and two months below the 1.0 grade equivalent; by the sixth grade they are between four and eight months below expectation. And by the ninth grade they are from two years, three months to two years, six months below expectation." While noting that "non-school (environmental) factors undoubtedly contribute to low achievement in priority schools," the report stated that "equality of educational opportunity cannot exist unless there are members from the black and white communities attending school together." Thus, the commission advocated "managed school integration," "pre-construction open housing agreements," and compensatory programs "as a supplement to but not as an alternative to school integration."[62]

Invariably, board response to these reports fell well short of the measures urged, exacerbating racial tensions that existed within the district. Until the 1960s, large city school districts were generally centralized, closed systems with autocratic administrative structures and rubber-stamp boards. Challenges to the authority of educational professionals, whether in the boardroom or the buildings themselves, were unusual and unwelcome. Like the American industries whose labor force they churned out, public schools faced few competitive pressures; unwieldy and unresponsive, they were often woefully unprepared to confront the conflicts that emerged in the 1960s.[63]

The Columbus Public School district was no exception. According to the 1968 Cunningham Report, the typical board meeting "proceeds rapidly in this way . . . the Superintendent reading in a loud clear voice, the Board members voting yeas when their names are called on each motion. The Superintendent does most of the talking and his recommendations are virtually always approved by unanimous vote . . . members of the board do not disagree in public. Last April, one member voted against a recommendation of the Superintendent and the curriculum committee; this reportedly was the first negative vote in years." Before the mid-1960s, the report said, "the Board was not accustomed to dealing with any organized opposition, and certainly not from the ranks of Negroes and the disadvantaged." Superintendent Harold Eibling and his powerful assistant, Cleo Dumaree, set an organizational tone of almost military rigidity, leading a loyal "old boys' network" of administrators resistant to and often resentful of externally imposed change. "Cleo Dumaree was an old warrior," said Superintendent Ellis. "He would train the new principals and they had to wear white shirts and clean their fingernails and put a tie on and look sharp and shine their shoes and wear clean underwear." "To be a Columbus administrator" at the time, said teacher Don Pierce, "you had to have the mentality of a Nazi soldier. You had to take orders and not question."[64]

Thus, when confronted with heightening black criticism, the district seemed unwilling and unable to provide satisfactory responses.

"A lot of the administrators were worn out," Ellis recalled. "They would go to meetings to try to listen to people and they'd get shouted down and they'd get called a racist and Cleo Dumaree would come home with his socks dripping wet from his sweat. He stood there and got assaulted verbally and threatened. It was kind of like a war zone." While the board did funnel funds to poorer schools for Title I and Head Start programs, it responded only superficially to demands for more integration in staffing, curricula, and student assignment. As a result, the Cunningham Report stated, "Critics of the schools who have taken the trouble to bring their criticisms to their elected representatives often leave Board meetings angry and frustrated because they perceive their appearance was treated with resentment and disrespect or, at best, indifference."[65]

These attitudes were echoed inside Columbus school buildings as well, creating a cycle of unresponsiveness that fanned animosities already smoldering in the black community. The mid-1960s movement from rights to remedies, beyond a mere transformation in policy, had marked a fundamental shift in psychology for many African Americans. Increasingly insistent demands for equality of respect accompanied the growing clamor for equality of results. This quest for identity and recognition consumed black culture and politics, from the "I Am a Man" placards of striking Memphis garbage collectors to the sunglasses and shotguns of Oakland Black Panthers. In public schooling, it manifested itself in the efforts of black parents, teachers, and students to shape education into something more representative of and responsive to these new concerns.

And so grassroots black activism ran headlong into deeply rooted district intransigence. On September 13, 1967, parents at mostly black Ohio Avenue Elementary, dissatisfied with the administration's reaction to the NAACP and Urban League reports, presented a list of twenty-seven demands to the board of education, among them breakfast and hot lunch programs, smaller classes, release of test scores, "intercultural" textbooks, "human relations" training for administrators and teachers, and a school lending library. In the face of board dissembling, and following the lead of "community control" movements that had arisen earlier in other northern cities, the parents organized a one-day student boycott of the school, the first in the district's history. There was, said Marian Craig, leader of the Ohio Avenue boycott, in a later interview, "a movement on the part of black parents to be involved in the total operation of schools where black students attend . . . whether in an all-black school or an integrated school."[66]

While Columbus would not experience the kind of conflagration that devastated black communities in Watts, Detroit, and so many other cities during the 1960s, the Ohio Avenue boycott, coinciding with a near riot on the Near East Side, signaled a striking rise in overt black-white antagonism in Columbus. Younger, more radical blacks, impatient with the outright slanders and perceived slights of discrimination, began openly challenging the assumptions of racial inferiority embedded in the American psyche and the operation of the Columbus schools, provoking defensive, fearful, and often angry reactions from white students and staff.[67] Every aspect of daily student life, from the "tracking" of students into vocational or college prep courses to the selection of a school's homecoming court, became a potential source of black-white friction. The drama of this worsening racial hostility played out most conspicuously in the larger junior and senior high schools, where neighborhood racial transition or common socioeconomic residential status made blacks and whites more likely to mix. "You could almost pinpoint the disruptions with where the boundary lines of housing were," said Damon Asbury, then the district's chief psychologist. "The schools that had difficulty were the schools that were in transition modes from being majority white students or predominantly white students to that range where the numbers were more equal."[68]

Between 1969 and 1971, high schools such as West (12 percent nonwhite in 1967), Eastmoor (13 percent nonwhite), Central (33 percent nonwhite), and Marion-Franklin (22 percent nonwhite) experienced boycotts, sit-ins, protests, even, in Central's case, the shooting of two black youths by a white student.[69] By early 1971, several of the system's schools were nearly out of control. Newspapers reported attempted firebombings at McGuffey Elementary and Monroe Junior High, while racial tensions temporarily shut down both Roosevelt Junior High and Central and led to the posting of police officers at Linmoor Junior High and Monroe. The disruptions peaked in late May, when black students at Linden-McKinley High, a racially balanced school located in a rapidly changing blue-collar residential area, attempted to replace an American flag standing on the school's stage with the red, black, and green of black nationalism. When white students resisted, administrators closed the building, fearing an all-out eruption. Attempts to restart school were scrapped in the face of continued conflict, and more than fifty Columbus police officers had to be stationed around the building as seniors returned for final exams.[70]

The most significant immediate consequence of the disruption at Linden-McKinley was the resignation of Superintendent Harold Eibling after fifteen years as head of the district. Wedded to a top-down, disciplined administrative style, Eibling had been unable to adapt to the manifold and messy pressures that threatened to engulf the system—racial tension, increasingly vocal black protest, nascent teacher unionization, and growing fiscal problems. Devastating ballot issue defeats in 1969 and 1971 indicated that Eibling and his administration had lost the confidence of the electorate.[71] Even more important, the events at Linden-McKinley had cost Eibling the backing of business leaders fearful that racial disruption would spill out of the schools and onto the streets that summer. These external pressures spurred the school board to bypass Assistant Superintendent Joe Davis, Eibling's heir apparent inside the administration, and hire an outsider less loyal to the status quo, one who, it seemed, might more easily be able to make changes within the district and rebuild bridges to the community. Thus, on June 15, 1971, the board announced that it had selected John Ellis, an ambitious young suburban superintendent with a Harvard doctorate and a fiery temper, to head the Columbus schools.[72]

The long-term fallout from the Linden-McKinley closing reached well beyond the superintendent's office, however. For many Columbus whites, media coverage of disturbances at the high school, particularly images of students running a gauntlet of police officers on their way to final exams, confirmed the conscious and unconscious anxieties that accompanied interracial contact. The words *Linden-McKinley* came to connote the unspoken fear and disdain with which whites viewed the burgeoning black presence in the schools, implicitly encapsulating the stereotypes—physical violence, deficient discipline, lax moral standards, declining academic achievement, and generally inferior status—that many whites associated with blacks.[73] In a matter of a few weeks, Linden-McKinley had become a sort of understood social footnote, a symbol that would be cited for years by white parents to justify avoiding sending their children to the Columbus Public Schools. Compounding the local impact of events at Linden-McKinley, meanwhile, was the national emergence of another word whose connotations came to supersede its content: *busing*.

From Rights to Remedies II: Busing and the Blurring of Brown Nationally, 1964–1972

With the passage of the Voting Rights Act in 1965, the already eroding moral, spiritual, and strategic cohesion of the civil rights movement dissolved. For a decade, the freedoms fought for had been so fundamental to American citizenship, so simultaneously small and vast, that the common purpose and shared sacrifice of the struggle dwarfed the divisions that did exist. As the tangible barriers of discrimination fell, however, the glue holding the movement together—the large, lumbering target of legal segregation—lost its force. Inevitable fissures emerged as the struggle for rights became a search for remedies, fragmenting the movement along generational, tactical, and geographical lines.

Accompanying these changes was a blurring of the stark morality of Selma, Montgomery, and the March on Washington. Non-discrimination—an ideal easy for northern whites to understand, difficult for them to oppose, and consistent with the nation's democratic mythology—splintered into two related concepts that were far more intellectually complex and psychologically messy. "disparate impact," the disproportionately negative effect that seemingly race-neutral policies have on African Americans due to the relationship between poverty, segregation, and educational attainment; and "affirmative action," the belief that this relationship can only be overcome by explicitly race-conscious remedies. As the hope of the Great Society faded into the flames of Watts, Detroit, and Vietnam, the practical application of these two ideas to policies affecting employment, taxation, and public education fueled a northern white backlash cultivated by Richard Nixon and George Wallace. Their 1968 and 1972 presidential campaigns developed what Thomas and Mary Edsall called "a new symbolic language for the politics of race . . . allowing politicians to mobilize white voters deeply resentful of racial change without referring specifically to race."[74] Throughout the 1970s, the most volatile word in this new vocabulary was *busing*.

Although the backlash against busing did not erupt nationally until 1971, its roots can be traced to provisions in the 1964 Civil Rights Act. Title VI of the act charged the Department of Health, Education and Welfare (HEW) with the responsibility of drawing up guidelines to ensure obedience to desegregation mandates, permitting HEW to deny federal funds if a school district failed to comply.[75] HEW's initial set of guidelines permitted school districts to adopt "freedom of choice" plans that allowed African Americans to transfer voluntarily to all-white schools and vice versa. Barely token desegregation ensued, as whites predictably refused to attend black schools and threatened blacks who sought to attend theirs.[76]

By 1968, stricter HEW guidelines, a strengthened Title VI, and a series of appellate court decisions tightened the noose around such plans, charging southern districts for the first time with the responsibility of actively integrating. While these developments turned the trickle of school desegregation into a stream, however, it was with the Supreme Court's ruling in *Green v. County School Board of New Kent County [Virginia]* that the flood began. Writing for a unanimous Court, Justice William Brennan declared that a school board operating a dual district had "the affirmative duty to take whatever steps might be necessary to convert to a unitary system in which racial discrimination would be eliminated root and branch." "Non-discriminatory" freedom of choice plans would no longer be tolerated by an impatient Court: "The burden on a school board today is to come forward with a plan that promises realistically to work, and promises realistically to work *now*."[77]

The following year, the Court demanded in *Alexander v. Holmes County Board of Education* that "every school district . . . terminate dual school systems at once." The Supreme Court's shift from nondiscrimination to affirmative action commenced the remarkable collapse of legally mandated public school segregation. In 1964, 1.2 percent of the 2.9 million black students in the South attended school with whites. As of 1968, that percentage had risen to 32 percent. By 1970, it was up to 85.6 percent, and two years later it stood at 91.3 percent. In four years, southern schools had become more integrated than those in the rest of the country.[78]

Still, white resistance to this process was substantial. Politicians protested, private academies multiplied, and racial violence sometimes flared.[79] Most galling to southerners was the use of buses to transport white students to formerly all-black schools, even though buses had been utilized for decades to carry African American children past nearby white schools. The school bus was quickly demonized as the obnoxious tool of overzealous federal judges and intrusive government bureaucrats. As one white Georgia parent told the *New York Times* in 1969, "My kids ain't riding no buses all over the country just to make the damned Supreme Court happy." Nevertheless, noted the Charleston (West Virginia) *Gazette,* "Massive desegregation was carried out peacefully in almost all of the 2700 school districts in the South, a good portion of it through busing." Their delay tactics defeated, southern officials generally resigned themselves to accepting desegregation's inevitability. "We have run out of time," said South Carolina governor Robert E. McNair. "We have run out of courts."[80]

Southerners still seethed, however, at what Senator Abe Ribicoff of Connecticut conceded was the "monumental hypocrisy" of northerners who "go home and talk liberalism to each other, but . . . don't practice it." In a statement at once reactionary and prophetic, Senator John C. Stennis of Mississippi warned his northern colleagues in early 1970, "If you have to [integrate] in your area, you will see what it means to us."[81]

As the Supreme Court pressed to bring *Brown* to school districts below the Mason-Dixon line, the Nixon administration sought to solidify an emerging coalition of conservative southerners and white working-class northerners by disavowing the kind of large-scale, court-ordered student assignment plans necessary to integrate urban districts in the North and South. Nixon had collected more African American votes in his unsuccessful 1960 presidential bid than he had while winning the presidency in 1968; he thus owed little to blacks and much to the historically Democratic South.[82] Almost immediately after taking office, Nixon ordered HEW to retreat from its successful assault on de jure segregation, shifting the primary responsibility for enforcing desegregation mandates to the Department of Justice. When Leon Panetta, then head of HEW's Office for Civil Rights, continued to exert pressure on the few remaining segregated southern school systems, he was fired. The administration's hostility to what it called "instant" integration was further illustrated when the Department of Justice sent its assistant solicitor general to argue against the NAACP in *Alexander v. Holmes*. The Legal Defense Fund denounced the move, declaring in a full-page newspaper ad, "Our government for the first time . . . has gone to court and asked that school segregation be allowed to continue." The Court's unambiguous ruling in *Alexander* was in part a scathing rebuff of the administration's legal backpedaling.[83]

On March 24, 1970, Nixon explicitly laid out his desegregation policy. The president's eight-thousand-word statement steered a middle course, expressing both his opposition to "deliberate," or de jure, segregation, and his belief that de facto segregation, "resulting genuinely from housing patterns," should not "by itself be cause for Federal enforcement actions." The statement also reiterated the president's opposition to "busing for racial balance" and his support for "neighborhood schools."[84] Nixon's message was that his administration would continue efforts to desegregate where dual districts were mandated by law but would not offer to remedy school segregation that appeared to be caused primarily by existing residential segregation. But with desegregation litigation moving from small, often rural districts to larger, more logistically complex urban areas, this distinction was becoming murky. Increasingly, court-ordered remedies necessitated substantial student transportation in order to overcome the legacy of segregated housing. As school desegregation spread to cities nationwide, its opponents found the once innocent yellow school bus a potent symbolic vehicle.

The genius of "busing" as a form of political shorthand lay in its versatility, its capacity to compress legitimate concerns and irrational fears into a single word whose racial neutrality lent it public legitimacy. By opposing busing instead of integration, whites could endorse the ideal of racial equality without supporting the most immediate means of achieving it.[85] At the same time, they were able to mask profound racial fear, resentment, and disdain with exaggerated arguments about a mode of transportation never questioned when it was used to facilitate rather than eliminate segregation. The emphasis on busing also shifted the desegregation debate away from the private- and public-sector actions that created segregation to the judicial decisions necessary to remove it, demonizing the federal courts while divorcing past from present and transforming white guilt into white victimhood.

At the same time, however, busing provoked a number of legitimate and troubling questions: Would it sever the schools from their surrounding communities? Would it drive whites from central city districts? Would its unintended consequences outweigh its anticipated advantages? While a morally tenable and ideologically consistent defense could not be mounted in support of denying, for example, black suffrage, such an argument could be manufactured in opposition to the shift from equal educational opportunity as a right to busing as a remedy.

Busing also exposed the class-based double standard of white liberalism: though the wealthy and the educated endorsed social change, they did not have to participate in it. Said a South Boston factory worker to Harvard sociologist Robert Coles, "They tell us we're trying to 'evade the federal court order' and we're 'racists.' But if rich people send their children to private school, they're not trying to 'evade' anything. Oh, no. They're just trying to give their children the 'best education possible.'"[86]

Finally, busing elicited a degree of uncertainty in many African American parents wary of sending their children into predominantly white environments hostile and unsympathetic to a black presence. This grassroots ambivalence underscored divisions that existed within the black leadership, a vocal portion of which argued that the push for integration implicitly endorsed white notions of African American cultural inferiority.[87] Absent a coordinated front, the moral momentum that propelled the Civil Rights movement proved unrecoverable.[88]

The vagueness and versatility of the word *busing* put supporters of school desegregation on the defensive, making it impossible for them to disentangle racist resistance from justifiable opposition in a manner stark and convincing enough to sustain public support. All too often, frustrated civil rights advocates found themselves battling straw men with straw men in a polarized duel of transportation statistics that deflected attention away from the very real problems of educational inequality. As a result, busing would become the perfect political wedge issue during the 1970s, providing rhetorical cover for the opening assault in a much larger conservative counteroffensive against the liberal programs and policies of the 1960s.

Still, as of early 1971, President Nixon's public position remained tentative. His 1970 desegregation statement had not endorsed de facto segregation but had deftly shifted the responsibility for addressing it to the judicial branch by saying that his administration had yet to be given guidelines outlining constitutionally permissible remedies.[89] On April 20, 1971, the Supreme Court responded by explicitly setting out acceptable remedial options in *Swann v. Charlotte-Mecklenburg Board of Education.* Writing for a unanimous Court, Chief Justice Warren Burger declared, "Once a right and a violation have been shown, the scope of a district court's equitable powers to remedy past wrongs is broad." Appropriate remedies could be "administratively awkward, inconvenient, and even bizarre," as long as they were effective in dismantling dual school districts. While "transportation" as an integrative tool had to be administered with careful regard to the circumstances of each case, the Court found "no basis for holding that the local school authorities may not be required to employ bus transportation as one tool of school desegregation." "Desegregation plans," the decision proclaimed, "cannot be limited to the walk-in school."[90]

On its face, *Swann* was a great liberal victory, a striking reaffirmation of *Brown*'s continuing relevance. Moreover, with two Nixon appointees, Burger and Harry Blackmun, participating in the unanimous opinion, it appeared to be a direct repudiation of the administration's tepid attitude toward desegregation. In the wake of the decision, a dispirited president announced, "The Supreme Court has acted and their decision is now the law of the land. It is up to the people to obey that law."[91]

However, the 9–0 decision masked deep divisions on the Court. Ambiguities and hedges throughout *Swann* reflect a ruling cobbled together by a new chief justice eager to compromise for consensus.[92] It took six drafts, circulated from early December 1970 to mid-April 1971, for Burger to achieve his aim. First, however, he had to satisfy a skeptical William Brennan that his ruling would not send supportive signals to intransigent southern school districts. In response to an early Burger draft that declared, "The Constitution, of course, does not command integration; it forbids segregation," Brennan called the chief justice's language "almost *haec verba* . . . the rallying cry of the massive resistance movement in Virginia, and of the die-hard segregationists for years after *Brown*." Brennan believed that opposition to integration was "at long last . . . crumbling in the

South," and he feared that "any tone of sympathy with local boards having to grapple with problems of their own making can only encourage continued intransigence." Brennan added, somewhat sardonically, "As our experiences with 'all deliberate speed' proved, tone is of primary importance." Still, as late as March 25, an exasperated Hugo Black threatened to dissent, writing, "I am of the opinion that it would be a mistake to give the appearance of a unanimity on the Court which does not actually exist."[93]

Finally, Burger agreed to uphold the Charlotte remedy on the condition that the Court's ruling avoid addressing de facto segregation. "We will not lack for cases on this in the future," he wrote before circulating his sixth draft, "and it is apparent that we will not achieve unanimity on it now." As a result, Burger's opinion expressly sidestepped the issue of "whether a showing that school segregation as a consequence of other types of state action, without any discriminatory action by the school authorities, is a constitutional violation requiring remedial action by a school desegregation decree." Thus, while *Swann* proclaimed busing a permissible remedial tool, the Court stopped short of applying the decision to northern segregation. Nevertheless, for cities outside the South, the handwriting was on the wall. As J. Harvie Wilkinson wrote, "With *Swann* and student busing, the school issue became a national one, because busing was meant not to remedy a peculiarly southern obstruction but to overcome the chief problem of the urban metropolis: racially separate patterns of housing."[94]

Any hope that *Swann* might quell the burgeoning busing controversy quickly faded. Protests, and sometimes violence, greeted desegregation plans around the country. As northern and western cases rose through the courts, antibusing sentiment steadily mounted in Congress, with liberals from affected districts quickly buckling to pressure from angry white constituents. Knowing that these were the voters who would carry him to a second term, Nixon shifted his desegregation stance from ambivalence to outright opposition. In an August 3, 1971, announcement, he stated, "I am against busing as the term is commonly used in school desegregation cases. I have consistently opposed the busing of our nation's schoolchildren to achieve a racial balance, and I am opposed to the busing of children simply for the sake of busing. Further . . . I have instructed the Attorney General and the Secretary of Health, Education and Welfare that they are to work with individual school districts to hold busing to the minimum required by law."[95]

The antibusing rhetoric escalated two days later when George Wallace declared his candidacy for the Democratic presidential nomination, vowing to make busing a prominent issue. Nixon, "at times almost obsessed by fear" of Wallace's conservative allure, responded by intensifying his own antibusing stance. Two days after a straw vote in the March 14, 1972, Florida primary indicated strong support for an antibusing constitutional amendment (as well as for Wallace, who finished far ahead of runner-up Hubert Humphrey), Nixon went on national television to reinforce his antibusing credentials.[96]

The politics of busing were made even more volatile in June 1972, when Sixth District Court judge Stephen Roth approved a desegregation remedy for the Detroit schools that involved fifty-three suburban districts. The remedy, immediately appealed, sent two ominous signals to northern whites: it indicated that cities outside the South would not long be immune to court-ordered busing, and for the first time it threatened seemingly safe suburban havens with school desegregation. Meanwhile, a similar district court order in Richmond, Virginia, was also winding its way to Washington.[97]

By November and Nixon's forty-nine-state landslide, busing had developed into the young decade's most wrenching domestic policy issue. Between *Swann* and the election of 1972, the dilemma of desegregation had become a battle over busing, and what had previously been perceived as a southern issue had been exposed as a national problem. With desegregation moving north and west, the seeds of civil disobedience had been sown, the divisive response of national public officials having legitimized the local opposition emerging in cities around the country.

The Avoidable Becomes the Inevitable: The Columbus Board of Education and the 1972 Bond Issue

In Columbus, the local elections of November 1971 had produced a board of education that reflected the divisions over desegregation developing nationwide. The new board consisted of four whites and an unprecedented three blacks, a racial and, for the most part, ideological split that would last the next six years. Caught in the middle was Superintendent Ellis, who sought to steer the schools gingerly toward integration while keeping his job safe, his career on track, and, if possible, his district out of federal court.

The leader of the board's antibusing faction was fifty-year-old Virginia Prentice. Prentice had worked her way through the ranks of the Columbus Council of PTAs, establishing a loyal political base among the city's white working class that made her the top vote getter in the 1969 board race, her first.[98] After utilizing Nixonian "law and order" rhetoric during the 1969 campaign, Prentice quickly converted her conservative code to the developing language of the antibusing movement, running four years later on a platform calling for "a common sense approach to education." Blacks, Prentice maintained, were using school desegregation to wrest economic and political control of Columbus from whites, a responsibility they were "not ready for" because they were "new to the political game." Dubbed "Mom" by affectionate PTA colleagues and "Ma" by disdainful black administrators, Prentice bore a striking physical and political resemblance to the archetypal anti-buser, Louise Day Hicks of the Boston Schools Committee; "popular legend has it," wrote the *Columbus Monthly*, "that [Prentice] is pleased with the comparison." "There will be no busing strictly for racial balance if I can help it," Prentice told a supportive audience during the summer of 1972. "Please remember that we are one vote away from it on the board. We have three members who are committed to full integration and four who feel that it is not the solution. Just pray that none of us four ever gets sick."[99]

Prentice's political ambition would eventually mitigate her extremism, pulling her slightly to the left of uncompromisingly conservative comrades Marilyn Redden and Paul Langdon. Langdon, fifty-seven in 1972, was the dean of the school board, having served since 1956.[100] While his position as assistant treasurer at Battelle Memorial Institute made him the board's expert on money matters, Langdon's social traditionalism more than his fiscal conservatism sustained the support of the Hilltop, the close-knit West Side neighborhood where Langdon lived. A fundamentalist Quaker who pressed to include creationism in the system's science curriculum, Langdon's religious conviction was matched only by his antipathy toward federal involvement in local affairs. Desegregation, he believed, was representative of a "fascist governmental attitude" and would spark a "mass exodus" of whites to the suburbs.[101]

The junior member of the board's antibusing bloc was Marilyn Redden, a mother of five, elected in 1971 after serving as president of the largely segregated Columbus Council of PTAs. Redden viewed the school board as a bulwark in the battle to protect an acceptable and endangered status quo. She was, for instance, the only board member to oppose expanding the school system's hot lunch program, arguing that by providing lunch to students, the district "encourages mothers not to be at home at noon."[102] Redden believed that desegregation equaled "socialization,"[103] and she used her oft-professed support for "voluntary integration" and integrated housing to mask the recognition that, absent government intervention, neither would occur in her lifetime. "The majority rules in this country," she declared. "I don't think minority rights are going to be trampled."[104]

By successfully weaving together race, religion, patriotism, and a profound mistrust of the federal government, Redden, Prentice, and Langdon presaged the rise of cultural conservatism and the Christian right. At the same time, however, they remained defenders of a disappearing era, traditionalists both resentful and fearful of Columbus's transformation from a big small town to a small big city. Busing embodied the racial and social ramifications of this transformation, signaling the contamination of home, school, and neighborhood and the pollution of the safety and sanctity of the status quo. Redden recalled the board adjourning from a long meeting one evening for dinner at the elegant Christopher Inn: "I'm, you know, a Midwest, farm country kind of girl, and I asked what escargot was. Dr. [Watson] Walker looked over at me and said, 'You don't know what that is?' And I said, 'No. And I'm not going to try it.' And he said, 'Well, I'll tell you what it is. It's snails. Try it, Marilyn, you might like it—just like busing.'"[105]

At the same board table but on the other side of the political spectrum was the three-member "black bloc": Marie Castleman, Dr. David Hamlar, and Dr. Watson Walker. After a decade of winning small victories against stiff resistance, Walker was growing frustrated with and callous toward his board duties, a change manifested in an increasingly caustic sense of humor. "It's obvious to me because of the divisions in this board," he declared after a particularly acrimonious vote, "that we need some outside advice, be it the state Department of Education or Jesus Christ himself." To avoid the emotions elicited by using buses to desegregate, Walker once told the board, "What we need is a train."[106] Another time, he abstained from a vote simply to break the monotonous predictability of the 4–3 result. And when Prentice complained in 1973 that she had sought unsuccessfully for four years to improve speech instruction in the district, Walker quipped that he had been trying for twelve years to remedy race relations and added that "you've gotten further than I have." Walker was also spending more time with his medical practice, often leaving or missing board meetings to perform surgery.[107]

Meanwhile, the crusading fervor Marie Castleman brought to her first term was quickly extinguished by a series of rejected policy initiatives. A social worker for the Veterans' Administration and magna cum laude graduate of Howard University, Castleman carried a more

ardent and Africentric attitude to the board table than her professional cohorts, Drs. Walker and Hamlar. During a meeting her first
year, she responded to Redden's defense of a white administrative
appointee by snapping, "Maybe if you were a soul sister you would
understand."[108] Castleman's early activism soon gave way to a somewhat sullen passivity, however. Despite serving for two terms, she
would never achieve much stature as a board member; ultimately,
her reputation would be based more on her penchant for falling
asleep at meetings than her effectiveness as a policy maker.

The burden of black leadership thus fell to David Hamlar, a native of Roanoke, Virginia. While none of the black school board
members favored court-ordered desegregation, all three viewed it as
the remedy of last resort. By making the greatest effort to keep the
district out of federal court, however, Hamlar also did the most to
ensure the school board's culpability once it got there. "If we're going to fight and bicker over every action," he angrily told the board
in June 1973, "court action is inevitable. . . . It's negative to hold off
and see what we can get away with." Courts in the South, he added,
"had to tell people to stop putting me off the bus before they finally
stopped putting me off the bus. . . . It took laws to improve that." By
sponsoring a series of voluntarily integrative proposals, Hamlar
hoped to give the board "something to fight with" in court. But as
each was rejected or watered down, they became part of a paper trail
publicly proclaiming the board's refusal to take affirmative steps to
remedy the effects of prior segregative acts. Hamlar said of the
board's white majority, "If they're against integration, I want it on
the record. When the court suit comes, I want the record to be clear
how we stand. If the courts feel we're doing all we should do, we
don't have to worry."[109]

Hamlar recognized that the antibusing bloc's intransigence would
almost assuredly land the district in federal court. "I'm almost willing to bet my life savings that we will get a suit within two years,"
he declared in mid-1972.[110] His fatalism was shared by the board's
fourth white member, Tom Moyer. A local attorney elected to the

board in 1969 at the age of twenty-nine, Moyer was a rising young Republican star with ties to U.S. Senator William Saxbe and Ohio governor James Rhodes. More of a business-oriented Republican (he was on the Columbus Area Chamber of Commerce's Downtown Area Committee) than a social issues conservative (he was also on the board of Planned Parenthood of Columbus), Moyer served as a swing vote and centering force on the board, often from his living room, where he would bring board members to discuss particularly delicate policy decisions.[111] As a lawyer and pragmatist, Moyer realized that the board had to take dramatic steps to forestall legal action. But as a young Republican with one eye on the next rung of the political ladder, he was unwilling to support such steps, arguing that the ideal of integration had to be weighed against the value and tradition of the neighborhood school. Though he managed skillfully to bridge the broadening gulf between board factions, Moyer fully understood that compromise could not keep the district out of court. As he told a Linden community group in May 1973, "I believe there are some people who want to see us in federal court on a segregation suit regardless of what we do. That's not an excuse for not doing anything, but I believe it will happen."[112]

Indeed, local civil rights groups dissatisfied with the board's response to the reports of the late 1960s were becoming increasingly impatient with the slow pace of integration. The NAACP stated that its objective was to "challenge [the] neighborhood schools concept, and end school segregation by all means available." Urban League policy, meanwhile, declared that only integrated education could be quality education. And the Columbus Area Civil Rights Council (CACRC) demanded "massive, countywide integration of the public schools," calling busing "the only practical means to achieve that end in the near future."[113]

The growing immediacy of such statements represented an effort to match the escalation of antibusing rhetoric occurring in Columbus and around the country, a cycle of polarization that paralyzed constructive dialogue by making compromise capitulation. The depth of this divisiveness first became apparent around the U-shaped table at 270 East State Street in mid-1972, as the school board wrestled with the issue of whether to place the largest bond issue in district history on the November ballot.[114]

Although racial volatility within the schools had dissipated somewhat in the year following the Linden-McKinley closing, the district was facing a crisis of another sort by the summer of 1972. With enrollment at an all-time high, voters had refused twice to okay funds for new construction to alleviate overcrowding. According to district figures for 1972–73, twenty-six secondary schools were on emergency schedules involving split sessions or extended days, and additional space had to be found for sixty-two classes in rented buildings and underutilized schools. Rapid residential development was overwhelming existing facilities, with thirty thousand new housing units having been constructed in the city the previous four years.[115] When the school district built Winterset Elementary in 1968, said Principal Glenna Palmer, there "weren't enough children to fill its nine classrooms." Four years later, apartment developments and home building on the city's booming northwest fringe had pushed the school's enrollment well past its three-hundred-student capacity, and eight classes had to be bused to two other elementaries.[116]

In addition to coping with this enrollment overflow, the district had to find the funds to meet new minimum standards adopted by the State Board of Education for school libraries, disabled access, and vocational education. "While it is true that superior facilities alone cannot guarantee a superior educational program," the district's official rationale for the bond issue noted, "it is also fact that inferior facilities will most assuredly doom an educational program to inferiority." Said the superintendent, "This is the space age, and the Columbus schools simply do not have enough space to do what ought to be done."[117]

The $89.5 million bond issue proposed by the administration was designed to fund construction of six new secondary schools and ten new elementaries, including four "developmental learning centers" (now known as "alternative" or "magnet" schools) for experimental programs. It would also "modernize or replace" several schools built in the nineteenth century, build or upgrade libraries in every school, create four "career centers" for vocational training, and provide additional space and resources for special education classes.[118]

While the entire board acknowledged the pressing need for new facilities, the three black members believed that integration should take priority over construction. With five votes needed to place a bond issue on the ballot, and unanimity considered essential when seeking the approval of increasingly tax-hostile voters,[119] the white majority could not dismiss the black bloc's basic demand: that the school board adopt a pledge making the promotion of integration official board policy.

The two factions wrangled bitterly over the wording and the intent of such a pledge. When black board members backed a statement that declared the goal of the Columbus Public Schools to be "to provide integrated educational experiences for all students," whites tabled the issue, calling "provide" too strong a word. Until that July 2 meeting, an editorialist wrote, "Columbus had been fortunate enough to escape open polarization. . . . Tuesday, the veneer was cracked and the entire community realizes the gulf between the black and white members of the school board is deep." As the July 20 election filing deadline rapidly approached, Ellis conceded, "I would be surprised if we have a bond issue on the ballot in this poisoned atmosphere."[120]

It was left to board president Tom Moyer to hammer one out. Starting at 7:30 on the eve of the board's July 18 meeting, Moyer managed to pull together language that satisfied both sides, securing unanimity shortly before convening the board at 4:00 P.M. the next day.[121] By 7–0 votes, the board approved the bond issue and adopted the following integration pledge: "It shall be the goal and policy of the Columbus Public Schools to prepare every student for life in an integrated society by giving each student the opportunity of integrated educational experiences. Such a goal does not imply the mandatory forced transportation of students to achieve a racial balance in any or all schools."[122]

After the meeting, reported one newspaper, "Those in the audience known to favor construction but strongly opposed to mandatory busing left with broad smiles." Black board members found the language of the integration policy weaker than they had wished. But the principle of integration was not the only pressure affecting their votes. Upgraded libraries, new buildings, and special programs would benefit African American children as well as white children. Millions of dollars of construction would create jobs for the black community. Perhaps most critical, however, was the influence of Republican mayor Tom Moody and the Columbus Area Chamber of Commerce. Worried that the board's all-too-public racial acrimony would scare off prospective business development, and intent on getting new schools to serve the subdivisions rising on the city's periphery, the Chamber urged the board not to link the bond issue to integration. When black members refused to back down, Moody made an "unprecedented" appearance before the board, imploring it to "resolve its differences however it can, as quietly as possible." [123]

Given these pressures, blacks chose to regard the integration policy that was finally approved not as an inadequate compromise but as a promising start, a significant first step toward the ultimate goal of ensuring equal educational opportunity for the district's African American students. [124] Pro-integration organizations that refused to support bond issues in 1969 and 1971 agreed to endorse the 1972 edition. "Even though the basic content of the building proposal varies little from previous ones," said Urban League president Napoleon Bell, "it was felt attitudes surrounding this proposal left doors open for innovative buildings and the beginning steps toward quality integrated education." The influential *Call and Post* was supportive but wary: "While we accept the fact that the facilities may be needed, we are unimpressed with the possibility that enough of the right people in the administration and the white leadership community had black folks in mind when the plans were conceived." The newspaper endorsed the ballot issue but cautioned blacks to "be prepared to fight for whatever change you believe is necessary." [125]

On the strength of a well-designed, well-financed campaign, the $89.5 million bond issue handily passed, winning an encouraging 55 percent of the vote. With its passage, the school board crossed a Rubicon. The district now had the money to embark on the largest building program in its history, siting schools and fixing attendance boundaries in ways that could either curtail segregation or set it in concrete. New construction had the potential to spread the system significantly, with school sites being carved out of cornfields in anticipation of encroaching residential development.[126] Unless the board took specific steps to foster integration, geographic sprawl and segregated housing patterns would ensure the need for extensive busing should the district be forced to desegregate in the future. Passage of the bond issue thus offered the board a final opportunity to veer from a path that increasingly seemed destined to end in federal court. "If we want to have quality integrated education," said Hamlar, "we have to make the choice right now."[127]

Shortly before the November 7 election, Ellis's administration had issued a blueprint of the district's bond issue plans. The thirty-three-page booklet, called "Promises Made," contained comforting words for both advocates and opponents of integration, sometimes in the same sentence. "New buildings will be located whenever possible to favor integration," it declared, inviting unresolvably conflicting interpretations of the words "whenever possible." The meaning of this statement was muddled further by the obliquely mentioned fact that sites for ten of the sixteen prospective schools had already been purchased. Though Ellis asserted in the booklet that "one way to help rebuild good faith [in the district] is to follow the principle that a promise made should be kept," he added that "it is possible, in fact probable, that slight modifications will occur." When the superintendent proclaimed, a day after the election, "We made promises and we want to keep them," the future of the Columbus Public Schools hinged on which promise would take priority: integration or construction.[128]

It did not take long for this question to be answered and for the cautious optimism of black board members to give way to disillusionment. Three weeks after the election, Marie Castleman proposed the creation of an advisory committee consisting of educators, lenders, bankers, businesspeople, real estate agents, and community leaders that would monitor the racial impact of new school sites and ensure the availability of open housing and equal employment opportunities in the areas where new schools were being built. "No educational system is independent of the social, financial, legal, political and religious institutions of our society," the proposal read. "Each affects the other." By addressing the racial effects of this institutional web, the committee would assist the district "in its effort to provide quality integrated education within the neighborhood concept."[129]

White board members immediately attacked Castleman's proposal, making it abundantly clear that construction, not integration, would be the priority promise of "Promises Made." "This motion," Prentice protested, "would withhold the building of schools for the purpose of bringing about social change." Moyer concurred, calling the proposal "in direct conflict with our present building program" and saying, "I won't vote for any recommendation which goes against the promises we made the voters." By contending that Castleman's proposal would undermine the newly approved building program, white board members implicitly acknowledged that they had no intention of using school sites or attendance boundary changes to facilitate integration. After the proposal was rejected, a reporter asked Castleman if the board was dragging its feet on racial issues. "Have they ever been lifted?" she answered. "There are no ifs, ands or buts about it," commented the *Call and Post*. "The Columbus Board of Education has once again openly betrayed the confidence of the black voters of Columbus."[130]

The board's response to passage of the bond issue of 1972 transformed the avoidable into the inevitable. With white members convinced of the district's innocence, black members certain of its guilt, and Superintendent Ellis caught in the middle, the Columbus Board of Education arrived at a policy-making stalemate, the district's inexorable slide toward desegregation accelerated by the growing impatience of integration's increasingly uncompromising advocates.

Between Integration and Litigation: John Ellis and the Road to District Court, 1973–1976

On June 21, 1973, the Supreme Court ruled in *Keyes v. Denver School District No. 1* that even though no "statutory dual system . . . ever existed" in the Denver public schools, the foreseeably segregative acts of board members and administrators constituted unconstitutional state action.[131] By rendering the distinction between de facto and de jure school segregation virtually irrelevant, *Keyes* threw open the door to desegregation in northern and western cities. Still, it was pure coincidence that the same day *Keyes* was issued, a coalition of three Columbus civil rights groups was at the Federal Courthouse on Marconi Avenue, filing a complaint with sixth District Court judge Carl Rubin. That complaint marked the start of twelve years of school desegregation litigation in Columbus, a case that would come to be known by the last name of its lead plaintiff, thirteen-year-old Gary L. Penick.

The alphabet-soup coalition bringing the suit called itself Project QUIET (Quality Integrated Education Tomorrow) and consisted of CACRC (Columbus Area Civil Rights Council), NWACHR (Northwest Area Council on Human Rights), and the local chapter of the NAACP. The complaint alleged the existence of illegal racial imbalance in the Columbus Public Schools and charged the Columbus Board of Education with a "lack of good faith in carrying out its adopted resolution for integrated educational experiences." It asked the court to order that building program funds be used to foster integration and called on Rubin to convene an immediate hearing. "If buildings are allowed to begin," the complaint read, "damage to plaintiffs' rights would be irreparable." The plaintiffs' attorney and former NAACP chapter president William "Wild Bill" Davis declared, "We're getting ready to build edifices which could set the pattern of attendance for two generations or more. . . . If the board doesn't start doin', we'll start suin'."[132]

With court consideration not expected for another year, however, the board had ample time to appropriate funds and initiate construction. Project QUIET attorneys attempted to seal off this opening by seeking a temporary injunction on the bond issue building program. Citing construction already approved for predominantly black or white schools, such as the $210,000 spent adding seven classrooms onto 100 percent white Devonshire Elementary, the plaintiffs argued that continued construction would create "segregated and unequal educational facilities" and leave the school board with fewer and fewer integrative options outside of busing.[133] "The nature of the suit will become moot if nothing is done," said NWACHR president Ken Connell. "This appears to be a classic case of how 'justice delayed is justice denied.'" Project QUIET's efforts were supported with sharpening anger by the *Call and Post*, which in an editorial accused the school board of "playing sadistic racial games with the black community" via a "construction program covertly planned to continue, forever, racial segregation of Columbus schoolchildren."[134]

Finally, on April 15, 1974, Judge Rubin held a hearing to determine whether an injunction should be issued. After listening to a handful of morning witnesses, the judge called both parties into his chambers just before noon recess to make a startling announcement. Enjoining the building program, he declared, would not address adequately the crux of the plaintiffs' case—the persistence of segregation in the Columbus Public Schools. "If plaintiffs are willing to file an amended complaint," Rubin continued, "that issue may be adjudicated in court."[135]

Rubin's all-or-nothing announcement swept away the legal center. There would be no gradually escalating complaints, no time wasted on peripheral issues; either file a full-scale desegregation suit, Rubin was saying, or stay out of my courtroom. Despite its lack of ambiguity, Rubin's ruling sent mixed signals to both sides. By forgoing an injunction, it enabled the district to proceed unobstructed with a building program already well under way. At the same time, by encouraging a significant expansion of the original complaint, the ruling implied that the plaintiffs had a compelling enough case to merit more sweeping review. Moreover, in requesting an amended complaint rather than demanding a new one, Rubin greased procedural wheels by allowing the Columbus case to maintain its place in the court's normal rotation. "It's a success for the plaintiff," Connell said, "when a federal judge asks you to file a more comprehensive case to seek a more comprehensive remedy." Proclaimed "Wild Bill" Davis, "We're throwing the gauntlet to the school board to develop an effective desegregation plan."[136]

The intransigence of the antibusing bloc, however, precluded such a plan, a reality that Superintendent Ellis understood keenly and accepted judiciously. Ellis possessed an impatient, sometimes combative intelligence tethered by personal ambition and political acumen; he was as respectful of the immovability of the board majority as he was aware of the inevitability of integration. As a Harvard graduate student in the early 1960s, he had helped formulate a voluntary desegregation plan ultimately rejected by Louise Day Hicks and the Boston School Committee. He thus understood the populist appeal and unwavering conviction of Virginia Prentice and recognized that directly challenging such conviction could divide the community and derail his career. Said David Hamlar, "I took it that we should do everything possible to get [desegregation] done. I never felt [Ellis] had the strength to fight people who thought it shouldn't be done." Unwilling to be martyred, Ellis adopted a mithridatic role, feeding the district small doses of integration to prepare it for the court order he saw coming. In doing so, said former PTA official and school board member Pauline Radebaugh, "John Ellis dragged Columbus kicking and screaming into the twentieth century."[137]

"The school board did not want to have me deal much with the process of desegregation," Ellis recalled. "They wanted us to hire the best lawyers we could and defend ourselves and hunker down and resist. They read the social history and the law differently than I did, and they didn't particularly want me to move in that direction. . . . So, I viewed my role as trying to move aggressively toward a state of integration without engaging in polarizing activities all the way. . . . My approach as the leader was to do as Confucius says: 'A journey of a thousand miles starts with the first step.' You have to get your toe in the water. You have to start somewhere rather than just stay in denial." That starting point was a little-publicized, seldom-used voluntary transfer plan created by the board in 1967 and nominally designed "to achieve better ethnic distribution." A northern form of the southern "freedom of choice" plans deemed insufficiently integrative in *Green*, the "Columbus Plan" allowed high school students to transfer to special programs at other schools, as long as racial balance was improved. But because the board refused to provide transportation, only 0.5 percent of Columbus high schoolers were enrolled in the program by 1972–73.[138]

As part of the behind-the-scenes bargaining needed to nail down black support for the bond issue, Ellis promised to expand the Columbus Plan to include transportation for special programs. However, when he also proposed in early 1973 to allow transfers solely to improve integration, white board members erupted. Such a move, Langdon contended, would "open Pandora's box." Prentice declared, "I don't want this board hung up on transportation for racial balance instead of for programs."[139] Eventually, the board agreed to allow transfers for racial balance but to offer transportation only for special programs. "It's a breakthrough to allow any transportation at all," said Walker. "[It's] token integration, but at least some integration."[140]

As the threat of a desegregation suit escalated, Ellis's administration continued to improve the Columbus Plan's publicity and enlarge its scope. "We were trying to get ourselves positioned so that we could prove that we were making efforts to integrate the school system," said Beverly Gifford, the district's public information director. "It came out of the fear that we were going to be in court and ordered to bus, and so we were looking for alternatives." To Ellis, however, the Columbus Plan served as more than what Watson Walker called a "Nixon-type delaying tactic . . . something to say 'Look what we're doing.'" "It was in my opinion a great teaching and learning device," Ellis said. "It was like having a pilot program before you do it on a massive scale. . . . There were schools that didn't have any black kids in them at all. Lots of schools. And we didn't have any buses rolling up with black kids on them going to white schools, nor did we have white kids rolling up to black schools. We didn't have any experience at all with that."[141] The Columbus Plan, Ellis observed, offered the district

> an opportunity to learn a lot of lessons on how to do things and how to confront things. . . . How do you welcome [children from another neighborhood]? How do you integrate them into the classroom? How do you work with the parents? How do you deal with the questions of athletic programs after school? How do you deal with the PTA when the parents are in another area? How do you deal with insuring that they don't end up resegregated back into the classroom when you group students? What do you do when there is a fight in the cafeteria? All those things Columbus had a chance to deal with in microcosm before they went to the macro system.[142]

The Columbus Plan exemplified Ellis's efforts to expand integration within the closely circumscribed space afforded him by the board majority. If it spawned only superficial integration, it was never intended or permitted to do much more.[143]

Ellis's administration took a number of other steps to nudge the system toward desegregation. In mid-1973, the superintendent negotiated a teacher integration plan with the Ohio Civil Rights Council that barely staved off a potentially bitter court hearing.[144] He established the district's first alternative schools in 1975, with specially designed curricula and carefully chosen faculties that drew students from around the city.[145] By creating community advisory panels and depending on younger, less hidebound staffers, Ellis found ways to circumvent the dutiful passivity of the administrative old guard and push through a number of moderately integrative proposals.[146]

Paradoxically, it was the ever increasing polarization over busing that ensured Ellis's security as superintendent. Desegregation-related violence in Boston and Louisville convinced local business leaders that antibusing intransigence could lead to similar situations in Columbus. If busing was bad, they reasoned, Boston was worse. As Tom Moyer warned his more conservative colleagues in late 1974, "School districts which have done nothing have had the doors torn off at the hinges."[147]

On September 30, 1975, the board majority, reacting to the prospect of an out-of-court desegregation settlement, denounced the superintendent for having sent administrators to study desegregation plans in other cities without board authorization. "It was obvious," said Ellis, "that there was a move at that time to do something to me—maybe fire me." Out of town on a business trip, Ellis was alerted to the potential coup by Beverly Gifford, who had him paged at the Atlanta airport. He immediately phoned Columbus reporters to explain his belief that "it was irresponsible not to plan for potential contingencies, just like you plan for [fires with] fire drills."[148]

Black board members and other integration advocates rushed to Ellis's defense. Teachers' union president Ted Thomas blasted the board majority's "head-in-the-sand attitude on the issue of desegregation." White board members, the normally more temperate *Call and Post* fumed in an editorial, were "motivated by racial prejudice of the most vicious type." "We are dealing with four dangerous white men and women," the newspaper warned.[149]

It was the backstage clout of Columbus business leaders, however, that quickly settled the issue. Publicly, chamber of commerce officials were circumspect, telling the board, "Contingency planning is logical and necessary in a situation as serious as this one." Privately, they were more forceful. "The business community, laid out in full glory," Ellis recalled, "came down pretty hard behind the

scenes on the school board and said, 'You leave Ellis alone. He's doing exactly what he ought to be doing.' They saved my neck."[150] In
doing so, the business community also tacitly endorsed Ellis's integrative efforts, creating a counterweight to the board's antibusing
faction that enabled community leaders to build a consensus around
the neutral goal of peacefully accepting the district court's decision.[151] Said Ellis, "After [Prentice] learned she wasn't going to be
able to fire me, she learned to try to live with me."[152]

On March 10, 1975, the NAACP intervened in *Penick v. Columbus Board of Education,* making Columbus part of what desegregation scholar Gary Orfield called the "most concentrated campaign
of urban school litigation" in the organization's history.[153] With the
NAACP's traveling team of expert witnesses and its nearly unblem-
ished record in desegregation suits, what had once appeared avoidable now seemed inescapable.[154] It is impossible to say whether John
Ellis was too realistic, too ambitious, or too weak to stand up to the
school board's recalcitrant majority; quite likely, given the circumstances, nothing could have kept the Columbus Public Schools out
of court. Regardless, by the beginning of the *Penick* trial on April 19,
1976, Ellis, along with many others in the community, could see
what lay ahead. "I had read the law carefully," he said. "I had stud-
ied other communities around the country. I had looked at our own
data and I realized that the court would find Columbus segregated
and would order some form of desegregation. There was no question
in my mind."[155]

Penick *Decided: The Ruling of Robert M. Duncan*

With the chamber's intercession on behalf of Ellis in late 1975, the
politics of school desegregation in Columbus reached an impasse.
The intransigence of the board majority, the bitterness of the board
minority, and the anxiety of the business community combined to
create an unspoken system of checks and balances that precluded

both volatile confrontation and dramatic compromise. When the white bloc rejected an NAACP offer to settle for a gradual, "stair-step" integration plan, a sense of uneasy anticipation settled over the dispute. The hopes and fears of a whole city thus came to rest on the shoulders of district court judge Robert M. Duncan.[156]

Still something of a cipher judicially, Duncan represented so many apparent contradictions that his very presence behind the bench had a moderating influence on the emotions surrounding *Penick*. Here was a Nixon appointee whose first major rulings resoundingly endorsed affirmative action; a law school classmate of school board attorney Sam Porter and an acquaintance of NAACP general counsel Nate Jones; an African American and a Republican. Equally comfortable in the social clubs of Columbus's white and black elite, Duncan had tasted both the bitterness of white racism and the benefits of white patronage. Above all, despite his powerful position, Duncan remained very much *of* the community: he lived in Berwick, an integrated neighborhood east of downtown; his wife, Shirley, taught kindergarten at Columbus's Oakland Park Elementary; and two of his three children would graduate from city public schools. To blacks, this signaled a comforting familiarity with the racial circumstances of the city and the school district; to whites, it meant that any decision made by Robert Duncan the district court judge would directly affect the life of Robert Duncan, the husband and father.[157] While more radical blacks saw an Uncle Tom and white antibusing extremists a double demon—a black jurist and a federal court judge—most of Columbus's moderate majority could seize on something hopeful amid the many contrasts in Duncan's biography.

Duncan was born on August 27, 1927, in Urbana, Ohio, a small town about fifty miles west of Columbus "where everything was segregated except the public school system and the library."[158] His was the generation that straddled *Brown*, the last to experience an America in which segregation was ritualized social reality. "In Urbana at that time," Duncan said, "you could still only go to the movie theater and sit at the left rear. Nobody ever told you to sit there.

You just automatically went there so as to *not* cause a problem." As a senior at Urbana High, Duncan was one of three black starters on the school's varsity basketball squad. After winning the district championship, the team returned to Urbana in search of a postgame meal: "We wanted to have something to eat but there was no restaurant in town [that would serve us]. This is our hometown! Well, we went to one and got put out. Then we went to a black restaurant and had hamburgers."[159]

Though equally segregated, Columbus, with its bustling black population, offered a young Duncan the excitement Urbana lacked: "I remember coming to Columbus when I was in high school and having my first ice cream soda. You couldn't go have ice cream sodas in places like Urbana." When he arrived at Ohio State, "The High Street area was almost completely de facto segregated. If you wanted to press the point and go in and sit around long enough, you could get something. But it was very reluctant and you got served very grudgingly. So we didn't generally go." Instead, Duncan recalled, "The entire social life of African Americans on this campus was on the East Side. Friday afternoon we would head for Long Street. Club Regal. Club Flamingo. Movie theaters . . . Sunday afternoon, all the [black] fraternities and sororities had meetings at the old Spring Street Y."[160]

Like many African Americans, Duncan looks back on the era before integration with a kind of qualified wistfulness:

> Although one shudders at the thought of ever returning to segregation, when you lived it on an everyday basis it was a rather well-organized separate society. It was fun and it was hierarchical. There were leaders in the community and there were people of great respect and there were people with a lot of money and there were people who had fine houses and, above all, there were some very nice places to go. . . . It wasn't day-to-day suffering. And although there's never been a day in my life I don't think about race, there were some days when you could almost say, "Yeah, I'm really glad to be a black law student in Columbus."[161]

But the piercing clarity of prejudice invariably punctures the haze of nostalgia. One of Duncan's most searing memories occurred as a third-year law student at Ohio State. He and classmate John Bowen became the first African Americans to pledge the school's law fraternity. When officials at the fraternity's Atlanta national headquarters found out, they informed the local chapter that accepting blacks violated the organization's constitution. "We got dumped out of the fraternity," Duncan recalled, "which was, to say the least, at that time traumatic. Nothing like that had ever happened to me before. . . . To show how schizophrenic society was in those days, about three months later, I got elected president of the class."[162]

Duncan spent seven years at Ohio State, where he majored in education as an undergraduate and received his law degree in 1952. That year, he passed the Ohio Bar and began his deferred military service. Though the armed forces had recently been desegregated, Duncan quickly discovered that the new policy had yet to be uniformly implemented:

> I go to Fort Hayes [in Columbus] and I am in a desegregated port of entry to the army. They put us on a desegregated train going from Columbus to Fort Meade, Maryland. Get off at Fort Meade and immediately go to a segregated part of Fort Meade to get our shots and clothing and all that kind of stuff. Stay there two days in segregated housing. Get on a segregated train in Fort Meade, all blacks together and all whites together. The train goes to Camp Breckenridge, Kentucky. And we get to Cincinnati on a train and we change trains. Now we are in a desegregated train going from Cincinnati down to Camp Breckenridge. We go now to a segregated area to distribute us where we're going to go. So then we get distributed out to desegregated Army facilities. This all happened in less than a week.[163]

Duncan returned to Columbus in 1955 with, in his words, "limited expectations," resigned to becoming a "competent practitioner, primarily serving a black clientele." His fortunes changed, however, when William Saxbe, a Republican from just outside Urbana, was elected attorney general of Ohio. Duncan's family had deep roots in the Urbana Republican Party, and "everybody in town" knew his grandfather, a porter and headwaiter at the city's hotel, and his father, a shoe shiner in the barbershop next door. When Duncan left Urbana for OSU, then-State Representative Saxbe arranged a job for him in the Ohio treasurer's office. A decade later, Saxbe hired the recently married lawyer to try workmen's compensation cases for the state, giving Duncan's pioneering career its first big boost and cementing his allegiance to the Republican Party.[164]

Over the next two decades, Duncan would become known as "the Jackie Robinson of the Ohio judiciary," turning the phrase *first black* into a permanent professional prefix: first black chief counsel in the Ohio attorney general's office (1965–66), first black elected Franklin County municipal court judge (1966–69), first black Ohio Supreme Court justice (1969–71),[165] first black on the United States Military Court of Appeals (1971–74), and, in the waning months of Watergate, Ohio's first black federal district court judge. As the *second* black district court judge to decide a desegregation suit, Duncan was mindful of but unfazed by the added scrutiny his actions would receive.[166] "I was always concerned about whether or not citizens in this community would think they're getting a prejudiced opinion from a judge who is black," he said. "On the other hand, I always thought, 'Well, if a black man didn't decide it, it would have to probably be some other ethnic person or group. So what the hell?'"[167]

More broadly, Duncan brought to *Penick* an acute sensitivity to both the case's gravity and its volatility. He frequently met informally with reporters to clarify important legal issues and explain impending procedures, even passing out pillows to make the hard courtroom benches more comfortable. "My approach to it," he said, "was 'I want newspaper people there.' I got really uncomfortable if I ever looked out there and didn't see any." A day before the trial began, the *Dispatch* ran a front-page photograph of the judge seated in his office, arms behind his head, feet resting lazily on his cluttered desk, a reassuring symbol of relaxed calm and an image in sharp contrast to the armed guards and metal detectors that greeted spectators entering the courtroom the next day. *Penick*, the judge assured the *Dispatch* on April 18, was "just another trial." As it opened the next morning, however, his assessment was far more sober. "This is an extremely important case in this community and the nation," he told a packed courtroom. "I pray that we will find a fair and just result."[168]

Thirty-six days of occasionally testy and often tedious testimony followed, spanning nearly two months. More than seventy witnesses and six hundred exhibits left Duncan and his clerks to wade through a 66-volume, 6,322-page transcript.[169] "It's going to be the toughest decision I've ever been called on to make," mused Duncan the day testimony ended. "We're dealing with the most valuable thing that all of us have—our children."[170]

It took Duncan just over six months from *Penick*'s September 3, 1976, closing arguments to hammer out a decision, a process delayed by a voluminous record and an unusually heavy criminal docket. Ironically, the bitter cold that would close the Columbus schools that winter ended up accelerating the completion of the ruling. In December 1976, Chief Judge Harry Phillips of the Sixth U.S. District assigned Duncan for two weeks to assist the busy Western District of Michigan in Grand Rapids. "It was sort of like eight below zero when I got there," Duncan recalled. "So my law clerks and I really couldn't do anything while we were in our spare moments. That's when we really did most of the writing of the opinion."[171]

At 10:00 A.M. on March 8, 1977, a week after the end of School without Schools and the departure of John Ellis, Duncan finally released his ruling. The thirty-six-page opinion and order quickly laid to rest months of speculation that overdue equaled uncertain: "[The] delay in reaching a decision," Duncan wrote, "should not be construed to reflect a hesitancy on the part of the Court in determining the basic result required by the evidence and the law. I am firmly convinced that the evidence clearly and convincingly weighs in favor of the plaintiffs."[172]

The lag between the end of the trial and the release of the ruling reflected a judge wrestling not with what to say but how to say it.

"This case was not close," Duncan confessed. "To find for the plaintiffs did not make me sit up nights."[173] Wanting to address both the Constitution and the community, Duncan faced the challenge of crafting an opinion that would be legally thorough without being hard to understand, emphatic without being accusatory, and sympathetic without being lenient. What emerged was a decision unusual in its compassion and humanity, the product of a judge forced by violations he could not deny to take on a role he did not relish. Revealing bits and pieces of Duncan's many masks—judge, African American, Republican, parent, civic leader—the ruling set a tone of resigned resolve that would eventually come to characterize the implementation of school desegregation in Columbus.

From the beginning of the decision, Duncan made clear his belief that the courts were ill suited to deal effectively with the complexity of racial segregation in America. In both the trial and the opinion, the judge decried what he later called the "punting syndrome," the tendency of politicians and policy makers to abdicate responsibility for "agonizing social issues" by kicking them into the courts and then blaming unelected judges for trying to resolve them.[174] "As I view it," he wrote in *Penick*, "the real reason that courts are in the school desegregation business is the failure of other governmental entities to confront and produce answers to the many problems in this area pursuant to the law of the United States. This Court is quick to admit that the litigation model is not the most efficient way to solve problems of far-reaching social impact, but our courts must always protect the constitutional rights of all our citizens." During the trial, Duncan had significantly injected himself only once into testimony, disbelievingly grilling twenty-year Ohio Board of Education member Wayne Shaffer about the state's failure to actively investigate segregation in Columbus. In the decision, Duncan reserved his harshest words for the state defendants. "As I understand [their] argument," he wrote, "they claim that they would have investigated had Columbus school officials so requested. This position borders on the preposterous. It cannot reasonably be expected that those who violate the Constitution will be anxious for an investigation in order that a remedy may be leveled against them."[175]

Duncan's judicial misgivings extended beyond the problems of addressing school segregation to the unintended consequences of remedying it. Developments around the country suggested that busing brought with it the danger of reducing *Brown* to a triumphant battle in a lost war. While media coverage of antibusing violence obscured the uneventful desegregation taking place in most of the country, images from cities such as Boston and Louisville symbolized mounting white resistance to African American advancement. And violence was only the most vivid manifestation of this resistance. By the mid-1970s, some sociologists, most notably the influential James Coleman, were making the controversial claim that school desegregation actually undermined integration by accelerating "white flight" from cities to suburbs.[176] This thesis raised the insidious paradox that, like a strain of bacteria growing immune to antibiotics, the disease of segregation might only be worsened by efforts to remedy it.

Meanwhile, the integration that *had* come to Columbus was proving no panacea for African Americans. The Columbus Plan, the district's voluntary transfer program, was coming under increasing criticism as a "black brain drain" that skimmed the academic cream from schools such as East and Linden-McKinley.[177] At the same time, the Ohio Civil Rights Council's teacher integration formula, fully implemented by 1975, seemed to be undermining discipline and morale at predominantly black schools, where experienced black teachers were often replaced by younger whites with little understanding of their new pupils' culture or circumstance. "The loss of more experienced staff," observed a consultant sent to study the plan, "has had a drastic and sometimes unmanageable impact on those schools severely affected." Moreover, the consultant reported, minority teachers sent to white schools "appear to be alienated, isolated, and have not been in many instances offered a full partnership in the educational process of those schools." Asserted East principal Ed Willis, "Many parents of inner-city children have expressed discontent and frustration at this agreement and view it as just another trick played on them by the white majority."[178] This conspiratorial vision of desegregation, not uncommon among African Americans, found its most vociferous local voice in radio-personality-turned-politician Bill Moss.[179]

Finally, any attempt to eliminate illegal segregation was going to cost money. In November 1976, Columbus voters rejected a 6.2-mill operating levy, forcing the board to make cuts in its inflation-ravaged budget that Superintendent Ellis called "virtually immoral."[180] Uncertainty over desegregation, along with more general antitax sentiment, clearly contributed to the levy loss, a link frequently emphasized by the board majority. Said Ellis, "Some people apparently were afraid that if they provided additional money for the schools, somehow we would use those dollars to buy buses and engage in forced busing."[181] *Penick* thus proved a twofold curse at the polls: opponents of desegregation who resented the issue's being in the hands of unelected judges could vent their frustrations by voting against the school levy; similarly, those who mistakenly viewed desegregation as a political choice rather than a judicial mandate believed that by voting down the school levy, they could vote down desegregation.

Duncan was keenly conscious of the wrongs that could result from even well-intentioned efforts to ensure constitutional rights. "A case such as this one is disturbing," he wrote, "because of the social costs which can be associated with the implementation of a remedy. Depending upon the school system involved, these social costs can include substantial expenditures of public funds, inconvenience and hardship for students, unrest on the part of various segments of the community involved, and flight by white residents from the desegregated school district, often resulting in more pronounced racial imbalance and in a loss of tax base." By tying legitimate worries about the consequences of remedial action to his unconditional duty to uphold constitutional rights, Duncan hoped to send calming signals of judicial flexibility and concern to the community. "While the plaintiffs must, and will, receive vindication for the deprivation of their constitutional rights," he wrote, "the social costs should not be forgotten in the formulation of a remedy." He added, "A desegregation remedy that may be so burden-some upon a school system as to impair its basic ability to provide the best possible educational opportunities, is no remedy at all." [182]

Like Justice Brennan in *Swann*, Duncan incisively understood the importance of tone. Convinced that confrontation could only hinder the effectiveness of a remedy, Duncan carefully crafted the language of his decision to be complex but uncomplicated and to es-tablish guilt without emphasizing blame. Knowing that blasting current board members would inflame their opposition, Duncan steered clear of condemnation, even going so far as to describe the "recent efforts of the Columbus defendants" as "in many ways highly commendable." "I tried to write the decision," he said, "to let people know that I felt no animus, that this is what the law de-cided and there was no other way to do this." [183]

With controversy inevitable, clarity was essential. "One of the things that I was always concerned about," he recalled, "was 'Will the people understand this case?'" To ensure that they did, Duncan largely spurned confusing and alienating legalese, making "a stud-ied attempt to write [the decision] at about the eleventh-grade read-ing level." [184]

Ultimately, of course, Duncan knew that his efforts to address the concerns of the community could neither convince nor convert. "I always had the feeling," he said, "that if this thing were ever put up to public vote, then it would probably lose. It was not something a majority of citizens would be in favor of." However, in what soci-ologist Jennifer Hochschild would call the conflict between democ-racy and liberalism in school desegregation, Duncan placed the awarding of constitutional rights above the rewarding of popular opinion. "The *Brown* principle," he wrote, "[is] still quite valid to-day, that unlawfully segregated schools are inherently unequal. Be-cause black children are expected and required to grow up, live and work in a majority white society, it is not only unlawful, it is unfair for public officials, by their actions or their inaction, to promote with segregative intent racially imbalanced schools." [185]

In order to prove that Columbus and state officials deliberately created and knowingly maintained an unconstitutionally segregated school district, NAACP attorneys during the trial traced an unbroken pattern of race-based decision making back more than a century. Utilizing a mass of historical sources and the most dramatic testimony of the trial, they had little difficulty demonstrating that by 1954, the year of *Brown*, "there was not a unitary school system in Columbus." The plaintiffs' pre-*Brown* evidence was the easiest for Duncan to interpret. It was also the most personal. "I knew all about this stuff," he said. "When I was doing my practice teaching as a senior [at OSU], the only place that an African American could do that was at Champion Avenue Junior High School." In *Penick's* most moving paragraph, Duncan wrote, "The evidence in this case harkens back to a previous era in the history of Columbus: a time fresh in the memory of some who testified at trial, when black parents and their children were openly and without pretense denied equality before the law and before their fellow citizens."[186]

The plaintiffs' claim that a dual district existed in Columbus at the time of *Brown* went undisputed by the defense. The case thus turned on a question of causation: what connection, if any, was there between segregation in 1954 and racial imbalance at the time of the trial?[187]

The defense contended that continued racial imbalance in the school district was solely the product of the city's undeniably segregated housing patterns. To keep up with Columbus's remarkable postwar growth, attorney Sam Porter argued, the district built schools at an extraordinary rate, siting them according to a racially neutral "neighborhood schools" policy. Any black-white imbalance that resulted was not the product of intentional board action, but of existing residential segregation, an independent variable beyond board control. Porter thus sought to prove that logistical necessity, not segregative intent, drove the board to build schools "where the people were." Citing the standard of proof set forth in *Keyes*,[188] Porter contended that absent such intent, existing segregation in the

Columbus Public Schools was not in violation of the Fourteenth Amendment. Moreover, he argued, the Columbus Plan and other recent actions amply demonstrated the district's good-faith efforts to enhance integration.

Duncan found the connection between city growth and school construction compelling. "That was the closest part of the case," he recalled. "The argument is that you built the new schools when the student population meteorically soared. You built the schools where the kids were. It's a good argument." Ultimately, however, "the greater weight of the evidence" presented by the plaintiffs convinced the judge that by act and omission, the school board had systematically and intentionally maintained the dual district that existed at the time of *Brown*. The defendants, Duncan wrote, had failed to prove "that the racial character of the school system is the result of racially neutral social dynamics or the result of acts of others for which defendants owe no responsibility." Nor, he added, had the defendants demonstrated "that the present admitted racial imbalance in the Columbus Public Schools would have occurred even in the absence of their segregative acts and omissions." In short, a generation after *Brown*, "nothing [had] occurred to substantially alleviate [the] continuity of discrimination of thousands of black students over the intervening decades."[189]

In his decision, Duncan extensively detailed the tools used by the board and administration to sustain segregation: new school sitings, optional and discontiguous attendance zones, gerrymandered pupil assignment boundaries, and race-based employment and appointment practices. The foreseeably segregative effects of these actions, the judge wrote, were compounded by the board's failure in the face of a significant degree of public notice to take adequate advantage of the integrative options it did have; "neither the magnet alternative school nor the Columbus Plan," he added, "will predictably provide students at [segregated] schools with their constitutional rights."[190] Race, Duncan concluded, could not be divorced from rationality in explaining the board's failure to fulfill its affirmative duty to establish a unitary system:

I am constrained, from certain facts which I believe to be proved, to draw the inference of segregative intent from the Columbus defendants' failures, after notice, to consider predictable racial consequences of their acts and omissions when alternatives were available which would have eliminated or lessened racial imbalance.[191]

Critically, Duncan concurred with the plaintiffs that residential segregation and school segregation were not, as the defense argued, independent of board decision making:

In Columbus, like many urban areas, there is often a substantial reciprocal effect between the color of the school and the color of the neighborhood it serves. The racial composition of a neighborhood tends to influence the racial identity of a school as white or black . . . The racial identification of the school in turn tends to maintain the neighborhood's racial identity, or even promote it by hastening the movement in a racial transition area . . . The Court finds that the school authorities do not control the housing segregation in Columbus, but the Court also finds that the actions of the school authorities have had a significant impact upon the housing patterns. The interaction of housing and the schools operates to promote segregation in each.[192]

Thus, the apparent racial neutrality of "neighborhood schools" only served to obscure and preserve the symbiotic efforts of housing developers and city school officials to maintain segregation. Furthermore, trial testimony revealed an overwhelming web of public and private policies supporting this relationship. Yet, while the plaintiffs painted a devastating picture of the complex and interlocking causes of urban segregation, only the public schools were on trial. Though equally complicit, bankers, lenders, developers, real estate agents, and federal officials were merely accomplices, the unindicted coconspirators of public school segregation.

Robert Duncan's *Penick* opinion was an unequivocal victory for Columbus blacks and an unambiguous defeat for antidesegregation whites, confirming what the former had known for generations while condemning what the latter had done for years. With the winners and losers of the litigation now decided, however, the case moved into its far messier remedy phase. In the order that followed his opinion, Duncan gave the city and state school boards ninety days to submit plans to desegregate the Columbus district. The antibusing intransigence of the white board majority had only made "forced busing" more likely to be included in these plans. To city leaders, this prospect evoked the chaotic spectacle of desegregation-related violence in Boston, stoking fears that a similar eruption could irrevocably mar Columbus's national image, derail its development potential, and cramp its expanding civic ambition. "A school desegregation problem," Judge Duncan wrote, "is one we could all do better without, but there is no denying that it is just that—a problem for our community—a problem that simply won't go away if left alone." [193]

2

"What We Must Do, We Must Do Well": Implementation, Desegregation, and the Divided Role of MCSC

On the morning of September 6, 1979, East High School principal Ed Willis greeted a phalanx of cameras, a crowd of reporters, and 240 tenth graders with these words: "Black people are not going back to Africa, and white people are not going back to Europe. We're going to East High School, and we're going to respect each other."[1] It was desegregation's first day in Columbus, and nowhere was its impact more dramatically felt than at East, for nearly four decades the flagship school of the black community. Busing had literally transformed the complexion of the school: its racial makeup, 99 percent black the year before, was now 55 percent white. Willis, however, would tolerate no racial turmoil. "I don't want to hear the word 'nigger,' and I don't want to hear the word 'honky,' or I'm going to deal with you," he told the morning assembly, no idle threat coming from a man 6 feet, 5 inches tall and 250 pounds.[2] For weeks, Willis had been working busily to ensure an uneventful opening: "I met with the teachers and told them, 'We can have a fight, but it can't be in September.' I met with the parents and told them, 'If you send me your kid at 7:30 in the morning, I'm going to send him back to you at 2:30 in the afternoon looking pretty much the same.'"[3] His efforts paid off. As the day progressed, East High saw no rocks, no riots, and no desegregation-related disorder. By noon, the national media were gone, and September 6 had become the most extraordinary ordinary day in the history of the Columbus Public Schools.

Because it involved such a radical racial transformation, East's opening served as a barometer for the rest of the system. Early reports from principals confirmed that desegregation was proceeding peacefully everywhere, and the day developed without significant disruption. "There were fights and there were verbal exchanges," remembered desegregation planner Calvin Smith, "but everybody seemed to keep more than their lid on." "We've gotten off to an exceptionally good start," beamed Superintendent Joe Davis. "I like to believe we've launched a winning streak."[4]

To a business elite that had come to equate peaceful implementation with successful desegregation, September 6 was a dazzling victory for Columbus, a potential civic calamity turned unexpected public relations coup. Fearful that a Bostonlike explosion of busing-related violence could permanently tarnish Columbus's image and cripple its promising economic prospects, city leaders had rallied the community behind the cause of public peace. In defining desegregation as an urban development issue rather than an educational one, however, the "growth consensus" that shaped political and economic activity in Columbus substituted civic order for civil rights.[5] Consequently, as the unifying urgency of September 6 dissolved into education's unglamorous daily routine, the kind of energy, effort, and resources committed to peaceful implementation could not be marshaled to confront the complex problems of desegregation's difficult "second generation."

"A Small, Boring Town in Ohio":
A Brief Biography of Columbus

To understand how Columbus's civic elite conceived of and confronted school desegregation, it is necessary first to understand the city's economic and social character. To do so, one must start with its geography. Flat, featureless, and wishboned by two slow-moving, inadequately navigable rivers, Columbus has always had one defining attribute: its central location. No Columbus existed when a group of prominent landowners from Franklinton, a trading post at the confluence of the Olentangy and Scioto rivers, offered the Ohio General Assembly a 1,200-acre tract on the Scioto's east bank to be used as the state's permanent capital. Seeking a conveniently central home, the legislature in 1812 chose the unsettled Scioto site over Dublin, Lancaster, Newark, Worthington, and Zanesville.[6] Columbus was thus created, and would continue to be shaped, by the convergence of government and development.

The state's new capital gradually grew into the agricultural, commercial, and political hub of central Ohio.[7] With the coming of canals in 1831, the National Road in 1833, and railroads after 1850, the city developed links to a larger flow of goods, evolving into a regional wholesale and distribution center. Still, situated in the center of the state, Columbus lacked the water access to markets and raw materials needed to attract the new industries emerging in towns like Cincinnati and Cleveland, and the primarily native-born southern and Appalachian farmers who settled the city did not actively seek such large-scale manufacturing. Moreover, the city's early elite, its wealth tied primarily to investments in real estate and commercial services, declined to risk the kind of start-up capital that manufacturing demanded. As late as 1860, Columbus's largest industry employed fewer than one hundred workers. "Small shops with limited assets," wrote historian Henry Hunker, "dominated the city's manufacturing until after 1870."[8] Columbus thus remained relatively small and resolutely rural until after the Civil War.

The 1869 opening of railroad links to the coal reserves of southeastern Ohio sparked an industrial and economic boom in Columbus. From 1870 to 1900, the city's population quadrupled while its manufacturing employment more than tripled.[9] By the turn of the century, Columbus had become a national leader in the production of shoes, railroad equipment, iron products, and carriages and buggies.[10] Critically, however, manufacturing never came to dominate Columbus the way it did Cleveland, Detroit, Pittsburgh, and the other cities of the "iron belt." Again, geography was in part destiny for the land-locked capital. Though Columbus was too far from primary shipping routes to develop into a major maker of goods, its central location made it a key crossroads for their movement.[11] The growth of governmental services accompanied the city's development as a distribution center. The prominent presence of local, state, and, after 1900, federal bureaucracies, along with the 1872 founding of Ohio State University, provided Columbus with a stable employment base. While Columbus stood as one of the nation's top forty industrial cities at the beginning of World War I, services and trade remained the largest sectors of its economy, even as manufacturing ranked first in Ohio.[12]

By the turn of the century, Columbus had developed into a city quite different from its neighbors on the Great Lakes and the Ohio River. With its comparative inaccessibility and relatively stunted industrial evolution, Columbus never became a magnet for immigration, leaving the city free of both territorial ethnic conflict and vibrant cultural flavor.[13] Columbus's service-based economy produced dependable, if unspectacular, growth, shielding central Ohio from cyclical shocks and fostering a conservative sociopolitical character largely bereft of the dynamism and disorder of ethnic politics or labor activism. If Columbus escaped the extremes of poverty that more industrial cities endured, it also never saw the accompanying excesses of wealth.[14] In the absence of the kind of vast fortunes that permitted deep-pocketed philanthropy, the growing city retained a small-town, cultural provincialism.

While Carnegies, Rockefellers, and Fords dominated the cities where their fortunes were built, their fortunes did not depend on the prosperity of these cities. The wealth of Columbus's commercial elite, however, remained uniquely and intimately tied to local investments—services, retail shops, real estate, banking—and, consequently, to the health of the local economy. "Who of us is not aware," asked the vice president of the Columbus Board of Trade in 1874, "that with the growth and prosperity of Columbus our own private interests are largely identified?" From its inception, the Columbus Chamber of Commerce actively involved itself in the politics of development, lobbying state and local officials to initiate municipal reforms and backing bond issues to pay for public improvements. Fearing the higher wages, labor unrest, and boom-and-bust upheavals that accompanied heavy manufacturing, Columbus's economic elite sought to maintain close control over a slowly but steadily expanding city, welcoming industrial development only warily.[15] Consequently, observed a 1976 Department of Development report, "growth was parochial, locally oriented and orchestrated by a power structure with a Southern small-town perspective consisting of bankers and merchants."[16]

The local dependence of Columbus business leaders bred a sense of civic loyalty and commitment to municipal matters born of economic self-interest. Embodying the often hazy distinction between public affairs, private profit, and personal power was Columbus's dominant dynasty, the Wolfe family. Beginning with the establishment of Wolfe Brothers Shoe Company in the late 1890s, Harry and Robert Wolfe built a central Ohio empire whose economic clout and political influence would span the next century. Shrouded in mystique and legend, Wolfe tentacles touched virtually every aspect of economic development in Columbus.[17] Through the family's media mouthpieces, the whims of Wolfe patriarchs could make or break political careers and proposed public policies.[18] Directly and indirectly, the Wolfes exerted unchallenged, if not unquestioned, authority over civic affairs in Columbus from the turn of the century to the onset of World War II, acting primarily on the premise that what was good for Columbus was good for the family and vice versa.[19] In the process, their devotion to orderly, controllable growth lastingly shaped the contours of Columbus's economic, social, and political development.

By 1930, Columbus had become the fourth largest city in Ohio, with a population of 290,564.[20] Because no natural barriers existed to restrain Columbus's sprawl, the annexation of undeveloped farmland had enabled what had been a "walking city" at the turn of the century to expand from fourteen to thirty-nine square miles. Unlike many of its northern urban counterparts, Columbus by the time of the Great Depression had not been encircled by a ring of suburbs. Although a real estate boom in the 1920s sparked suburban growth, Columbus remained the only incorporated city in a county that contained eighteen villages and eighteen townships. By contrast, Cleveland in 1930 had already been hemmed in by forty-eight independent municipalities and Lake Erie.[21] While the depression and World War II completely stalled Columbus's expansion between 1930 and 1950, the combination of locally dependent leadership, lack of industry, and landlocked location paradoxically left the metropolitan area underdeveloped enough to allow the city itself to spread significantly and without impediment after the war.

The depression had a less devastating effect on central Ohio than on other areas of the country, but its impact was still substantial. Columbus's real estate market collapsed, major civic projects were dropped, and not enough tax revenue could be raised to finance necessary new services. Total employment in Franklin County fell 10.4 percent from 1930 to 1940, even as the county's overall population rose 7.7 percent. The manufacturing sector of the region's economy suffered the biggest hit, falling 33 percent in Columbus from 1929 to 1935 and 26 percent in Franklin County from 1930 to 1940.[22]

With business activism declining, chamber of commerce executive Delmar Starkey took advantage of the lull to stack the chamber's board with representatives from small firms eager to attract new manufacturing plants and the subcontracting spin-offs they would bring. After becoming chamber president in 1937, Starkey bypassed the city's traditional leadership and began clandestinely pressing for industrial expansion. With America's entry into World War II imminent, Starkey's negotiations bore spectacular fruit: the selection of Columbus as the site of a federally financed, $14 million Curtiss-Wright aircraft plant.[23]

The opening of the Curtiss-Wright plant in 1941 proved an economic watershed for Columbus. At peak production, the plant employed twenty-five thousand workers, almost ten times more than any other area firm and approximately 15 percent of all Franklin County employment. The federally funded factory also sparked Columbus's first major wave of industrial unionization, breaking the hold of established, nonunionized firms such as Buckeye Steel and driving up wage levels in some economic sectors. Most important, Curtiss-Wright and the ripples it sent through the local economy lured thousands of southern black and Appalachian white job seekers to Columbus, creating both a postwar pool of available semi-skilled labor and an unprecedented drain on city services.[24]

In 1945, with production at Curtiss-Wright winding down and GIs returning from the war, Mayor James Rhodes called a handful of handpicked business leaders into his office to discuss the formation of a "citizens' committee" devoted to passing bond issues to fund desperately needed infrastructure improvements. A generation had passed since the city's last major capital improvements effort. Sudden economic growth and rapid population increase had stretched existing services to their limits. Schools were falling apart, hospitals were needed, roads had to be built, and a severe drought had prompted concerns about the city's water supply. Rhodes told his guests that if Columbus hoped to stave off civic catastrophe without inviting out-of-control growth, a carefully constructed campaign had to be waged to gain voter support for a dramatic expansion of services and infrastructure. Out of this meeting, the Metropolitan Committee was born.[25]

The creation of the Metropolitan Committee commenced two decades of coordinated private-sector influence over the allocation of public funds in Columbus. Between 1945 and 1967, an "executive committee" of twelve to fifteen invited business leaders decided what bond issues would appear on which ballot and then personally stumped for their passage.[26] Planners from the city, the chamber of commerce, and the Development Committee for Greater Columbus were enlisted as de facto staff and directed to develop the details of the bond packages the committee sought. The city and county officials responsible for formally placing these issues on the ballot,

wrote one historian, "agreed to accept whatever the Metropolitan
Committee recommended."[27] Backed by the visible and invisible
clout of Columbus's most powerful business leaders, voter approval
was almost assured.[28] The committee's campaign strategy, recalled
its unofficial chairman, Paul Gingher, was as follows: "You bring in
every group in the city. You neutralize or capture any potential opposition. The newspapers assign reporters to you, give you all the
space you need, all the propaganda you want. It was massive. The
packaging of the proposals was important. It was a matter of putting
enough things together for enough people."[29]

In eight elections over twenty-two years, Columbus voters approved forty-five Metropolitan Committee–endorsed ballot issues
that, when combined with the government matching funds they se-
cured, were worth hundreds of millions of dollars.[30] This money
financed the civic hardware of a burgeoning metropolitan area: new
schools, sewer lines, hospitals, streets, recreation centers, parks, freeways, water and sewage treatment facilities, and municipal buildings. It also underwrote the expansion of Port Columbus Airport,
the construction of Veterans Memorial Coliseum, and the improvement of existing infrastructure. In concert with the city's aggressive
annexation policy, capital improvements fund, and almost countywide water and sewer service monopoly, local business leaders were
able to facilitate a suburban boom without sacrificing the growth of
the city itself. By 1970, Columbus's population had grown to 539,469,
spread over 144 square miles.[31] (See map of postwar annexation patterns in Columbus.)

The Metropolitan Committee represented the intimate relationship between politics and development in Columbus at its most cooperative, coordinated, and effective. By forging consensus on basic
projects needed to maintain the city's geographic and economic
growth, it also papered over the potentially paralyzing factionali-
zation of a business community that often disagreed about the direction this growth should take. While the Wolfe family remained
dominant, power in Columbus became more diffuse after World
War II. From 1946 to 1963, the Starkey-led chamber of commerce

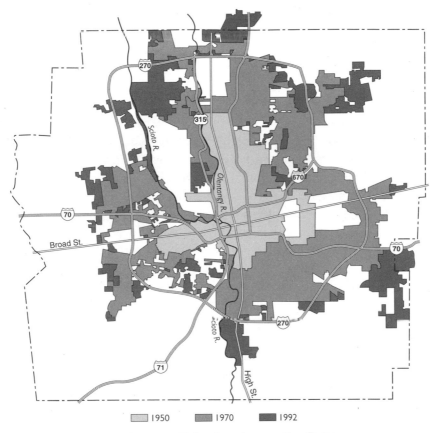

Map 2. Postwar Columbus Annexation Patterns
Source: Columbus Development Department

continued, with limited success, to pursue major manufacturing plants.[32] Meanwhile, fierce disputes emerged, one between the Wolfes and a faction led by developer John Galbreath and Nationwide Insurance over the location of downtown urban renewal, and another between the Wolfes and the Lazarus family department store dynasty over the securing of federal funds for a new dam and reservoir.[33] Thus, even as individual executives fought to direct development in

ways that would maximize their private economic interests, the
Metropolitan Committee allowed Columbus's oligarchy to pursue a
common agenda of publicly funded projects designed to sustain the
city's growth. "We had one rule," Gingher noted. "We wouldn't support any issues that benefited one vested interest or one end of
town. We only supported the things that everyone recognized were
needed."[34]

The Metropolitan Committee eventually disbanded because,
said Gingher, "the main purpose of putting the city on its way had
been accomplished."[35] Indeed, Columbus had survived the growing
pains of the postwar years to reach a kind of infrastructural maturity: freeways were completed or planned, adequate water and sewer
facilities were built, and city services were in place to meet the
needs of Columbus's increasing business and residential sprawl. By
the 1970s, the capital of Ohio had become an oasis of prosperity
amid the despair of the "Rust Belt." Unlike Akron or Pittsburgh,
Columbus had a diversified employment base that could smoothly
adapt to the nation's transition from an industrial to a service-based
economy.[36] Unlike Detroit and Cleveland, it had escaped the 1960s
without experiencing the kind of urban conflagration that could have
hollowed out its inner city, accelerated middle-class flight, and decimated its tax base. And, unlike virtually all major northern cities,
its growth was not choked off by a surrounding ring of suburbs.[37]
Columbus's bond rating was high,[38] its tax rate low,[39] and its unemployment level consistently below the national average. It was, in
short, a uniquely healthy city with promising economic prospects.

Still, like a teenager caught between awkward adolescence and
confident adulthood, Columbus remained a city in search of an image. If the 1950s and 1960s had been about becoming a major city,
the 1970s and 1980s would be about becoming a "major league"
city. For, despite its economic stability, Columbus remained undeniably, almost proudly, bland. "We do everything at almost a B-grade
level," Republican mayor Tom Moody told the Chicago Tribune.
"We may not be first class in anything."[40] While Cleveland became
the butt of countless "Mistake on the Lake" jokes, Columbus could

not shake its reputation for being, in the words of the *Wall Street Journal*, "an overgrown hick town." "[I have] yet to find an American city bereft of even one decent restaurant," humorist Calvin Trillin once observed, "although I've heard some good arguments about Columbus, Ohio." Even Johnny Carson took a swipe at the city, saying, "The most exciting thing we've ever done for [Christopher] Columbus is to name a small, boring town in Ohio after him." "Columbus," summarized a local reporter, "hasn't the distinctive pungence of the South, sprawling confidence of the West, or decline-and-fall syndrome of the East. It has, in people and environment, a wonderful, godawful irritating solidity, productiveness, conservatism, and smugness."[41]

To a new generation of business leaders emerging in Columbus during the 1970s, however, the city's lack of personality was no laughing matter.[42] The baby boom was over, jobs and people were fleeing the Snowbelt for the Sunbelt, and global competition had begun to threaten the assumed permanence of American prosperity. With both private and public resources becoming more scarce, competition to attract them intensified. Lacking stunning scenery or perpetually sunny weather, Columbus had only its elusive, undefinable "quality of life" as a promotional tool to lure the white-collar, corporate, and high-tech "growth" jobs local business leaders sought.[43] To succeed in an increasingly competitive municipal marketplace, Columbus civic leaders came to believe that their city needed both a more identifiable national image and a more ambitious self-identity. "Columbus is a good, clean, honest, stodgy city," said Ohio State economist Paul Craig. "We don't cheat, but we don't dream, either." Concurred Sherwood Fawcett, president of Columbus-based Battelle Memorial Institute, the world's largest private research foundation, "If you look at some other cities, such as Seattle or Kansas City or Atlanta, you see a dynamic thrust, a spirit that you can't help but feel. Business is good and Columbus is prosperous, but I don't feel that spirit here."[44]

Throughout the 1970s, Columbus civic leaders studied, disputed, and fantasized about the jewels that would give their sleepy city some sparkle.[45] They envisioned bustling downtown shopping, a busy convention center, top-quality cultural institutions, and everyone's ideal, a major-league sports franchise. Declared Clyde Tipton, president of Battelle's convention center development corporation, "This is the time to sit down and say, 'What do we want Columbus to be like when it grows up?'"[46]

For executives of the city's largest locally dependent companies, individual power, personal pleasure, and corporate prosperity were all bound up in the answer. Yet, while they bickered over the engine of the area's imminent ascent, Columbus business leaders carried the customs of the Metropolitan Committee into the 1970s, cooperating reflexively to preserve the conditions that made Columbus conducive to growth. As a result, they were able quickly to achieve consensus on how to confront the most ominous obstacle to Columbus's continued progress. To become "another Seattle" or "another Atlanta," the city had to avoid becoming "another Boston." "The most vexing issue to most Columbus business leaders is a social one," observed a *Dispatch* reporter, "the peaceful desegregation of the Columbus schools."[47]

"You Can't Take an Ostrich Approach": Boston, Busing, and the Creation of MCSC

By the early 1970s, the domination of Columbus's traditional patriarchs had begun to diffuse. No longer did they possess the virtually unchallenged power to set major civic priorities. New voices with new agendas—African American leaders, community activists, social service organizations, suburban interests—had an increasing impact on local affairs. Yet the influence of the oligarchy had not really waned, it had merely reconfigured to accommodate a broader range of actors and ideas. Media control, social pressure, campaign contributions, and interlocking corporate boards were just a few of the tools Columbus's business elite could use to define the boundaries of permissible political activity. As such, they exerted a sort of "third rail" authority over local matters; the Wolfes might not single-handedly be able to initiate a major project or make a political career, but they could certainly still torpedo one. Thus, even as a more diverse group of municipal movers was emerging in Columbus, access to real power remained dependent on allegiance to the cooperative culture of civic influence established by the Metropolitan Committee, a culture built around the gospel of growth.

"Virtually all U.S. cities," writes urban sociologist Harvey Molotoch, "are dominated by a small, parochial elite whose members have business or professional interests that are linked to local development or growth. These elites use public authority and private power as a means to stimulate economic development and thus enhance their own local business interests."[48] Alarmed by sharpening municipal competition, Columbus's elites by the time of *Penick* had come to define "growth" as the steady expansion of economic activity, municipal boundaries, and civic stature. Public-private cooperation was geared toward sustaining all three elements simultaneously; remove one, it was believed, and the other two would falter. Potentially divisive ideological extremes were muted by this tripartite definition, which served as an interpretive screen through which business leaders filtered major municipal matters. Given the tacit boundaries set by the city's most influential individuals and institutions, political parties in Columbus never veered far to the left or right of this centrist growth consensus.

Although different interests competed within this consensus, certain assumptions went unchallenged. Because disruption could damage property and property values, tarnish Columbus's image, and generate the kind of uncertainty that could spoil the city's favorable business climate, the imperative of civic order was perhaps the most fundamental. Strikes and other labor-related disturbances historically had little impact on Columbus, with its comparatively weak manufacturing base. Racial turbulence, on the other hand, posed a very real and potentially wrenching threat to the stability of any large, urban area. As far back as the 1920s, in the face of a massive Ku Klux Klan resurgence, white business leaders in Columbus had backed efforts to thwart racial violence and promote a baseline degree of comfort for African Americans. "There has always been some level of rather satisfactory communication between the black community and the power structure," said Robert Duncan. "The power structure in Columbus traditionally gives the black community just enough to keep it relatively happy. Whenever you push, they just sort of give up a little and they take you off guard." "They fight bush fires to keep them from becoming wild prairie fires," observed *Call and Post* general manager Amos Lynch, a chamber of commerce executive in the 1960s and 1970s. "We do things in this community to keep things from happening. We take people up to a point and we give them what it will require to allow them to survive but not to grow. . . . Enough to keep the stomach from collapsing, one side to another—as long as you're doing that, the [black] community remains very apathetic."[49]

Due at least in part to an activist chamber of commerce's efforts to reach out to moderate African American leaders, Columbus escaped the urban uprisings that scarred scores of cities during the 1960s.[50] Declaring in its 1967 annual report that "there is no question that the chief issue before our community is the problem of the socio-economically disadvantaged," the chamber brought together white CEOs and prominent figures from the black community to form the Problems of the Inner City Committee (POTIC). Though some within the chamber tagged the committee "im-POTIC," it did contribute to Columbus's relative civic calm during the long, hot summers of the late 1960s.[51] "When Dr. King got killed," Ed Willis said, "buildings were burning all over the United States, and in Columbus we were setting bonfires, we were burning leaves. It's just not a militant city." "The business community," said John Ellis, "felt that Columbus was a vibrant city with a bright future, but if chaos reigned in the streets and in the schools, businesses would be threatened and the image of the community would be damaged. . . . They couldn't tolerate riots. They couldn't tolerate burnings and lootings and vandalism and they couldn't tolerate the minority community marching in the streets and shouting, 'We shall overcome.'"[52]

By the middle of the 1970s, however, the "domestic Vietnam" of school desegregation threatened to undermine the city's history of relative racial harmony and, in turn, jeopardize its promising economic outlook. "When I came here in 1974," said WBNS-TV news director Bill Vance, "my perception was that Columbus was a town which had been wrapped in cellophane, and the late sixties and early seventies just sort of washed around it as a result. But something as pervasive and as important as schools can wipe that kind of thing away."[53]

It was the traumatic implementation of busing in Boston that galvanized city leaders to confront the controversial issue of school desegregation. On June 21, 1974, Federal District Court judge Arthur Garrity ordered a two-phase desegregation plan for the Boston Public Schools. Vowing to resist, Louise Day Hicks and the recalcitrant Boston School Committee unrepentantly dismissed the court's remedy. Meanwhile, working-class whites in two passionately territorial ethnic enclaves, South Boston and Charlestown, braced to fight Garrity's plan. As the September 12 opening of school drew near, other city leaders—Mayor Kevin White, Massachusetts governor Francis Sargent, the Boston area business community—made no attempt to brake the momentum of the antibusing movement.

As the cameras rolled, whites greeted the first black busloads to arrive in South Boston with rocks and racial slurs. The violence and anger of opening day escalated in the ensuing weeks, inflamed by antibusing protests and a white student boycott. In October, a Haitian immigrant driving through South Boston narrowly escaped after being dragged from his car by a mob of angry whites; the next day, riot police clashed with young blacks in Roxbury, leaving thirty-eight injured. Lamented the *Boston Globe*, "What we prayed wouldn't happen has happened. The city of Boston has got out of control." The following week, racial violence at Hyde Park High forced Governor Sargent to call out 450 National Guardsmen. And in December, 135 African American pupils were trapped for four hours

inside South Boston High by thousands of screaming "Southies" reacting to rumors that a white student had been stabbed. Only by
sending decoy buses to the front of the school were police able to
evacuate the students safely.[54]

The violence in Boston laid bare the hypocrisy of northern race
relations. From the city that was both the "Cradle of Liberty" and
the capital of liberalism, the nation's historical and intellectual hub,
stark images of racial warfare were broadcast nightly to the world,
eliciting uncomfortably easy parallels to Little Rock seventeen
years earlier and amplifying doubts about desegregation in the
minds of many Americans, black and white.

Noting that only four of the eighty Boston schools involved in
Phase I of the remedy experienced substantial disruption, desegregation advocates argued that the media's coverage distorted busing by
magnifying the violence that occasionally accompanied it. "It seems
there is an angry mob of white parents in the doorway of every
school in the nation either anticipating or reacting to a court order
to desegregate," wrote one scholar. "But there has been much more
peaceful school desegregation than violent." The United States
Commission on Civil Rights criticized the "sensationalized report-
ing of violence in South Boston," maintaining that "for every
Boston . . . there are a dozen other communities which have received no headlines and attracted no television coverage, where desegregation is proceeding without incident."[55]

Yet by assuming that the scope of the resistance was more important than its televised ferocity, such responses misinterpreted
the national impact of the disruption in Boston. To cities facing imminent desegregation orders, that *any* violence occurred was more
relevant than how much occurred, and that *any* of it was televised
was more consequential than how it was televised. "The ugly racial
flare-ups centering around Boston schools," wrote the *Call and
Post*, "have touched a sensitive nerve with many area people who
feel that if it can happen in Boston, it may happen here."[56] Columbus civic leaders believed that while Boston could survive the enduring stain of such graphically negative publicity, a growing city
still seeking a national identity, a city like Columbus, might not.

By shifting public focus from the effectiveness of busing to its peaceful implementation, events in Boston shaped the parameters of debate in Columbus, transforming a troublesome educational and racial dispute into an urgent economic development issue. "Boston," recalled Mayor Tom Moody, "was an every night thing on television for us." To the business community in particular, the specter of Southie provided spur and subtext for desegregation preparation. The potential for violence loomed like a guillotine over Columbus's economic future, threatening the image of civic stability critical to new business development. "Boston is the prime example of lack of forward planning," Buckeye International CEO Rowland Brown told a chamber of commerce–sponsored gathering of one hundred area executives in April 1976. "It will take years to remove the scar tissue from the past many months of strife over schools in Boston, and in the meantime, Boston's image in the rest of the world has been badly damaged. . . . You can't take an ostrich approach—every city which has tried this has regretted it."[57]

A series of alarming events nationally compounded the local anxiety provoked by the violence in Boston, which continued sporadically through the Bicentennial. OSU professor Charles Glatt was assassinated in Dayton while working on that city's desegregation plan. Desegregation-related riots occurred in Louisville. And rancorous legal battles continued in Cleveland and other cities. Meanwhile, the national NAACP had arrived in Columbus, with Nate Jones confidently declaring that intentional segregation had "been proven in Boston, Dayton, Detroit and will be in Columbus." As awareness of the school district's legal destiny grew, so did dismay over the school board's increasing antagonism. Warned Jones, "One of the great ironies is that the staunchest adherents of law and order create a climate of resistance to a court order."[58]

Goaded by the absence of constructive school board leadership, decision makers in Columbus began mobilizing to neutralize the tempest that so often seemed to accompany school desegregation. Business leaders rallied behind Superintendent Ellis's contingency planning efforts, securing his job in the face of the board majority's incipient coup. Democrats and Republicans tacitly agreed to keep the issue of school desegregation out of the potentially charged 1975 mayoral race, which pitted white Republican incumbent Moody against the city's first black mayoral candidate, Dr. John Rosemond.[59] Also that fall, a group of clergy and laypeople formed the Coalition of Religious Congregations (CORC), which called on members of Columbus's religious community "to pledge themselves to pursue peaceful and productive approaches to the difficult issue of desegregated education."[60]

The Columbus Area Chamber of Commerce's School Issues Committee, meanwhile, was quietly conducting a study of school desegregation in other cities that would become the business community's blueprint for confronting the controversy. "The objective of the Chamber," the committee's report recommended, "should be to help bring about community acceptance and support of *whatever* decision is reached by the court."[61] In other words, the role of the area's economic elite should be the same regardless of Judge Duncan's ruling: ensure civic order. The chamber, the report suggested, should work proactively to remain neutral. Any perceived ideological bias could provoke resentment in the community, confrontation in the streets, and a backlash at the cash register. The historical, legal, and educational issues that desegregation involved were too complicated, controversial, and emotional to touch. Peace, however, was as easy to support as busing was to oppose.

Further research revealed that effective leadership, information, and communication were critical for community acceptance of a desegregation remedy. The experience of other cities, reported Battelle Memorial Institute researcher George Rosinger, demonstrated that these elements could best "be achieved with a *coalition* of concerned interest groups."[62] "We should help form a committee to promote peaceful accommodation to whatever decision Judge Duncan may reach," chamber chairman Robert Lazarus Jr. told an assembly of top executives, "and then work as an equal among a committee of equals." In early 1976, a committee of ten organizations already independently involved in planning for desegregation began meeting to formulate a coordinated strategy. "We grew out of a widely-felt community need to have some organization to implement what many people believed to be a forthcoming desegregation plan," chamber of commerce representative John Henle said. "We decided, 'Columbus is not going to go through the idiocy of a Louisville or a Boston.'" Said Sam Gresham, then an urban policy planner and political organizer, "The business community knew there was a change coming. But how to adapt to that change was not to resist it, it was to control it."[63]

The committee tapped Rowland Brown to pull together a broad-based group of community leaders charged with preparing the city for the outcome of the trial. Brown was at once an obvious and complex choice to organize such a group. Chairman of both the Urban Education Coalition, a local public-private advisory group, and the Citizens Council for Ohio Schools, an independent public school watchdog, he was a knowledgeable and passionate advocate of urban education.[64] At the same time, as a corporate CEO and a member of numerous local boards, he could flow easily among the city's business elite. Yet while Brown was the individual in Columbus best equipped to bridge the ideological gap between advocacy groups and corporate executives, he also embodied the tension that would ultimately break the community-wide coalition apart: the gulf between peaceful implementation and successful desegregation.

To the bulk of the business community in central Ohio, desegregation was an economic issue, not an educational one.[65] "They didn't want a PR black eye on the city of Columbus that would stop the growth that was in their economic benefit," said Gresham. "The overriding concern of the business community was: 'We don't want anything that's going to tarnish the image of the city of Columbus. We are a growing town. We're still fighting to get our name on the weather map.'" Agreed John Ellis, "The business community did not like the Boston image: that the view of your city could be dramatically altered for the worse on a permanent basis; that your image would be bad; that you would lose your people; that you'd lose your economic base; that you'd lose power because of population changes. That was one of the big fears. That was one of the few countervailing fears to the pernicious fear of racial integration."[66]

As head of Buckeye International, Inc., a manufacturing firm with nearly four thousand employees worldwide, Brown's corporate credentials allowed him to communicate credibly with business-people either ambivalent toward or hostile to desegregation. "In general," he said, they "didn't particularly have a strong view with respect to the appropriateness of court-ordered busing as a solution to the problem. They were very much concerned [about] what had happened in Boston, Detroit, Cleveland, and other areas." In a letter to Mel Schottenstein, prominent lawyer, developer, and head of the Columbus-based Yassenoff Foundation, Brown outlined "the economic impact an unsuccessful implementation would have" on central Ohio: "Borderline businesses would move out of the area, new businesses would not want to locate here. Property values would not be at realistic levels. Columbus values would go down while property values in areas outside Columbus would go up. This means less revenue for the city, therefore the possibility of reduced city services. With business moving out and people moving out, jobs would be lost. The entire Central Ohio area would be a less attractive place to live. Many businesses look at the quality of the school system in a given area as an indication of the strength of the area."[67] By tying continued economic stability to the unpredictability of implementation, Brown convinced business leaders that the funding of a temporary, community-wide coalition was indispensable to the preservation of peace.

However, while Brown understood his corporate colleagues' view of desegregation as an economic minefield, he also carried a deep personal commitment to the concept of integration as an educational ideal. Brown considered court-ordered desegregation a foregone conclusion in Columbus. As such, he regarded it not as a looming disaster but a golden opportunity, a unique chance to generate enduring areawide interest in the city schools. With good luck and skillful maneuvering, he believed, a temporary coalition formed to ensure peaceful implementation could be transformed into a permanent organization devoted to fostering quality integrated education. "I consider the ultimate goal of this group much more than just 'cooling it,'" he told fellow committee members in mid-1976.[68]

Thus, while ideological neutrality was necessary to sustain the support of the business community, Brown himself was a well-established champion of integration. Moreover, though admired, Brown was never fully embraced by the entrenched power at the center of the city's corporate elite, which perceived the graduate of both Harvard and Harvard Law as an East Coast liberal with shallow roots in the community. "I remember once at a dinner party the night after the Michigan–Ohio State football game," explained attorney John Elam, then chair of the chamber's Quality Education Committee. "Rowland said, 'I don't understand. People are talking about The Game. The Game—that's Harvard-Yale!'"[69] To compound this perception, Brown was linked to a liberal chamber leadership coming under increasing fire for neglecting economic development in favor of a kind of noblesse oblige social activism.

All of this meant that Brown had the capacity to convince but not the clout to convert. Only the danger of disruptive implementation could persuade business leaders to contribute their resources, money, and civic prestige. Conversely, Brown's more long-range vision was already shared by the service organizations and advocacy groups whose representatives would be responsible for the day-to-day work of the committee. Thus, in shaping a diverse, broad-based coalition, Brown had to balance conflicting conceptions of just what such a coalition's mission should be. The statement of purpose subsequently adopted by the group, which by late 1976 had named itself the Metropolitan Columbus Schools Committee (MCSC), endorsed both peaceful acceptance of the district court order and quality education in the Columbus schools.[70] In embracing both while maintaining a conspicuous neutrality, MCSC's formal guidelines endowed the organization with the flexibility to respond to fluctuating circumstances, enabling it to hold together an inherently unstable alliance for the next four years.[71] At the same time, by pragmatically endorsing peaceful implementation rather than successful desegregation, MCSC's mission statement tacitly acknowledged that the two had essentially become synonymous.

Backers of both visions of MCSC laudably wanted to see the buses roll in Columbus without incident. Beyond issues of basic safety, however, their motivations for participating in the coalition fundamentally diverged. Those who considered desegregation an educational good regarded peaceful implementation as a necessary first step down the long, unexplored path to "quality integrated education." On the other hand, those who viewed desegregation as a potential development disaster (and "effective desegregation" as an oxymoron) envisioned peaceful implementation as the relieving conclusion of an emergency effort to preserve Columbus's potential for growth. With peaceful implementation the starting gate for one faction and the finish line for another, the goal that brought MCSC together contained the seeds that would break it apart.

"Raising Hell Is No Way to Raise Our Children": Setting the Boundaries of Dissent

Response to Judge Duncan's March 8, 1977, *Penick* ruling revealed the extent to which a "law and order" consensus had already been reached in Columbus. Major newspapers, civil rights organizations, city hall, MCSC, and the chamber of commerce all called on the school board to accept the decision and proceed quickly and quietly with developing a desegregation plan. Though the board voted 4–3 the following week to appeal, it also agreed unanimously to begin formulating a remedy.[72] "I dislike using children as pawns in a chess game," Virginia Prentice declared. "I want to make it crystal clear, however, that the judge has ordered us to desegregate the schools, and I urge the citizens of this community to obey the law."[73]

The months immediately following Duncan's decision were marked by the conspicuous quiet of a city holding its collective breath. The judge's firm but flexible ruling offered few specific clues as to just how extensive a remedy had to be to pass constitutional muster. Moreover, by granting remedy-formulating responsibilities to new superintendent Joe Davis rather than outside consultants, Duncan temporarily placated school officials already resentful of court control. "I did not want Columbus to be incapable of developing its own remedy plan," Davis recalled. "I didn't want to force the court to choose a consultant. I thought it was in the best interests of the community if the people of Columbus had to look no further than the administration, whose salaries they were paying, to say, 'It's our plan, and we're here to live with the consequences.'" "This is a unique city," declared board president Steven Boley. "Columbus can devise a Columbus remedy by Columbus people that works."[74]

Confrontation, meanwhile, was channeled into 175 district-sponsored Community Input Panels (CIPs). Opinions at CIP meetings, desegregation planner Calvin Smith said, "ran the gamut from 'don't do a damn thing and go to prison before you do it,' to 'do whatever the judge tells you and do it better than anybody has ever done it.'" By promoting the illusion of citizen participation, CIPs served as civic steam vents for the more than four thousand individuals who attended. "Some people may not like the final plan," Davis said, "but no one will be able to say they were not heard while it was being drawn up."[75]

As details of the board's desegregation plan began to emerge, however, the facade of community tranquillity crumbled. Davis had charged a committee of six black and ten white administrators with developing a remedy by June 6 that satisfied three criteria: "Meet the requirements of Constitutional law. Be educationally sound. [And] identify the human, material, and financial resources required for implementation." By early May, district officials had conceded that the system's geography and demographics made it impossible to fulfill these commands without increasing transportation substantially beyond the seventeen thousand students already bused. Still, it seemed a shock when Davis presented the outline of a three-phase, $21 million remedy that involved the transfer of nearly half the district's students. A *Dispatch* headline screamed, "40,000 Pupils in Columbus Would Be Uprooted by Plan."[76]

On June 10, the board majority officially voted to submit a $23 million plan phasing in the busing of 39,730 students over three years.[77] The plan eliminated predominantly black schools but left a ring of twenty-one all-white schools along the district's rapidly developing periphery. White board members qualified their invocations of order with declarations of disgust. "I have gone through many hours of mental anguish trying to accept what I must do," Redden grieved. "I have voted not to approve, not to defend, but to submit this plan. I ask all fellow citizens to work with me to uphold the law." Said Prentice, "I do not propose to like it because I do disagree with the original premise. However, the judge did order it and I expect the citizens of this city to abide by the court's decision."[78]

Desegregation advocates contended that the board majority's plan barely followed even the letter of the law. The white bloc, they argued, had adopted obstructionist tactics used by recalcitrant school boards across the country: submitting insufficiently desegregative plans that placed undue burden on African American students; inflating budget numbers to inflame public criticism; and demanding unnecessary delay in the name of adequate preparation time.[79] NAACP attorney Leo Ross blasted the submitted plan's "pockets of privilege" and accused the board majority of "dragging its feet." The *Call and Post* declared its opposition to any remedy that "would create an enclave of publicly funded white private elementary schools." "'With all deliberate speed' was acceptable in 1954," the paper editorialized, "but too slow in 1977. It is time, indeed overtime, for the school board to begin talking about a desegregation plan that is equitable and educationally sound, rather than a plan that is the minimum or less than what the court will accept." Agreed David Hamlar, "They're asking primarily what the judge will accept, rather than what is the best plan for the desegregation of the system. They lost the case in court. They're trying to win it in the remedy phase."[80]

Working with African American administrators on the planning committee, black board members put together an alternate plan that desegregated every school to within 15 percent of the district's 32 percent black enrollment. Board president Boley permitted the minority to submit the plan to Duncan but denounced it as an effort to introduce "massive busing" and racial quotas and an attempt to induce socioeconomic change via the public schools. "Our function is to educate," he asserted, "not to socialize."[81] Indeed, the white majority resisted deliberate efforts throughout the planning process to effect economic as well as racial integration. "Some of the school board members," said Hamlar, "even said things as derogatory as, 'Why put these kids in an area where the other kids have cars or nice clothes? When they see that, they will want to have those things, even if they have to steal them to get them.'"[82]

The antagonism escalated in late June when Duncan tabbed OSU dean of education Luvern Cunningham to be the court's "special master."[83] White board members, "surprised and appalled" by the appointment, criticized the author of the 1968 OSU Advisory Commission Report as an eager integrationist. The NAACP countered by saying that "the only thing that would please the defendant would be the appointment of an individual opposed to school desegregation." That same week, the Supreme Court remanded Dayton's desegregation decision, calling for more specific findings from the district court. Justice Rehnquist's ruling in *Dayton* expressed doubts that the "incremental segregative effect" of the Dayton school board's violations was sufficient to warrant the systemwide remedy that had been ordered and implemented. Rehnquist's declaration that the Dayton remedy was "entirely out of proportion to the constitutional violations found by the District Court" sent a hopeful signal to the Columbus board majority, prompting it to submit a revised plan concentrating only on the eleven schools specifically cited in Duncan's opinion.[84] While Langdon praised the new plan as the "least disruptive for parents," NAACP attorneys labeled it "hot air," "nonsense," and "ludicrous." "It would be better for the city as a whole," commented the *Citizen-Journal*, "if this board would accept the peaceful desegregation of the school system, instead of frantically grasping at legal straws to avoid its responsibilities." With remedy hearings scheduled for mid-July, the simmering quiet of spring had given way to the incendiary rhetoric of summer. "Busing the city schools' students to achieve racial balance," wrote one reporter, had become "the hottest topic in Columbus."[85]

MCSC, meanwhile, had kept a low profile since the release of Duncan's ruling, using the lull to organize a resource center of desegregation information, a speakers' bureau, and a twenty-minute audiovisual presentation called "Desegregation: A Challenge to Columbus." The committee structured its strategy around an attitude survey of registered Columbus voters conducted in the immediate aftermath of the decision. The survey identified a large local population ambivalent either in its approval or disapproval of the court order, and it recommended that MCSC concentrate on preventing this "swing vote" from shifting in the direction of disapproval. Critically, the survey found that while "'busing' and 'neighborhood schools' continue to have the same symbolic content in Columbus as they have had elsewhere . . . a majority in all parts of the city want to see the Board obey the law and white parents *not* use demonstrations as a tactic." Still, the survey said, for MCSC to ensure peaceful implementation, it would have to move swiftly to prevent the white board majority from assuming "a leadership role around which opposition [could] coalesce."[86]

Given its mission of neutrality, however, MCSC could do little to counter what its Steering Committee's April 27 minutes called "statements by certain school board members in opposition to busing that could be considered inflammatory or at least prejudicial to public acceptance of a Board plan." The May 11 minutes reflected the committee's belief that speaking out too soon could link MCSC permanently to a remedy plan that school officials privately acknowledged would contain far more busing than the community seemed prepared for, which would taint the perception of MCSC as "a peaceful leader," further alienate an already suspicious board majority, and possibly open the organization to blame if hostility to busing helped defeat a fall school levy. On the other hand, urged Steering Committee member Carol Lister, "We must act now because there is a vacuum in the community and it is fast becoming filled by words on the issue from the opposition."[87]

Indeed, as busing in Columbus moved from possibility to probability, organized and increasingly vocal resistance began to emerge. With the active support of board members Langdon and Redden, North Side homemaker and Walden Elementary parent Kaye Cook founded a local chapter of the National Association of Neighborhood Schools (NANS) in mid-May. Around the same time, Worthington real estate broker William Halley organized Citizens Against Forced Busing (CAFB). Both groups stressed change through peaceful legal and legislative means. "We're not a bunch of rednecks trying to lynch somebody or cause a riot," said Halley. "We'll try to change the law. We're a vast majority. That's the American system." Likewise, said Cook, NANS "is a peaceful, non-violent group" dedicated to "the neighborhood, color-blind school [as] the only way to achieve integration."[88]

The week after the school board submitted its initial remedy plan, however, grassroots antibusing rhetoric began to grow more inflammatory, hinting at actions beyond peaceful protest. During a packed rally at Salem Elementary, Halley responded to a woman seeking "something [she] could do within the law to keep [her] child in school here" by declaring "there is nothing short of confrontation one way or the other that will do any good." In a letter to the *Dispatch*, Cook wrote, "The purpose of NANS is to stay forced busing as well as federal intervention in schools either by a Constitutional amendment or by other means as may be necessary to accomplish this objective." Just as MCSC's official neutrality cloaked the integrationism of its leaders, the professed pacifism of antibusing groups seemed to disguise more disruptive designs. Chillingly, after touring Columbus in mid-June, University of Louisville Desegregation

Training Institute director Anthony Gamboa observed, "The divisiveness that exists in Columbus, Ohio is identical to the divisiveness that existed and continues to exist in Louisville and Boston."[89]

With the school board "falling apart" over remedy planning and a potentially volatile antibusing movement emerging, MCSC decided that city leaders needed to assume a more visible stand. During an open meeting in early June at the chamber of commerce between Rowland Brown, Mayor Moody, and several city council members, city council president M. D. Portman stated that the council stood unanimously behind the "MCSC objectives" and would "do all possible to make Columbus a model city."[90] Two weeks later, Moody told a group of seventeen representatives from CAFB and NANS, "My role as mayor of the city of Columbus is not to take sides in this, but to keep peace in the community. The only side I'm taking is the side of the law." While acknowledging his own ardent opposition to busing, the mayor, typically not given to such uncompromising language, declared, "I must enforce the law and I don't give a damn about the consequences. . . . Fight if you want in the courtroom, but not in the streets. The minute you begin to fight [in the streets], black or white, I will lock you up and put you both in the same jail cell." The economic future of Columbus, the mayor said, hinged on the preservation of peace: "If you could walk through Louisville and see the abandoned mall that two years ago was vibrant, you would see what I mean."[91]

If Moody's warning reflected a stepped-up sense of urgency among city leaders, it took a civic disaster dress rehearsal to pull MCSC itself from behind the scenes. A Fourth of July KKK rally on the steps of the Ohio Statehouse spiraled into violence when Imperial Wizard Dale Reusch returned the taunts of hundreds of demonstrators chanting "Ku Klux Klan—Scum of the land!" "The air was filled with flying debris, swinging fists, and flailing flagpoles as the battle was joined," the *Call and Post* detailed. The mini-riot shook an already jittery city. "If that is the way Columbus is going to accept desegregation," said state senator Michael Schwarzwalder, a central Ohio Democrat, "we will injure ourselves, our children, and our community for many years to come." Lamented the *Citizen-Journal*, "We have been branded nationally as a city which has turned to violence over the issue of school desegregation. We cannot let the extremists tear our city apart."[92]

The KKK disruption spurred MCSC to move forward with the opening salvo of its privately funded public relations campaign: a full-page ad in the July 27 edition of Columbus's two daily newspapers. The dramatic ad pictured an assortment of cans, rocks, and sticks in front of a STOP FORCED BUSING sign. The caption declared, "RAISING HELL IS NO WAY TO RAISE OUR CHILDREN." "Strong language?" read the copy. "That's what it seems to take to wake up some Columbus citizens to the fact that all this overreacting, screaming, and rumor-spreading is hurting our schoolchildren and our community. The funny thing is that all this carrying on and jumping to conclusions is based on confusion, myth, and unfounded rumors about a desegregation plan that, as yet, is no plan at all. . . . No matter what the decision contains, we trust the people of Columbus will accept it and join together in peaceful, positive support to make it a benchmark and a model for the entire country."[93] The ad, which MCSC Community Awareness Program chair Carol Lister conceded was "a bit of a bombshell," sent antibusers scrambling to reassert their right to peaceful resistance, exactly the response MCSC was seeking. "It was designed to capture people's attention, which it did," Brown explained. "We wanted those who oppose court-ordered desegregation to clearly disavow any resort to obstruction or 'raising hell.'"[94]

A week later, MCSC ran a second, "more upbeat" ad. "Let's make it work, Columbus," it urged over a set of children's blocks spelling out "education." "Desegregation is the most crucial challenge Columbus has ever faced. We've learned too valuable a lesson from the disastrous mistakes made in Boston, Louisville, and other cities to make the same ones in Columbus." Noted Brown, "We didn't say anybody was wrong, but how they went about trying to prove they were right was critical." Combined, the two ads braked the antibusing momentum that had been building in the city, sending an unmistakable warning to enemies of school desegregation that opposition was allowable, but disruption was not. "I think the message was pretty clear," Moody said, "that if you try to start something over this, you're going to end up in trouble and you're not going to lead a popular movement."[95]

With civic order seemingly threatened, Columbus's elite-driven growth consensus, in the form of MCSC, had responded, demonstrating once again its capacity to define the boundaries of permissible dissent. Anyone who stepped beyond these boundaries, said David Hamlar, risked being "smacked down." "We thought we might as well hit the papers with a splash," recalled MCSC executive director Don Pierce. "It was a message, and the message [was] that it's going to be peaceful, and the business community—your bosses—are behind the peace. You may disagree with it and you have a right to disagree, but we're not going to have a Boston. I think basically MCSC's job was done then. I think that set the tone."[96]

"Feeling Like a Yo-Yo": Rehnquist's Stay and the Uprooting of MCSC

Sandwiched between the two MCSC ads was Judge Duncan's July 29 ruling declaring the remedies submitted by the Columbus and state boards "constitutionally unacceptable."[97] "The entire Columbus Public School System was unconstitutionally segregated," the judge wrote. "The law requires, then, that the remedy have the hope of desegregating the entire system." After Duncan's ruling, Superintendent Davis said, "it became apparent that there could be no privileged sanctuaries in the school system."[98] Finally, on October 4, Duncan approved a Columbus board plan that desegregated every school in the system to within 15 percent of districtwide black enrollment. The judge ordered implementation the following September, reluctantly dismissing NAACP requests to begin desegregation that January. "The delay is unfortunate," he wrote, "but not to delay is unreasonable. When balanced against a more orderly and better planned fall implementation . . . the January implementation does not in my view merit the substantial risk of getting the desegregation process off on the wrong foot."[99]

Having already authorized an appeal of Duncan's *Penick* decision, the board voted 4–2 to contest the judge's remedial order as well. The appeals were consolidated, and oral arguments were heard by a three-judge panel in Cincinnati on February 15, 1978. The Sixth Circuit judges had little sympathy for Sam Porter's efforts to undercut Duncan with the "incremental segregative effect" dictum from Justice Rehnquist's *Dayton* I opinion. Before the board attorney began, Judge George Edwards warned, "You ought to know you have a big job here. You have to demolish the detailed, thorough and well-reasoned opinion of Judge Duncan." Throughout Porter's presentation, the judges peppered him with caustic questions and openly sarcastic comments. "We got bombed!" Porter, the scion of the city's largest law firm, recalled. "That's one of the worst professional experiences I've ever been around. It was *awful*. They were just all over me. The presiding judge got so mad at me he turned his chair away and wouldn't even look! It was terrible."[100]

In the panel's unanimous July 14 decision, Judge Edwards declared the *Dayton* defense inapplicable and the approved remedy appropriate. "It was not just the last wave which breached the dike and caused the flood," he wrote. "Beyond doubt the sum total of . . . violations made the Columbus school system a segregated school system in violation of the Fourteenth Amendment and thoroughly justified the District Judge in ordering a systemwide remedy."[101]

The Sixth Circuit's unambiguous ruling seemed to lift what MCSC vice chair Frank Lomax called "the cloud of uncertainty" surrounding school desegregation in Columbus. In its aftermath, the city and school district steeled for fall's apparently inevitable implementation. Stepping up police training and intelligence work, Moody declared, "We are prepared for the worst and hopeful the worst never comes. Columbus will abide by the law, and recognize the tinder box situation." While MCSC readied its massive public relations program, the school board voted unanimously to approve a Redden-sponsored "peace pledge" proclaiming its "total commitment to obeying the law." "We are hopeful that the Columbus example will prove one for other cities facing court-ordered desegregation to imitate, not to avoid," the *Dispatch* wrote. The editorial's headline captured the business community's nervous vigilance: "Obeying Court Order Key to City's Image." [102]

In early August, 83,000 students received their assignments for the 1978–79 school year; 42,000 would be sent to new schools, 37,000 would be bused. The nation's fourteenth-largest city school system, gradually girding for desegregation since late 1977, now worked feverishly to move an estimated 22,000 desks and chairs, 2,000 boxes of equipment, and 500,000 textbooks. At a gathering of administrators a month before the first day of school, Superintendent Davis declared, "We are prepared." [103]

The board majority, however, had one last legal card to play. On August 1, Sam Porter petitioned Supreme Court Justice Potter Stewart for a stay of implementation. When Stewart rejected the request without comment the following day, Porter went "justice-shopping," filing the petition next with a sympathetic William Rehnquist. Convinced that the scope of the remedy ordered in Columbus far surpassed the nature of the violations found in *Penick*, Rehnquist saw the school board's request as a gateway through which to mount an all-out challenge to a decade of desegregation law. If successful, he could transform the concept of "incremental segregative effect" into controlling precedent, effectively precluding the possibility of systemwide remedy. [104]

On August 11, Rehnquist ordered an indefinite stay of implementation pending the Columbus school board's petition for Supreme Court review. Not even the power of protocol could prevent the justice from reversing Potter Stewart's original rejection. "While I am naturally reluctant to take action in this matter different from that taken by [Stewart]," he wrote, "I am of the opinion that the Sixth Circuit in this case evinced an unduly grudging application of

Dayton." In a memo to the Court, Rehnquist justified the authority of his action while tacitly acknowledging its audacity: "It is my understanding that an applicant for a stay may go from Justice to Justice, and that even though he is turned down by eight of the nine Members of the Court, the ninth member nonetheless has the authority to grant it. Obviously, for a ninth Justice to go in the teeth of the recorded views of his eight Brethren would smack of arrogance, but that goes to the question of the wisdom of the action rather than the authority for it."[105] Though John Paul Stevens agreed to the NAACP's request that the Court convene a special session to review Rehnquist's stay, the majority of the justices, vacationing around the country, were ambivalent toward or opposed to such an extraordinary action. Cautioned Burger, "Justices cannot get involved in a continuing 'ping-pong game.'"[106]

Rehnquist's order, recalled Porter, was "the only stay that was ever granted that stopped the process" of implementation. "We were in shock," commented one school administrator. "It was like putting the brakes on a speeding train."[107] The following day, an overjoyed board majority voted to revert to a "status quo" school year.[108] Antibusing activists volunteered to do anything from stuffing envelopes to moving furniture to get the schools "back to normal" by September 7.[109]

Black leaders, on the other hand, expressed a mix of outrage and anxiety at an action they viewed as a local manifestation of a national conservative backlash against African American advancement. Upon learning of the stay, said Columbus Youth Services Bureau director and MCSC Youth Task Force chair Clifford Tyree, "I experienced feelings that I had felt only on three previous occasions—the death of President John Kennedy, Dr. Martin Luther King, and Senator Robert Kennedy—the feeling of anger, disbelief and frustration." "I'm worried about what the mood of Columbus and the mood of the state and the mood of the nation is," said Hamlar. "The only protection minorities have is the court, and when the court starts turning on them, it's almost like backing a guy in the corner. He's got to fight his way out." Stated Columbus NAACP

President Tom Fullove, "Our efforts to wipe out segregation and discrimination in Columbus, Ohio are starting to take a beating. Segregation is the water for a growing fervor of discrimination, racism, unemployment and poverty. If black people have not recognized this yet, then we had better start learning how to 'Shuffle' and 'Yes sir boss' again in order to live in this town." [110]

Caught in the middle, meanwhile, was an MCSC thoroughly surprised by and utterly unprepared for Rehnquist's stay. For the better part of a year, the organization had been working on two fronts to ready the city for desegregation that September. A multifaceted public relations campaign had been assembled that included an onslaught of television, radio, and print ads scheduled to begin ten days before the start of school. At the same time, MCSC task forces established programs designed to foster positive leadership within desegregated schools and productive communication between communities linked by the remedy.[111] By postponing desegregation indefinitely, however, Rehnquist's stay forced MCSC to shelve the PR offensive and suspend the task force programs. Robbed of any immediate role, MCSC suddenly found itself facing troubling questions about its identity and its future. "It is undoubtedly frustrating, feeling like a yo-yo," Brown told an August 16 special meeting of the Steering Committee. "If our purpose was to deal with frustrations of the community, we must first deal with our own frustrations." [112]

To some on the Steering Committee, Rehnquist's stay warranted a fundamental shift in the group's mission, from promoting quality education and peaceful acceptance of federal court orders to pressing actively for integration within the Columbus Public Schools. "'Busing' is a fake [issue]," Capital University president Thomas Langevin argued. "We are for peaceful, integrated, quality education." In his poststay statement to the press, Rowland Brown declared, "We have a strong commitment to achieving higher quality education and greater opportunities for integrated educational experience in Columbus. We have never accepted the proposition that quality education had to suffer by reason of school desegregation in the school system." [113]

Others, however, argued that the organizational integrity of MCSC should not be compromised by individual impatience and frustration. "People should not confuse their personal philosophy with the functions of MCSC," Steering Committee member John Henle cautioned. "It is important to realize that people here wear at least two hats—this Committee plus a strong interest in integrated education; but I would like to stress that it is important for everybody in the group to re-read the purpose of the Committee. We have been subject to the attack that this group is pro-busing and interested in speedy integration. Its purpose was to respond to court orders." MCSC could use its official commitment to "maintaining quality education in metropolitan Columbus" to justify its continued existence.[114] The problem, as Henle recognized, was finding a way of translating this commitment into action without jeopardizing MCSC's already precarious position as a neutral coalition devoted to the promotion of civic peace.

Indeed, while MCSC had effectively conveyed the message that disruption and demagoguery would not be tolerated in Columbus, its stated neutrality left it largely powerless to counter criticism. As a result, antibusing leaders on the board and in the community were able effectively to portray MCSC as what one writer called "some kind of pro-busing *bête noire,* dominated by suburban liberals whose kids would never see the inside of a public school."[115] Particularly feisty was the telegenic head of NANS, Kaye Cook. Over the course of a year, Cook had become the main mouthpiece of the antibusing movement in Columbus, positioning NANS as a law-abiding champion of nondiscrimination and freedom of choice. In the process, she developed a public prominence far out of proportion to the size of her organization. Describing one televised debate with Moody, Cook recalled, "During the cutaway, he said, 'You're really good. When this whole thing is over with, I'm going to have you working for me.' I looked at him and said, 'Mayor, when this thing is over with, you might be working for me.'"[116]

That Cook's debate opponent was Moody, himself an avowed critic of busing, demonstrates one of MCSC's unexpected problems:

the absence of a pro-desegregation organization in Columbus to counter the accusations of antibusers.[117] This void was due in part to the participation of so many civil rights groups and African American community leaders in MCSC. On a deeper level, however, it reflected the basic fact that there simply *were* no "probusing" advocates.[118] In fifteen years of antisegregation protest, no black leader had ever demanded or endorsed busing as an end in itself. Rather, blacks viewed busing as one tool among many at the disposal of school officials charged with providing equal educational opportunity.[119] The anger that followed the stay was directed not at Rehnquist's suspension of busing but at a school board that seemed to expend far more effort avoiding its constitutional charge than answering it. Asked Curtis Brooks, executive director of the Columbus Metropolitan Area Community Action Organization (CMACAO), "How can we teach [our children] to respect the 'Star Spangled Banner' if our leaders are still whistling 'Dixie'?"[120]

Black anger at the school system's persistent refusal to integrate, however, masked a growing ambivalence about desegregation itself. Earlier in the decade, white resistance seemed only to fortify black determination to gain equal access to the resources of the school district. "The huge overwhelming majority [of blacks]," said Duncan, "figured that the South Boston situation just presented another fight and we had to go out and win that kind of a fight: 'Those people are the enemy and we've got to overtake them to get across this line into this promised land.' And what's in the promised land? I don't think anybody thought too much about that."[121]

A decade of opposition, however, had transformed the language of public debate over desegregation; concern for equal educational opportunity seemed increasingly overwhelmed by contempt for "forced busing," "neighborhood schools," and "racial balance." Twenty-five years after *Brown,* many blacks were beginning to ask themselves if desegregation in bad faith might be worse than no desegregation at all. Will Anderson, director of the district's pre-desegregation staff development programs, used an apocryphal conversation with a bigoted white teacher to explain this hollow, haunting sentiment: "'Did you go through the [staff development] training?' 'Yes, I went through the training.' 'Were you sensitized?' 'Yes, I was sensitized. I'm going to try to teach those niggers better.'" With growing legitimacy, some blacks argued that desegregation was inherently destructive; school board member and antibusing zealot Bill Moss consistently characterized "so-called desegregation" as a conspiracy designed to sustain white supremacy by inflaming racial tensions and robbing blacks of control over the education of their children. Following a forum on the question "Is desegregation good or bad for the black community?" a *Call and Post* reporter concluded, "Consensus in the black community seems to be that desegregation per se is not what is important. What is important . . . is what happens in the classroom. What's being taught, who's doing the teaching, how those persons are responding to the needs of students and the quality of available facilities, the community seems to believe, are more important questions to be answered."[122]

For many Columbus African Americans, an enduring and inertial faith in the benefits of integration ultimately outweighed justifiable misgivings about the process of school desegregation.[123] The ambivalence that existed, however, meant that no organized opposition would emerge to combat the crusading ardor of the antibusers. "[It] would have made it easier," Henle said, "if there was a parallel on our left to the anti-busers, because then some of the kooks would be throwing their barbs at them." Instead, MCSC became, by default, the designated villain of antibusing forces on the board and in the community. By the time of Rehnquist's stay, MCSC had been successfully painted as a "pro-busing, pro-desegregation advocacy group."[124]

The difficulty of sustaining a claim to neutrality in the face of this perception of partiality straitjacketed MCSC's poststay movements. Absent the urgency of imminent desegregation, it could find neither the mandate nor the money to expand its role. Since its inception, MCSC's cash flow had come from separate streams emblematic of the divergent visions within the organization. Federal grants underwrote its major grassroots efforts, the Youth Task Force and Cooperating Neighborhoods programs. Local, private sector donors, meanwhile, funded the Community Awareness Program, MCSC's elaborate public relations campaign.[125]

Efforts to merge the two streams in the lull following Rehnquist's stay, however, proved futile. With the pressing imperative of peaceful implementation temporarily relaxed, local business leaders were reluctant to pay for programs designed to enhance acceptance not of the court's orders, but of integration itself. Moreover, MCSC's welcome had been worn down by both the drawn-out time line of desegregation and the relentless criticism of antibusers. Describing how doubts about MCSC's continuing relevance made it difficult to pry more money from local foundation and chamber of commerce coffers, Brown told the Steering Committee, "Our problem is not in the staff but at the trustee level. They are tired of hearing from me. [Executive Director Don Pierce] and I are told we have a vested interest." Though he "personally" agreed that the organization's endeavors should extend beyond implementation, John Henle confirmed that the chamber held "a narrower view of MCSC's role: work toward peaceful acceptance of school desegregation."[126] As a consequence, MCSC operated for the first half of 1979 on a bare-bones budget of $20,000.

Rehnquist's action had lifted not just the urgency of desegregation's imminence, but also the sense of its inevitability. "No matter how you slice it," Brown told the Steering Committee, "our present School Board wants to suppose there is no desegregation in sight." The leaders of MCSC's task forces agreed: "In some segments of the Columbus community, the stay has created the illusion that desegregation will never occur in Columbus. This misconception has resulted in apathy and the assumption by some that the issue is now and forever dead."[127]

Steering Committee members feared the stay might dangerously relegitimize radical opposition to desegregation. "The potential for non-compliance, major civil disobedience, and violence remains," one private report read. "The situation is now more serious since community involvement in the desegregation process could be more difficult in the future." "In September," asserted an MCSC application for federal funds, "the community—while not liking the idea of busing—was ready to accept the idea of peaceful implementation. Now, after the stay, a prevalent attitude appears to be summed up in this statement, 'See, even a Supreme Court judge says that Duncan's decision is wrong.' Without organized community effort and leadership, the once well-prepared groundwork will yield unproductive results that will produce only community discord."[128]

Penick's April 24, 1979, Supreme Court hearing only exacerbated the fears and frustrations of MCSC officials.[129] Guided by sympathetic questions from Rehnquist and Lewis Powell, Sam Porter confidently laid out the board's claim that the violations cited by Judge Duncan "were isolated findings that . . . cannot support a system-wide remedy." Arguing for the first and only time before the high court, the school board's attorney redeemed himself for the debacle in Cincinnati a year earlier. "Porter's reception in the Supreme Court," wrote NAACP attorney Paul Dimond, "was considerably more friendly than the one he suffered at the hands of the Sixth Circuit. As I listened at counsel table, I had the sinking feeling that the decision had already been made." "When we left," Porter recalled, "they carried me out on shields. They thought I'd won that case. I did too."[130]

By early summer, many had come to believe that a rightward-leaning Supreme Court would further delay, drastically curtail, or even reverse Columbus's desegregation remedy.[131] For the first time, MCSC was forced to confront the discouraging prospect of promoting public acceptance of a court decision with which the desegregation advocates on the Steering Committee fundamentally disagreed. "If a finding of liability would be reversed," warned John Henle, "a strict interpretation of our statement of purpose would be that the schools had done nothing wrong. In the event that happens, we will have a lot of personal problems." "These meetings are getting more depressing," Anti-Defamation League representative Carol Lister complained in mid-May. "We have to establish a demilitarized zone in this room."[132]

Demoralized by public criticism and paralyzed by a lack of private support, MCSC officials fretted that months of inactivity had crippled the group to such an extent that it could not even respond effectively to a favorable ruling. "Our situation is like planting a tree and nurturing it for two years," said OSU president Harold Enarson, "then pulling the tree out by the roots, [replanting] it and expecting the tree to flourish." [133]

"What We Must Do, We Must Do Well": MCSC and the Campaign for Peaceful Implementation

The wait for word from Washington continued through June, the days passing agonizingly without a decision. Speculation grew that the delay signaled deep divisions on the court, that the justices were in a battle over the soul of school desegregation a quarter century after *Brown*. Finally, shortly after 10:00 A.M. on July 2, the last day of the Supreme Court's 1979 spring term, the ruling came down.[134] "For the reasons set forth in the opinions filed with the clerk," Justice Byron White announced, "the judgments of the Court of Appeals for the Sixth Circuit are affirmed."[135] Writing for the majority, White declared that, "the [Columbus] board's conduct at the time of the trial and before not only was animated by an unconstitutional, segregative purpose, but also had current, segregative impact that was sufficiently systemwide to warrant the remedy ordered by the District Court." Deferring to Duncan, White found "no apparent reason to disturb the factual findings and conclusions entered by the District Court and strongly affirmed by the Court of Appeals."[136]

Though by no means the definitive statement some expected, the Columbus ruling, along with the Court's accompanying Dayton decision, arrested at least temporarily the antidesegregation course the court had taken for the previous five years.[137] "These are the

decisions that determine which century modern America cele-
brates," commented the *New York Times*, "the post-Reconstruction
abandonment of black Americans, starting in the 1870s, or the birth
of liberty heralded by the 1770s. . . . Columbus showed a pattern of
segregative choice that the justices could not condone." Twenty-
eight months and one false start after Robert Duncan's original order, the highest court in the land had sanctioned the systemwide
desegregation of the Columbus Public School District. Wrote the
Citizen-Journal, "The federal suit charging Columbus schools with
illegal racial segregation was filed six years ago. Many of the facts
cited during the local trial go back for decades. It is time for Columbus to get on with desegregating its public schools—justice demands it." [138]

At a closed-door meeting with the school board on July 12, Duncan pronounced fall implementation "unavoidable." Three weeks
later, the judge firmly rebuffed the board's last-ditch pleas for delay,
formally declaring that "full implementation of the remedy plan
must commence for all grades in September, 1979." [139] Neither cost
nor convenience, he admonished, could obstruct the "timely vindication of Constitutional rights." Ironically, the speed with which
the district dismantled desegregation in 1978 boomeranged in 1979,
as Duncan responded to the board's logistical laments by dryly sug-
gesting that it "call upon the experience gained in the rapid resched-
uling of students last year after the Supreme Court stay order was
entered." In his conclusion, Duncan returned to the melding of civic
and Constitutional concerns that had so animated his original order:
"The plaintiffs' day for the enjoyment of rights according to our law
has arrived. Any further delay will only make more burdensome an
already arduous undertaking. We of this community must get on
with it with a view to the day when this court's involvement in the
affairs of the Columbus school district will be concluded. The
sooner the better." [140]

As abruptly as Rehnquist's stay had uprooted MCSC, White's
opinion replanted it. "MCSC is in business," Brown told a rejuve-
nated Steering Committee on July 2, "and what we are being asked

to do is exactly what we are structured to do." With MCSC as the institutional rallying point, the mechanisms of the city's growth consensus immediately produced a flurry of activity aimed at ensuring civic order. Businesses "loaned" executives to MCSC to assist with public relations and administrative tasks. Banks donated money for a full-page newspaper ad. Foundations and corporations kicked in the additional funds needed to fine-tune MCSC's Community Awareness Program. Politicians predicted peace, the police department prepared for violence, and the board of education unanimously restated its "total commitment to obeying the law."[141]

Having exhausted all avenues of legal protest, antibusing board members publicly embraced the goal of peaceful implementation. "I didn't give a hang if we did anything or not," Redden recalled. "I was almost ready to defy the court—that's how adamant I was that we were doing the wrong thing. [But] we are to obey the courts, we are to obey those over us, regardless of what they are. . . . That was the only thing that kept me from going out on a limb."[142] Virginia Prentice, whose itch for higher office had moderated her once unflinching opposition to desegregation, captured the reluctant resolve of the board majority with a phrase that would become the district's implementation credo. Standing before an MCSC-sponsored assemblage of business, political, and community leaders, Prentice proclaimed, "What we must do, we must do well!"[143]

With implementation imminent, hectic preparations commenced to ready the district for its September 6 opening day. The Columbus Council of PTAs organized thousands of volunteer "soothers" to greet students at bus stops and welcome them at schools, while the Coalition of Religious Congregations pledged to have at least one clergy member meet the buses at every building. Principals and teachers held open houses to introduce parents to their children's new surroundings. "Activity buses" began running with the opening of fall high school sports practice; drivers were given special training and a thirty-three-page handbook emphasizing their importance as front-line representatives of the district. Finally, well aware of the danger of misinformation, the administration resurrected FACTline, a telephone information bank eliminated by budget cuts earlier in the year. For a month after Duncan's August 2 order, its four phones were inundated with four to five hundred calls a day.[144]

FACTline also doubled as the "nerve center" of a "community information and rumor control plan" linking 270 East State Street, the district's central administrative offices, with the Columbus police department.[145] Officials considered a positive police presence essential to peaceful implementation, particularly in light of the department's painful legacy of police brutality and its historically antagonistic relations with the black community. "The demeanor of police officers was a very substantial problem," said Moody. "There was a lot of work to be done simply to change the vocabulary and the approach of these officers."[146] After studying police tactics in Louisville and Boston, the department assigned over half of its entire force to twelve-member security teams.[147] The officers received at least seven days of special training, including psychological and sensitivity orientation designed to familiarize them with the unique circumstances of school desegregation.[148] At a daily cost to the city of $300,000, the department's specially equipped force would be dispersed throughout the district during the first few days of implementation. Its ultimate goal, noted Desegregation Task Force chief James Rutter, was to go unneeded: "We trained for [violence] and are prepared for it. But if we don't have to use that money, we're not going to."[149]

Meanwhile, the school system's transportation planners worked intensively to re-reconfigure the district. To desegregate every school to within 15 percent of the system's 35.6 percent black enrollment, an estimated 35,636 students would be bused, twice as many as the year before. Two thousand bus pick-up points—triple the 1978 total—were designated, most within sight of the rider's front door. The district's transportation routes, Joe Davis liked to point out, totaled 31,000 miles a day, the equivalent of six times around the earth every week.[150]

It was amidst this blizzard of behind-the-scenes activity that MCSC finally assumed center stage, dusting off the media campaign Rehnquist's stay had shelved the year before.[151] As opening day approached, the faces of five Columbus elementary school students, three white and two black, began appearing all over the city. Gazing from forty-six billboards and two thousand posters, all earnest eyes and plaintive smiles, the innocent quintet accompanied a simple slogan: "We All Look Up to You." The same phrase was repeated in 738 radio spots and 62 television ads, the final line of a ubiquitous jingle that became the theme song for Columbus school desegregation:

> Think of us Columbus, and give us kids a break.
> Stop and think it over, our futures are at stake.
> Remember we'll be learning from what we hear and see.
> So think about the kind of kids you want us kids to be.
> Think of us Columbus, no matter what you do.
> Remember this September, we all look up to you.[152]

The messengers were small, but their message was powerful. "It was kind of a guilt trip," said John Henle. " 'Don't screw up these children's future.' "[153]

Developed by Hameroff-Milenthal, a local advertising agency, the positive yet pointed media blitz was the centerpiece of MCSC's $300,000 Community Awareness Program.[154] "We treated it much like a campaign," Brown explained, "a campaign for education and non-violence." Like a political party, MCSC utilized every available outlet to take its message to the citizenry: PTAs, cheerleaders, churches, talk and call-in shows, company newspapers, unions. Even the legendary Woody Hayes, Ohio State's former head football coach, was pressed into service, telling an assembly of student leaders, "When you win, you win together." In the process, the committee sought to create a climate in which complying with the court order was considered both a parental obligation and a civic duty. "The smartest thing MCSC did," said Brown, "was to develop the idea that the people of Columbus, the parents and everybody, had a responsibility not to let the children down. We had the vast majority of the people in the city, including parents who were very disturbed by busing, feeling like they owed it to the children not to vent their spleen."[155]

MCSC's media offensive even seemed to make antibusers long for school desegregation, if only as a way to escape the omnipresent advertising jingle. "Whenever I hear the phrase 'we all look up to you,'" read one letter to the *Dispatch*, "I grab my nearest bottle of aspirin. Yes, it actually gives me a headache. Why? Because they are pushing this busing ad down our throats. I hope when school does start, this disgusting commercial will end." The *Dispatch* called Nicole Arena, a red-haired, freckle-faced fifth grader featured in the television spot, "better known right now in these parts, probably, than [TV stars] Loni Anderson or Catherine Bach." Anyone unable to recognize the phrase "we all look up to you," commented the *Citizen-Journal*, "qualif[ies] as a hermit."[156]

The coda to MCSC's campaign was a final full-page newspaper advertisement funded by the city's three largest banks.[157] So different from the bombshell two years before, the ad pictured a child's drawing of smiling stick figures, an old-fashioned schoolhouse, and an American flag. Scrawled in crayonlike letters over the binder-paper background was the message, "New faces, new places, but school is still school." For the national media descending on Columbus, the campaign had become as significant a story as desegregation itself, a lesson in transforming urban controversy into civic mission. "Columbus is going to take a test tomorrow," Joe Davis declared the day before implementation, "and the whole nation will be watching. I have every reason to believe we shall pass this test and demonstrate that Columbus is a city to be reckoned with in the future." Though police reports warned of disruption from outside extremists, desegregation planner Damon Asbury later said that "we had had very little happen in the community to suggest that there was going to be any kind of violence." By the time the buses rolled, said Moody, "it is my gut feeling as a politician that we ended up with over 90 percent of the people in Columbus understanding that obeying the law and making the best of it was the smart way to handle things. It became popular to be peaceful."[158]

"Declare Victory and Disband": Peaceful Implementation, Successful Desegregation, and the Demise of MCSC

In an employee newsletter sent out a week before opening day, Superintendent Joe Davis wrote, "To my knowledge, we are the only major city in the country that will be implementing a full-scale remedy plan this fall, and it is inevitable that we will be the focus of a great deal of attention." Indeed, as desegregation dawned on a clear, muggy Thursday, it was greeted by a media barrage unprecedented in the district's history. To cover what WTVN-TV news director Mark Pierce called the "most important thing to happen to Columbus in many, many decades," the three local television outlets dispatched at least six news crews apiece, while the *Dispatch* sent out over thirty reporters and photographers. Combined with the cameras, lights, and microphones of the national press, they formed a teeming media presence that seemed everywhere opening day. As the first bus arrived at Buckeye Junior High, Principal Larry Metz quipped, "Finally the students outnumber the reporters."[159]

If the national media had come to Columbus anticipating controversy, they uncovered only calm. Early reports phoned from relieved principals to an anxious Davis indicated that desegregation was proceeding peacefully throughout the district. Eastmoor High: "Everything started off smoothly. Roof's still on and windows are still in." Mifflin High: "So quiet the volunteers have nothing to do. Beautiful start." Brookhaven High: "Not at all different; just a different bunch of kids."[160] Pauline Radebaugh, then a school board candidate and

FACTline volunteer, recalled the scene in the administration's downtown "war room" as the day developed without disruption:

> We had desks for *Time, Life, U.S. News and World Report*, the wire services, all the major networks, radio and television—and all these people were in there. They were primed. They've got open lines, hot lines all over the country. They started getting antsy around 6:30 [A.M.]. They almost had nervous breakdowns by 8:00. They were chewing nails by 9:30. By 10:00, they were ready to leave: "You haven't done anything!" They had cars out on Fifth Street ready to roll to take them everywhere they wanted . . . to follow the riots and the violence. And they were disappointed. They were completely gone, out of downtown by noon. They couldn't find any stories. You know, "Columbus can't give us the headlines that Boston and everybody else did." [161]

"They were so used to the fact that when you don't have conflict you don't have a story," Rowland Brown said, "[that] they simply packed up their bags and left, even though they had shot thousands of feet of stuff." [162]

The uneventfulness of September 6, said Brown, was "almost unbelievable." The specially equipped officers of the Desegregation Task Force spent most of their time throwing footballs, reading, and playing cards. "We saw the police reading comic books and *Playboy* magazines because there was nothing for them to do," said PTA volunteer Eleanor Zeller. Boredom reigned in the war room, as well. "Phones were ringing and [reporters] kept coming in to see what we were talking about," Radebaugh recalled. "And I will never forget—I was answering one call and it was about vacation time. Some parents were double-checking because they had reservations to make, and this [reporter] said, 'Jesus Christ, all they want to know about is vacation!'" "Columbus is a unique city," said the school board's Steven Boley, "and I knew our citizens wouldn't react like those in Boston, Louisville, or Detroit." [163]

Other than a few minor logistical blunders, even common opening day chaos largely failed to materialize. "Usually the first day is kind of ragged," observed Willis. "But everyone has been working hard to make desegregation go. This is probably the smoothest first day that we've had in the nine years I've been here." From OSU basketball twin towers Herb Williams and Granville Waiters at Champion to the "flower ladies" at Binns Elementary, thousands of volunteers met students at bus stops and greeted them at schools. "Some of the students," the *Cincinnati Enquirer* reported, "appeared more frightened by the onslaught of adult volunteers—both black and white—than the prospects of attending a new school." Recalled MCSC Youth Task Force chair Cliff Tyree, "I have never experienced a day like that in my life here in Columbus. There was a feeling like, almost festive, of love and concern. . . . I said 'we should bottle this.'" [164]

Meanwhile, the "outside agitation" dreaded by school administrators and city officials never appeared. That, said Brown, was more than mere good fortune: "We were told several groups were coming up from Tennessee and Kentucky to raise hell. As it turned out, the state police were alerted. Whether these various steps by law enforcement officials were legal or not, the fact is these folks were 'discouraged' from coming farther north." Only a pair of bomb hoaxes and a handful of picketers hinted at the disruption dreaded for half a decade. "The beauty of the day the buses rolled," said Moody, "was that it was nothing." [165] In a tribute to the triumphantly mundane, the headline in that evening's *Dispatch* proclaimed: "Opening of Schools Is Normal." [166]

Both locally and nationally, the lack of a story in Columbus became the lead story about Columbus. "The fact that nothing had happened," *Dispatch* editor Robert Smith said, "was just as big news as if something had happened." The city's response to implementation was heralded as an inspiring demonstration of constructive leadership and community goodwill. The *Akron Beacon-Journal* gushed, "What happened in Columbus . . . should have dealt a blow to cynics and restored the faith of doubters in the basic goodness of civilized people. Children attended classes peacefully, with no more trauma than ordinarily accompanies an opening day, and with the support of the community. . . . In a world so often torn by selfishness and dissent, a city of half-million that can put aside individual differences for the good of the community and its children offers an encouraging example for all." Kudos also came from Cleveland, where an even more bitterly fought busing order would begin the following week. "The Columbus experience," commented the *Cleveland Plain-Dealer*, "shows busing can go smoothly even though it is initially opposed." Said Moody, "People across the country were saying, 'We don't know how it happened, but it worked in Columbus. They got away with it.'" [167]

In a kind of accidental alchemy, surprised city leaders saw an assumed civic stain metamorphose into public relations gold. A letter to Rowland Brown from John Hamill, president of First Trust Company, captured the business community's bewildered delight at the revelation that any good could come from desegregation: "I believe that the important message that must get across to the community and to any new businesses coming to town is that while we have busing, the impact of it will not ruin the notion that Columbus is a good city in which to live. I don't mean to whitewash the situation regarding desegregation of the schools but if, in fact, busing is not as terrible as most believe, it is then that message that has to be promoted." Somehow, peaceful implementation had not only preserved Columbus's encouraging growth prospects, it had enhanced them. "The city of Columbus has done something that probably promises more for the future of Columbus than anything else we could possibly do," Moody told a Kiwanis Club luncheon. "If we can continue this, we will not set back Columbus for three or five years. We can keep the community healthy for investment." Chamber of commerce president Al Dietzel affirmed that the beginning of busing had not impaired business recruitment. "I haven't heard anything negative," he said. "In fact, it's been to the contrary. There have been a lot of comments nationally over the way desegregation began. It's been a credit to the school system and the citizens. It speaks well for the community." Noted a *Dispatch* story, "While there will be years of debate over how busing has affected the education of Columbus students, no one argues that Columbus got a king-size helping of 'positive' national publicity." "The people who were looking at us for business dealings didn't stay away," said Moody. "[Peaceful implementation] enhanced our reputation outside the city a great deal more than the people who live here know." It also boosted Columbus's self-image, as Rowland Brown observed: "The city came away feeling very good about itself. This made it, during the eighties, a more attractive place than other cities. . . . It was quiet testimony to the character of the city." [168]

Many factors contributed to desegregation's uneventful implementation in Columbus. [169] Foremost among them, however, was the capacity of the city's powerful, business-led growth consensus to absorb dissent by marshaling its sweeping influence behind the cause of civic order. As the institutional manifestation of this consensus, MCSC justifiably received much of the acclaim bestowed on Columbus in the afterglow of implementation. Assistant attorney general Drew Days III issued a "rare" Justice Department statement expressing "congratulations to the citizens of Columbus, Ohio and to the Metropolitan Columbus Schools Committee on their splendid efforts to ensure a peaceful transition to desegregated schools." MCSC, one reporter wrote, "turned out to be a bigger story than desegregation itself. . . . Columbus may have just had the finest experience of any major city in starting school desegregation." And in its 1979 Annual Report, the Columbus Area Chamber of Commerce boasted, "We were one of the primary supporters of the Metropolitan Columbus Schools Committee, which affected a nationally unprecedented peaceful implementation of this city's school desegregation plan." [170]

The applause was a gratifying reward for the individuals who had guided MCSC through a tumultuous three years. "Since June '76," an appreciative Brown told the Steering Committee shortly after opening day, "we've come a long way." Yet Brown and his colleagues also understood that this distance had only taken MCSC to the starting line, that civic order could not be confused with "successful desegregation": "Peaceful implementation of desegregation was a positive beginning for the school system. MCSC realizes that peaceful desegregation is not the same as successful desegregation. Successful desegregation is an ongoing process requiring continuing adjustment and assistance in the transition from the logistics of desegregation to effective education in an integrated setting." In other words, while a tranquil start to the school year was imperative, the real challenges lay ahead. As the headiness of opening day dissipated, concerns reemerged about desegregation's perplexing but predictable "second generation" complications, the obvious and invisible clashes that arise when ingrained prejudices meet unprecedented racial and economic diversity. The building-level problems MCSC officials observed were confirmed by Damon Asbury, director of the district's desegregation monitoring office: escalating discipline problems; declining teacher morale; diminishing parental involvement; and racially disproportionate suspension, expulsion, corporal punishment, extracurricular participation, and special education "tracking" statistics.[171] All of these intractable dilemmas were developing in a school system that had not passed an additional operating levy since 1968, a district whose science textbooks still wondered if humans would ever set foot on the moon.

Desegregation advocates in MCSC believed that its postimplementation momentum should be channeled into addressing these issues. "There is a continuing need," a November internal report declared, "for an agency, independent of the school system, to operate a program dealing with second-generation desegregation problems."[172] For the next several months, committee members brainstormed the structure and purpose of such an agency. Should it be a school district watchdog? A desegregation monitor? An educational research group? Should it advocate specific issues, develop grassroots programs, or nurture school-business partnerships? And, the most basic question, should it proceed as MCSC or assume a new name and different mission?

Initially, committee leaders maintained that MCSC had the community credibility to proceed under a broader mandate. "MCSC is perceived as a functional, viable coalition of people interested in schools," Brown said. "We have created an image of an institution that can do Columbus some good." Moreover, officials noted, "We are the only citywide organization dealing with schools right now in the desegregated setting outside of the system."[173] However, it was business community participation that had legitimized MCSC and business community money that had sustained it. Consequently, business community support would be essential if MCSC were to continue in its existing incarnation.

Only a few weeks after the opening of school, signs began to appear signaling that such support would not be forthcoming. In the years between the formulation of MCSC and the implementation of desegregation, a significant shake-up had taken place at the chamber of commerce that marked the completion of a generational and attitudinal shift among Columbus's business elite. With the blessing of a new line of old names, an emerging crop of aggressive young entrepreneurs—impatient with the low-key leadership of President Kline Roberts—had commandeered the chamber. Roberts, they believed, had for too long emphasized social issues at the expense of the chamber's primary mission: economic development. Meanwhile, municipal competition had increased and Columbus's growth had slowed. A new brand of unabashed boosterism was needed to sell the city, and the chamber was its logical headquarters. "After two decades of boom expansion," *Dispatch* reporter David Lore wrote in late 1977, "the local economy appears to be returning to the moderate growth patterns which marked the pre-war years. At the chamber, businessmen seem to be saying the ride is over. It's time to get out and push. And many don't view Roberts as a pusher." Lore's article, part of a six-part series on the changing nature of city leadership, served as a public warning of Wolfe family opposition to the longtime chamber head. An unmistakable omen, it marked the beginning of the end of Roberts's tenure; by late 1978, he was gone, replaced by Al Dietzel, executive director of the local United Way.[174]

With Dietzel as president and dynamic young developer Jack Kessler as chair of the board, the chamber of commerce quickly signaled its new direction. "We did an analysis and found a relatively small amount of chamber money actually goes to economic development," Dietzel announced, promising a fourfold increase. During the fall of 1979, the chamber launched "Columbus, We're Making It Great," an extensive advertising and marketing campaign designed to sell the city to outside businesses and promote civic pride. Stated the chamber's 1979 annual report, "We believe we have laid a solid foundation for a newer, bolder Columbus Chamber for the 1980s. . . . In essence, we do not intend to be a passive observer."[175]

The emergence of this new boosterism pushed MCSC's allies at the chamber of commerce out of favor.[176] With them went any hope of securing private-sector support to maintain or expand the committee's activities. To a business leadership that had always equated peaceful implementation with successful desegregation, MCSC's was a mission accomplished. The goal of preventing "another Boston" had little to do with struggles in the classroom and everything to do with battles in the street; consensus could be built around programs seen as promoting civic order, not programs perceived as promoting desegregation. "The business people in this community," MCSC vice chairman and Urban League executive director Frank Lomax lamented, "are saying, 'Okay, we got the buses rolling; it's over.' That's simply not right. There's a long, long way to go yet." "Perhaps too many of us think of our program only in terms of community awareness and billboards," Brown scornfully suggested. What Brown and Lomax saw as the beginning of the fight, however, business leaders viewed as the end of a war. "My belief," said John Elam, the chamber's MCSC representative, "is that—as in Vietnam—this group should declare victory and disband."[177]

It was evident by the end of 1979 that the Columbus Area Chamber of Commerce had no interest in extending its imprimatur to either a reconstituted MCSC or a reconfigured successor. Tellingly, the chamber's endorsement was conspicuously missing from MCSC's final application for federal funds.[178] Said Lomax, "The people who don't pay attention to the system . . . assume the job is already done." Absent the cash and clout of the business community,

MCSC itself clearly could not continue. Instead, vowed John Henle, "a generation of new ideas . . . will arise from [its] ashes." By April 1980, Steering Committee diehards had reached a "consensus . . . that within a year MCSC should cease to exist, but should be replaced by another vehicle concerned with broader issues in public education." Eventually, Brown believed, "some other organization" would emerge "to meet . . . a growing demand by business, labor, religious and civic groups to play a more direct role in the future, not only of the Columbus Schools, but of education in Central Ohio in general."[179]

No such phoenix would arise, however, to take MCSC's place. "The people of this area respond very well, shoulder to shoulder, in emergencies," Moody observed, "[but] we let things slip away from us in our calmness and smugness."[180] Impending implementation had created a sense of unifying urgency in Columbus that the daily routine of desegregation could not inspire. For four years, two often overlapping visions had coexisted within MCSC: one viewed school desegregation through the prism of economic development, the other through the lens of human development. Only the former, however, could galvanize the growth consensus that shaped political and economic activity in Columbus. Despite the efforts of its adherents to preserve such a fragile and fragmented coalition, the glue that held MCSC together dissolved on September 6, 1979. Over the next nine months, unable to secure either federal funds or sufficient local support, MCSC—and the immediacy that had sustained it—gradually, inexorably disintegrated.[181] Finally, during the summer of 1980, without fanfare and without declaring victory, it noiselessly disappeared.

Though one can easily regard MCSC's demise as an opportunity lost, there is no guarantee that its continued existence would have produced constructive contributions to urban education in Columbus, particularly given the dogged resistance of educational bureaucracies to the scrutiny of outsiders. More than anything else, the history of MCSC reveals both the broad power and the narrow limitations of the business-led growth consensus that governs Columbus.

By successfully rallying the community behind the laudable goal of peaceful implementation, city leaders displayed their capacity to define both the parameters of public debate and the boundaries of permissible dissent in Columbus. At the same time, however, the equating of peaceful implementation with successful desegregation—the prioritization of civic order over civil rights—implicitly exposed the assumption that economic development and efforts to ensure equal educational opportunity are inherently incompatible.

3

Like Squeezing the Center
of a Balloon: Busing, Housing,
and the Consequences of
the Common Areas

The canon of the modern civil rights movement is replete with powerful symbols of dramatic confrontation: the federal troops in Little Rock, the fire hoses in Birmingham, the burning buses in Boston. The sensational theater of overt racism, however, all too often obscures the true backstage banality of unequal opportunity. The many tools used to preserve racial and economic segregation are elusive, adaptable, fluid, and disposable. They are seldom unambiguous and commonly cannot be traced to discrete human agency. In part because they are so amorphous, they do not fit comfortably with the heroes, villains, triumphs, and tragedies that transform discrimination into common cause.

In Columbus, where no violence accompanied school desegregation, the ever-present threat of confrontation became the focal point, and its absence as the buses rolled quickly assumed the needed role of dramatic denouement. As a result, when the shadow of this threat finally lifted, the complex problems that came into view seemed to many to have been produced by desegregation itself. Busing thus became the catchall culprit for the Columbus Public School District's ills.

The belief that school desegregation is to blame for public education's problems has hardened into conventional wisdom in Columbus. Yet desegregation failed to ensure equal educational opportunity not because it was inherently detrimental to learning, but because it was intrinsically incompatible with new residential real estate development. Even before the first buses rolled in Columbus, the threat of desegregation had redefined the parameters of single-family housing in the city, essentially turning the boundaries of the Columbus school district into a residential development redline. The myriad resources that follow new housing development—the financial as well as the "social" capital—were both exiting and avoiding the city school system by 1979; busing simply solidified and intensified this ongoing process. Moreover, because the borders of the city school district and the borders of the city had been diverging since 1965, suburban school systems had come to serve a major portion of Columbus by 1979. For the growth consensus that had done so much to preserve the peace before desegregation, the existence of these "common areas"— Columbus territory served by suburban school districts—provided a residential development safety valve, disengaging Columbus's growth from the growth of the Columbus schools. In essence, the long-term health of the city schools was sacrificed to preserve the expansion of the city itself.

The product of this process has been a decline in the status of the Columbus Public Schools, from development necessity to development barrier and, ultimately, to development hazard. The main characters, however, are not only the individuals involved, but also the seemingly tangential tools they used to facilitate this abandonment, tools as varied and obscure as school boundary laws, municipal annexation procedures, water and sewer service extensions, and "For Sale" signs.

"The School District Didn't Change": The Creation of the Common Areas

With no natural borders to restrain its sprawl, Columbus expanded rapidly after World War II primarily by encroaching on and then absorbing surrounding fields and farmland. The procedure by which this unincorporated territory was brought into the city is known in Ohio as annexation. Annexations are typically initiated by property owners who hope to improve the marketability or developability of their land by gaining access to the services provided by a contiguous, incorporated city or village. To begin the process, a petition laying out the area to be annexed must be signed by a majority of landowners within that area and submitted to the three-person Board of County Commissions.[1] If the annexing municipality can demonstrate its capacity to provide adequate services, the petition is generally approved. Following a series of formal procedures, the land in question is officially incorporated into that municipality.

Though annexation seems a fairly prosaic process on paper, it is, in fact, fraught with politics, conflict, and emotion. Before 1955, public schools were perhaps the primary source of controversy. Until that year, state law mandated that school district territory transfer accompany municipal annexation. So, for example, if a Clinton Township farm was annexed to Columbus, that property automatically had to be transferred to the Columbus Public School District. While the requirement that municipalities and their school districts have coterminous boundaries simplified maps and reduced administrative paperwork, it also complicated development, linking land transfers to the emotional bond between a community and its schools. Holdouts residing in areas to be annexed often put up fierce resistance, claiming allegiance to the local school district already serving their children. Or, if the property in question was particularly tax rich, the school system that stood to lose the land would accuse the annexing municipality of a revenue-motivated territory grab. As a result, annexation frequently generated bitter battles between rural residents and urban, progrowth interests and between small townships and larger municipalities.[2]

The creation of the State Board of Education in 1955 was intended, in part, to facilitate development by detaching the school district issue from municipal annexation debates.[3] After 1955, school districts seeking to absorb municipally annexed land had to petition the twenty-three-member state board for approval; while coterminous boundaries were still preferable, after 1955 they were no longer automatic. Consequently, it became possible for territory to remain in its original school district despite being annexed to a municipality served by a different district.

During its first decade, the state board emphasized jurisdictional consolidation, favoring large schools and large school systems. This emphasis gave the flourishing, fiscally sound Columbus Public School District an advantage over smaller, poorer neighbors. From 1957 to mid-1964, the state board rejected only four of Columbus's forty-four annexation requests, enabling the district to keep pace with the determined expansionism of exuberant Democratic mayor Maynard Sensenbrenner.[4]

Narrowly elected in 1953, Sensenbrenner took over a straining city whose stagnant boundaries contained too many people and too little available land. With residential and industrial development spilling into the unincorporated townships of Franklin County, Columbus for the first time faced the Cleveland-like prospect of encirclement by its rapidly growing suburbs. If surrounding municipalities captured too much of the advancing sprawl, Columbus's capacity for long-term expansion would be choked off.[5]

Swiftly and decisively, Sensenbrenner concluded that the city's best defense was an assertive offense. With the enthusiastic backing of the Wolfe-owned *Dispatch*, the Columbus Area Chamber of Commerce, the Metropolitan Committee, and the area's developers, the mayor embarked on an aggressive effort to gobble up unincorporated land. "Sensenbrenner made annexation his thing," said Kline Roberts. "Columbus would not be surrounded like Cleveland or Cincinnati. He even threatened to annex Cleveland."[6]

In the campaign to corral new development in Franklin County, Columbus's most effective weapon was its near monopoly on water and sewer services. The city already supplied utilities to several surrounding suburbs, and only it possessed the infrastructure, the expertise, and the economies of scale necessary to service the area's unclaimed growth safely and efficiently.[7] Seizing on these essential services as leverage, the Sensenbrenner administration in 1954 declared annexation to Columbus a precondition for the extension of water and sewer lines. To access utilities, developers had to bring their land either into the city itself or into a suburb whose service area was carefully controlled by Columbus. As a result, the city was able to stave off suburban encirclement while securing a substantial portion of Franklin County's new development. Having grown only forty square miles in its first 142 years, Columbus more than doubled in area from 1954 to 1959, becoming the largest city in Ohio by the end of the decade.[8]

After the city's growth surge stalled somewhat under one-term Republican mayor Ralston Westlake,[9] Sensenbrenner returned to office determined to resume the expansionism that had become his hallmark. By 1964, however, the dynamics of development had shifted. The region's rapid growth was moving farther toward the fringes of Franklin County, outstripping even Columbus's steadily enlarging borders. New housing, employment opportunities, and freeway construction worked symbiotically to draw a ballooning middle class to communities outside the city. From 1950 to 1960, for example, the population of Hilliard on the west side of Franklin County grew 923 percent, that of Reynoldsburg on the east side 976 percent; other suburbs would develop as spectacularly over the next three decades.[10]

Along with this physical and demographic growth came an increase in suburban political clout at the municipal, county, and state levels. Because interjurisdictional battles could only chill metropolitan economic development, Columbus city leaders recognized that cooperating with their neighbors had become not merely desirable, but also necessary. Thus, in 1964, Sensenbrenner administration city services director Warren "Hap" Cremean began entering Columbus into a new round of water and sewer service contracts with adjoining Franklin County municipalities. "Thereafter," explained Harrison Smith Jr., central Ohio's foremost annexation attorney since the 1950s, "each of the contracting suburbs could grow up to a predetermined size and over a specific area, and the remaining [unincorporated territory] could be annexed and served only by Columbus."[11] While these contracts preserved both the city's service monopoly and its ability to expand, they also would prove overly generous, opening the door for the outer ring of suburbs to eventually capture far more development than was originally anticipated.

Some local leaders viewed the city-suburban collaboration represented by Cremean's new service contracts as the first step toward the eventual "metropolitanization" of the entire region. Metropolitanizing Franklin County meant transforming it into a single, more efficient economic unit by eliminating jurisdictional fragmentation, administrative redundancy, and service duplication. For a time, area officials considered applying this idea to the county's school systems. "Within the next ten to fifteen years," Columbus school superintendent Harold Eibling suggested in 1966, "the citizens of Columbus may see . . . a school district reorganization in Franklin County designed to include the Columbus City District and all other suburban and local school districts in one large Franklin County Metropolitan School District." The 1968 Cunningham Report urged an even shorter timetable: "The metropolitan area of Columbus should have a Metropolitan School Authority within five years," it declared.[12] Yet while the drive toward metropolitanization took hold in some areas of local governance, it was derailed before reaching the realm of public education by another dynamic shaping city-suburban growth: race.

By the mid-1960s, civil rights had become the nation's most pressing and controversial domestic issue, and public education stood at the center of the debate. Nationally, the Civil Rights Act of 1964 had granted the Department of Health, Education, and Welfare the authority to investigate segregation in local school districts, and

African American community control movements had emerged in cities around the country. Locally, the proportion of blacks in the Columbus Public Schools was gradually rising, with racial turnover in central city neighborhoods producing more black-white contact and heightened interracial conflict within individual school buildings. Black parents and civil rights groups, meanwhile, had commenced their increasingly vocal calls for systemwide integration. By 1965, the connotations of the Columbus Public Schools had subtly begun to shift: a city school system was just starting to become an "inner city" school system.

As a consequence, racial intimations infected the already controversial school district land transfer issue. For the better part of its first decade, the State Board of Education had favored the efficiency of large school districts like Columbus in its transfer rulings. By the mid-1960s, however, consolidation's political pitfalls were beginning to overshadow its economic virtues. Migration from the cities had multiplied the influence of suburban interests in the electorate and on the state board, providing an increasingly sympathetic ear to arguments that Columbus's annexation efforts robbed burgeoning suburban school systems of potentially tax-rich property. Parents fleeing urban areas for the sanctuary of new subdivisions became particularly incensed when territory transfer meant their new home would no longer be in the school district they had originally sought. Meanwhile, desegregation suits brought against two Ohio school boards had raised but not resolved the question of the state's responsibility to remedy de facto segregation.[13] Growing suburban clout thus combined with the threat of integration to produce an abrupt reversal in the state board's attitude toward territory transfer in Franklin County. On August 8, 1965, the all-white board rejected eight of the Columbus Public Schools' nine transfer requests.[14] This quiet triumph of expediency over efficiency marked the beginning of the city of Columbus's disengagement from the Columbus Public Schools.

After 1965, the size of the city and the size of the school district began to diverge sharply. While the Sensenbrenner administration accelerated its annexation efforts, what school superintendent Eibling called the state board's "inconsistent rulings" on territory transfers chilled the school district's ability to keep pace. "There were bloody battles to block Columbus," Hap Cremean recalled. "Believe me, it got rough. But we always had the pat answer: the [disputed territory's] school district didn't change." In 1967, the state board declared a temporary moratorium on territory transfers, directing individual districts to reach permanent boundary agreements that would eliminate the uncertainty engendered by potential annexation. The moratorium soon dissolved, however, with only one such compact having been reached.[15]

By the beginning of the 1970s, additional factors had come to inhibit the Columbus school district's ability to expand. Land annexed by the city was generally underdeveloped and sparsely populated. With the school system's fiscal credibility already in decline, it was difficult for the board to justify pursuing residential development with comparatively little property tax payoff.[16] At the same time, heightening racial tension and increasing overcrowding threw into question the district's ability to serve adequately its existing population, let alone the additional students new home building would eventually generate. Given its strained race relations and facilities, the district recognized that it could not persuade an already averse state board to endorse further expansion.

There remained, nonetheless, one final test of Columbus's ability to confront the growing influence of suburban resistance. On April 12, 1971, the state board approved the transfer of the insolvent Mifflin Local School District to Columbus. Under normal circumstances, suburban officials would have quietly applauded the city schools' absorbing Mifflin's 42.5 percent black enrollment; certainly, their districts would not have accepted the students without a fight. The storms of protest that accompanied the Mifflin transfer instead concerned the Columbus schools' compensation for taking over the bankrupt district: 8.7 square miles of territory served at the time by seven different suburban systems. Most controversial was the transfer of the "Golden Finger," a tax-rich, 910-acre sliver along Route 33 northwest of downtown that contained dozens of industrial and commercial establishments and just a handful of Grandview Heights students.[17]

For the next five years, suburban officials fought the transfer deal in both the state legislature and the state courts. Calling the agreement a "plunder" and a "land grab," Republican state representative Alan Norris from suburban Westerville failed twice to pass legislation that would have made school territory transfer contingent on the approval of voters in the annexed district.[18] Meanwhile, the suburbs' legal challenge wound its way through the state courts, culminating in a 1976 Ohio Supreme Court ruling upholding the jurisdictional authority of the State Board of Education.[19] The Golden Finger transfer finally took place that bicentennial fall, having paralyzed the Columbus schools' annexation aims for five years.

If the state board's mid-1960s policy shift hindered the city school district's ability to keep up with municipal growth, the Mifflin–Golden Finger controversy extinguished it. Columbus school administrators understood that the initiation of any major territory transfer not involving tax-poor property or a significant population of African American students would meet with a frosty response from state board members and hostile obstructionism from suburban residents and elected officials. Testifying before the Ohio House Education Committee at a 1975 hearing on Rep. Norris's proposed territory transfer bill, Columbus administrator Howard Merriman sardonically observed, "It was all right for Columbus to annex a troubled, financially unsound district, which had lost accreditation, which has buildings in sad need of repair, additions and remodeling, which had a minority population of consequence—but not all right to annex areas from other districts."[20] Faced by then with full-scale desegregation and worsening fiscal problems, Columbus school officials could no longer stomach spending years in state courts and legislative hearing rooms in a laborious quest for land and students they lacked the money to serve. Moreover, politically ambitious board members such as Steven Boley and Virginia Prentice recognized that a drawn-out transfer try might alienate the growing portion of

Columbus voters who lived in suburban school districts. By the implementation of desegregation in 1979, the boundaries of the city and the city school system, essentially coterminous just fifteen years earlier, had dramatically diverged: The Columbus Public School District served only 109 of the City of Columbus's 180 square miles.

"DeSegregation Means DeUrbanization": Race, Penick, and Development

When the "common areas"—Columbus territory served by suburban school systems—began to emerge in the late 1960s, they had little immediate impact on development patterns in Franklin County. Passage of the Fair Housing Act of 1968 barely dented residential segregation, and the neighborhood schools along the city school district's flourishing fringe remained securely all-white. For two decades, developers had cooperated closely with Columbus school administrators to coordinate school and housing construction, a collaboration that continued through the early 1970s. New schools helped sell new subdivisions, and new subdivisions represented continued economic growth; this relationship was underscored by the heavy-hitting support of city leaders so critical to passage of 1972's $89.5 million bond issue, the largest commitment of bricks and mortar in the school district's history. "In the last four years," stated the endorsement of the city council and Mayor Moody, "30,000 dwelling units have been built [in Columbus] but not one school. . . . Inasmuch as the economic well-being of this community and its people is contingent upon its educational system, it is imperative every effort be extended in supporting this proposal." In the afterglow of the district's election-day triumph, Superintendent John Ellis declared, "The building program will enable the school system to be a valuable partner in the growth and progress of the city."[21]

Ellis's understandably enthusiastic prediction turned out to be wholly inaccurate. Though it seemed at the time a dramatic reaffirmation of the Columbus public school system's indispensability, the 1972 bond issue instead marked the end of twenty years of district-developer reciprocity. Never again would city schools be used to sell new subdivisions; never again would they be treated as a boon rather than a barrier to Columbus's growth. After 1972, the Columbus Public School District quickly and irreversibly came to be seen not as indispensable to development but as incompatible with it.[22]

Like squeezing the center of a balloon, the prospect of school desegregation drove single-family housing development out of the Columbus schools and into surrounding suburban systems. Combined with the Supreme Court's *Keyes* decision, which opened the door to desegregation in northern, urban school districts, the filing of *Penick* in 1973 injected a degree of uncertainty into the central city home-building market that chilled capital investment. With real estate agents no longer able to guarantee prospective home buyers a predictable neighborhood school assignment, bankers, developers, and builders were unwilling to risk their resources on new construction within the boundaries of the city school system. Once the developments that drove the 1972 bond issue were completed, single-family home building within the Columbus school district ground to a halt. "From 1970 to 1972," said Carl Klein, research supervisor for the Planning Division of the Columbus Development Department, "probably 50 percent of the subdivisions [in Columbus] were platted in the Columbus school district. That falls to 20 percent in '73 and '74, and then it drops down."[23] A 1983 Development Department study stated that "since 1975, new [single-family housing] construction in the Columbus school district has been reduced to the point of insignificance." Observed Klein, "It's clear that first [desegregation] was being talked about, and then it was being pursued, and that seemed to have a triggering effect."[24] Indeed, it was the *threat* of desegregation, not desegregation itself, that transformed the Columbus Public School District into a virtually unbreachable barrier to residential development.

During the early and mid-1970s, sociologists such as James Coleman began to raise the controversial argument that school desegregation exacerbated the ongoing American exodus from cities to suburbs. In order to escape busing, they contended, middle-class whites fled urban school systems for the sanctity of surrounding suburban areas, ultimately leaving desegregated districts poorer and more segregated than before. "The emerging problem with regard to school desegregation," Coleman wrote, "is the problem of segregation between central city and suburbs; in addition, current means by which schools are being desegregated are intensifying that problem rather than reducing it."[25] Because school district and municipal boundaries were coterminous in most major cities, outmigrants had to flee to—and inmigrants settle in—separate suburban jurisdictions to escape court-ordered busing. By depleting municipal tax bases, Coleman and others argued, this process of "resegregation" accelerated the decay of urban schools and the decline of large American cities.

Columbus's unusual growth patterns, however, allowed it to escape this kind of municipal decline. More Sunbelt sprawl than Rust Belt bulk, the city was, in one resident's words, "a suburb without an urb." Through its annexation and water-sewer policies, Columbus had avoided the "white noose" of suburban encirclement; by the early 1970s, in fact, the city had expanded so rapidly that several neighboring municipalities had become "inburbs," suburbs entirely surrounded by Columbus territory.[26] Most important, the growth of the common areas meant that much of the developable land on the city's periphery remained outside the Columbus Public School District and, consequently, beyond the reach of desegregation. The Supreme Court's 1974 *Milliken* decision, which essentially sanctioned white flight by braking busing at urban school district borders, ensured that the common areas would remain securely served by suburban schools.[27] As a result, Columbus, unlike many other cities, was able to sustain its economic and geographic growth in the shadow of imminent desegregation. Rather than drive development out of the city, the threat of busing merely defined where it would occur within the city. The boundaries of the Columbus Public School District thus became the "redline" within which new residential development—and the economic activity that followed it—would no longer take place.[28]

For the developers, builders, and real estate agents who had worked so closely with the school district through the bond issue of 1972, it was an ideal scenario for a housing market faced with impending busing. They could still build homes in the city, taking advantage of less-restrictive zoning, smaller, lower-cost lots, and guaranteed water-sewer service with quicker, cheaper tap-in. At the same time, they could use the threat of busing as a marketing tool, promoting the perceived safety and stability of overwhelmingly white suburban school districts. "Developers had the best of both worlds," said Calvin Smith, director of the Columbus schools' desegregation monitoring office, "because they could still develop in the City of Columbus, but develop in other school districts [which] were not being desegregated and wouldn't ever have to fear that."[29]

By 1977, developers had begun openly peddling the desirability of "not Columbus." Said Smith, "They knew that if they didn't market their other developments as being in specific school districts, they wouldn't appeal to a certain clientele." Realtors promoted suburban schools in their sales efforts, with ads, billboards, and "For Sale" signs that for the first time displayed the name of the district serving each property, as long as it was not Columbus. Whereas in 1970, individual Columbus schools were identified as repositories for poor and minority children, by mid-decade, the district as a whole had been so branded. "It wasn't that big a deal whether you went to [Columbus] North High School or you went to [suburban] Worthington back in 1958," observed Jim Hyre, Columbus superintendent from 1982 to 1987, "and it wasn't that big a deal in 1968. But in 1978, North was closed, you had to go to [predominantly black] Linden-McKinley. You were in that assignment pattern. That issue became a major item."[30]

Mostly the messages were subtle.[31] An ad in the April 10, 1977,

Columbus Dispatch preyed upon the urgency of parents seeking to pull their children from the city schools by dropping carefully coded intimations of racial exclusivity. "DeSegregation means DeUrbanization," the ad read. "Consider raising your family in the Northcountry. . . . After our initial conversation, we'll go on an orientation tour of the Northcountry and check out the properties of special interest to you or I'll list your special requirement and call you when something comes available. Whether you're anxious to find something or just looking, we know everything that's available in the Northcountry." Occasionally, however, the signals were less ambiguous. "Don't Bus, Come Live with Us," urged one developer. In a particularly egregious episode, HER, the area's largest realtor, "put up billboards portraying cannibals cooking missionaries, with the caption, 'Feeling Crowded?'" "Of course, the cannibals were all black and people in the pot were all white," recalled Beverly Gifford. "It was terrible." When city councilman Jerry Hammond complained, HER quickly removed the billboards and apologized, claiming that any racial implications had been unintended.[32]

While developers capitalized on looming desegregation to sell new subdivisions, suburban officials exploited *Penick* as well, using the fear of urban schools as both carrot and stick in their late 1970s levy campaigns.[33] Despite soaring inflation, antitax anger, and a statewide school funding crisis, every suburban district in Franklin County approved a levy between November 1976 and November 1978.[34] Threats of insolvency and, consequently, consolidation with Columbus "had a tendency to soften the tax attitude of people in the suburbs," said Westerville superintendent Harold Rowe after his district passed an 11.3-mill levy in 1977. Another suburban superintendent, who said he would deny the quote if attributed, was referring to Judge Duncan's decision when he told a *Dispatch* reporter in late 1977, "You know as well as I do why levies failed in November and passed this spring."[35] Suburban officials, said Robert Weiler, cochair of Columbus's 1979 levy campaign, "used Columbus in every way possible. The threat that their kids would go into Columbus was probably the greatest motivation for supporting the suburban schools. How do you think the suburbs got their bond issues passed? 'If we don't pass it, we'll go into Columbus.'"[36]

While the controversy surrounding school desegregation contributed to suburban levy victories, it tipped the tally the other direction in Columbus school votes. With antibusing activists voicing explicit levy opposition and white board members indicating tacit disapproval, resentful city voters vented their various frustrations at the ballot box.[37] Forty-four additional operating levies were approved in Franklin County from 1969 to 1981, but none in the Columbus school district.[38] Between 1976 and 1979 alone, Columbus failed four times to persuade voters to approve new moneys, despite strong support from the chamber of commerce and the mayor's office.[39] Changes in state law magnified the impact of these levy losses. In 1976, the Ohio legislature passed a property tax rollback law intended to protect home owners from inflation.[40] By reducing millage to counter inflationary growth in property values, the rollback stabilized tax rates for Ohio home owners. As a consequence, however, school districts needed revenue growth from either new construction or higher taxes to keep pace with rapidly rising costs. Older, central-city systems were thus forced to go to the voters more frequently just to meet mandates or maintain existing programs, while ballot issues in expanding suburban districts often involved new facilities and additional services. Staggered by the one-two punch of inflation and levy defeats, the Columbus Public School District had to take out an embarrassing $8.6 million loan from the General Assembly's school bankruptcy fund in 1978 simply to stay open.[41] Operating at state minimum standards from 1976 to 1981, Columbus endured $28 million in budget cuts and a staff reduction of 888. Superintendent Joe Davis described the district's fiscal distress as "the most perilous financial times the Columbus Public Schools have faced since the depths of the Depression."[42]

Columbus's skeletal budget thus stood in sharp contrast to the fiscal stability of adjacent districts, part of a desegregation-related development spiral that accelerated city-suburban educational disparities. To suburban school systems, more single-family home buyers meant a broader base of voting middle-class taxpayers with children in the public schools, a corresponding increase in commercial development, and the tangible financial and intangible psychological advantages of expansion; all of this, in turn, attracted more single-family home buyers, continuing the cycle and perpetuating the exodus of residential development from the city school district. Columbus, meanwhile, was left with a stagnating tax base, an increasing proportion of economically disadvantaged students,[43] and a shrinking core of voters with school-age children.[44] These factors interacted with the prolonged *Penick* process, undermining the city school district's ability to compete with its suburban neighbors for middle-class families lured to central Ohio by its reliable economy. Commented Davis, "If a guy gets transferred in from Pittsburgh, he's not going to want to move into a district that is facing controversy over desegregation and doesn't know if it can keep its doors open."[45]

Despite the administration's initial denials, some desegregation-related middle-class flight did occur, particularly from the district's white northwest fringe. "Every time the NAACP makes a statement, we lose twenty-five kids," cracked one northwest Columbus principal. Ultimately, flight from the Columbus schools conformed to the pattern exhibited by most desegregated urban districts: the number of outmigrants surged from the year of the verdict through the year following implementation, stabilizing soon afterwards.[46] Much of the system's steep enrollment decline, however, must be attributed to baby bust birth rates. Only three of sixteen Franklin County school districts saw enrollment grow between 1973 and 1983, and several, including lily-white Upper Arlington, lost a larger percentage of pupils than Columbus did.[47] Over time, therefore, the district's most vexing problem proved not to be flight—existing home owners escaping Columbus—but middle-class "avoidance"— new home buyers never locating in the city school system.

Whether real estate interests drove or followed the housing market beyond the Columbus Public School District is a chicken-and-egg question.[48] With profitable development dependent on a combination of information, anticipation, and access to capital, the post-1972 plunge in platted Columbus school district lots indicates a real estate community steering its investments toward safety. Anticipating the probable outcome of *Penick*, developers quit building houses within Columbus Public School District boundaries because they had every reason to believe, based on past practices and national trends, that the market could not reliably support them. "Developers are going to develop and builders are going to build where they can sell homes," said local developer Don Epler. "Other parts of the country had experienced [desegregation], and the general development and building community [in central Ohio] knew that it was going to affect their sales."[49] In desegregation's shadow, class, race, and education intersected with Columbus's fiscal instability and student assignment uncertainty to make suburban school districts more appealing to middle-class home buyers.

By anticipating the market, however, developers also shaped it. While Columbus Public School District boundaries continued to contain a large stock of attractive existing homes, after around 1975, prospective buyers could only look to suburban school systems for *new* homes. Though the aggregate number of housing units within Columbus school borders grew 18.1 percent during the 1970s, practically all of that increase occurred in the years surrounding the 1972 bond issue. By mid-decade, a consensus clearly had been reached that city schools were an unacceptable investment risk. With the herdlike momentum that inevitably governs development, this consensus had become virtually ironclad by desegregation's implementation. As a result, between 1980 and 1990, the total number of housing units inside the Columbus Public School District actually dropped 2.1 percent; during the same span, aggregate housing units in the city of Columbus increased 17.5 percent. Population statistics further illustrate this trend. From 1970 to 1990, the municipal population served by Columbus schools dropped 11.5 percent, while the population of the city as a whole rose 14.7 percent. Moreover, the proportion of the city's population living in the common areas grew from insignificance to 23 percent during those twenty years.[50]

Hence, a vicious circle emerged: because real estate interests perceived no post-*Penick* market for new homes in the Columbus school district, there ceased to be development; and because there was no development, there ceased to be a market.

Developers argued that their decision making was driven by money rather than color, that they aspired to minimize risk, not racial mixing. "They don't develop to try to segregate," said Robert Weiler, chair of a large local development company and a Columbus school board member from 1985 to 1991. "They develop to sell houses. Their only motive is profit." Recognizing that such a contention can be both accurate and disingenuous, however, is fundamental to understanding the relationship between development and desegregation.[51]

School desegregation as it came to be carried out was the product of a progressive liberal paradigm of racial inequality, one that viewed racism manifested in segregation as a malignant but curable historical cancer. If equal rights could contain the cancer, then integration would eventually eliminate it. Premised on this ideal, the modern Civil Rights movement proved extraordinarily successful; in one generation, it substantially succeeded in lifting the political, legal, and social controls that for centuries had sustained America's racial caste system.

As public racism became more offensive, however, private discrimination grew more defensive. The controls that the Civil Rights movement eliminated had been designed to address the twin fears that had historically sustained white racism: the fear of physical retribution and the fear of social (and sexual) pollution. In its efforts to eliminate public barriers to black "encroachment," the Civil Rights movement reignited these deeply ingrained white fears; the shift from rights to remedies, with its goal of winning state sanction to compel black advancement, fanned the flames.

As the most individually intrusive of the remedies attempted, busing for school desegregation provoked the most volatile response. Because it was intended to effect more than mere token interracial contact, it amplified the fundamental axiom of post-*Brown*

racial dynamics: what is integration to whites is isolation to blacks;
what is integration to blacks is invasion to whites. By eliminating
the certainty and security of the neighborhood school, busing shattered the sanctuary provided by continued residential segregation,
exposing white children to the perceived hazards associated with a
significant black presence: physical danger, educational devalua-
tion, sexual promiscuity, lax discipline, and so on.[52] In doing so, it
revealed the force of race and racial fear as permanent, structural
features of the American marketplace, a paralyzingly nebulous enemy that the liberal black-white alliance that drove the Civil Rights
movement was neither adequately prepared to confront nor flexible
enough to combat.[53]

The reciprocal relationship between residential segregation and
the neighborhood school had long made education a fundamental
locational element of new development. To America's suburbaniz-
ing white middle class, good neighborhoods meant good schools and
vice versa, and neither was compatible with anything more than
minimal integration. "We can solve a housing problem, or we can
try to solve a racial problem," observed William Levitt, the nation's
most influential postwar home builder, "but we cannot combine
the two." While lifting the legal structures of residential segregation
largely eliminated overt discrimination from the housing market, it
did little to abolish the role of race in determining the desirability of
an area. Race was no longer a discrete locational sales point, like
proximity to shopping or a good view. Instead, it became an unspoken but understood element of other market variables—superficially race-neutral factors such as safety, quiet, comfort, status,
stricter zoning, and school quality were all imbued with seldom-
stated racial implications, conscious and subconscious assumptions
shared by whites regardless of class or political persuasion. The
profitability of residential development thus continued to depend
on the relative racial exclusivity of neighborhood and school, even
as the methods of ensuring exclusivity grew more elusive.[54] Consequently, the maintenance of a certain degree of housing segregation
was not, as Robert Weiler implied, incidental to profit; it was in-
trinsic to it.

By divorcing urban schools from the private market, busing as a remedy for unequal educational opportunity provided both an incentive and an escape hatch for the abandonment of desegregated systems. In Columbus, the threat of busing injected a districtwide dose of uncertainty that proved poisonous to development. The unintended consequence of such an unwieldy, race-conscious remedy was to sharpen the equally race-conscious, but far more nimble, fluid, and subtle responses of the market. Almost instantaneously, *Penick* shaped and solidified residential development patterns in Columbus, transforming the entire city school district into a "no new housing" zone. Other private and public resources inexorably followed—sewer lines, water mains, roads, property taxes, political clout, commercial development, employment opportunities—creating a cycle in which the exodus of resources worsened the district's existing woes, in turn accelerating the exodus of resources. By no means did this process have an instant, neutron bomb–like impact; rather, its effect was gradual, foreseeable, and, absent both the immediate economic incentive and the political will to confront it, irreversible.[55] By 1979, even before the "forced busing" of a single Columbus student, the structures that would sustain this cycle of abandonment were already in place.[56]

Because of the existence of the common areas, however, the threat of desegregation in Columbus drove development only out of the school district, not out of the city. While city leaders flexed their civic muscles to confront the growth-threatening emergency of implementation, they remained conspicuously silent about a jurisdictional discrepancy that allowed 40 percent of the city to be served by suburban schools. Such an oddity could scarcely proceed unnoticed by Columbus's development-based growth consensus, and the post-*Penick* shift in development patterns demonstrates that it did not. The complicity of city leaders in the expansion and development of the common areas indicates that, from the beginning, they viewed desegregation itself as incompatible with growth. The common areas thus proved a unique and effective safety valve, preserving both public-private and city-suburban cooperation in the economic and geographic growth of the metropolitan area.

By ensuring Columbus's capacity to expand, the common areas also safeguarded the influence of the city's white business elite over major civic matters. Reducing the proportion of African Americans in a city—and, consequently, their political clout—is often a primary motivation for aggressive annexation or for consolidation with neighboring municipalities; Richmond and Indianapolis can be viewed as examples of this strategy.[57] Columbus, however, seems to be the only city where municipal annexation was pursued while school territory transfer was not, a combination that preserved a "safe" white majority in the city even as it more closely clustered blacks in the city schools.

Columbus's growth consensus never entirely forsook the Columbus Public School District, which was still too healthy and educated too much of the region's labor force to abandon entirely. The chamber of commerce continued to fund and run levy campaigns, and the rhetoric of civic leaders consistently stressed the impact of urban education on the prosperity of central Ohio. Still, business community backing for the desegregated district manifested itself not in the warm handshake of wholehearted partnership, but in the desperate clasp of emergency support, holding the district up while the ground gave way beneath it. Urban League executive director Frank Lomax lamented this crisis-driven perspective in a report bemoaning the slow dissolution of MCSC: "Some express the notion that since the Columbus Public School system is becoming blacker and poorer, no one is demanding quality and excellence from the system and by implication, [people are] satisfied with mediocrity. Therefore, as long as the system is fairly orderly and quiet without too much notoriety, let it alone, the sentiment goes. This feeling is justified on the basis that the business community can now assume a laissez-faire attitude because of the proximity of the surrounding fifteen school districts that will provide our available labor pool of future employees."[58]

The presence of the common areas enabled desegregation to proceed without handicapping Columbus's growth. Along the way, however, the Columbus Public School District had come to be considered a barrier to the residential development key to the city's expansion. By the time the buses rolled, the entire Columbus Public School District had been branded by the same unspoken assumptions of inferiority and second-class citizenship that stigmatized the poor and minority students it was disproportionately responsible for educating.[59] As a result, the interests of the city and the interests of the city schools began to diverge; thereafter, anytime the two conflicted, the city as a rule won out, and the good of the city school district could be sacrificed for the growth of the Columbus metropolitan area.

"It Isn't Cool to Annex My School": Annexation, Moratorium, and the Declining Status of the Columbus Schools

By the end of 1979 in Columbus, the fear of burning buses and bomb threats had quietly given way to the day-to-day trials of desegregation's second generation. With the issue finally out of the "fishbowl" (the nickname of the district's central office) and into the classroom, the administration and school board could begin to focus on other urgent problems.

One such long-deferred dilemma was annexation. In late 1978, the question of the common areas had been raised briefly by Superintendent Davis in a report to the community called "Choices for the '80s." "Choices" offered two possibilities for using territory transfer to bolster the destitute district's tax base and offset its continuing enrollment slide: (1) aggressively pursue new annexation, or (2) seek legislation that would make city and school district boundaries coterminous. Though the report offered only options, merely raising the issue was enough to provoke swift reaction from suburban schools. Groveport-Madison board member Richard Kettell initiated an effort to forge a coalition of suburban districts threatened by annexation, saying they should not remain "sitting under the sword, continually faced with the question of what Columbus is going to do." Before the controversy could catch fire, the school board shelved the issue, turning its attention to the more pressing problems of desegregation planning and levy campaigning. Shortly after the start of busing, however, the specter of annexation was raised again, with Davis warning that "at some point, the board will have to look at it."[60]

In the spring of 1980, as the district braced for another painful round of school closings, that prickly point finally arrived.[61] The previous fall's elections had produced an unprecedented four-person turnover on the board, and three of the new members—Gary Holland, Carole Williams, and Pauline Radebaugh—had pressed the annexation issue hard during the campaign.[62] "Whatever is in the city," Radebaugh maintained, "should be in the school district as a matter of principle and practicality." Said sitting board member Bill Moss, "We are surrounded by increasingly hostile white suburban districts while we continue to close schools and disrupt the educational process in the central city." District officials recognized that any attempt to annex the rapidly developing common areas would spark a storm of protest, making political, judicial, business, and state board support unlikely. Without cooperation, Davis cautioned, "It's an exercise in futility. [We would just] be spinning our wheels."[63] However, some school leaders believed Columbus held a powerful trump: the threat of a metropolitan desegregation suit.[64] Because the Columbus schools educated over 90 percent of Franklin County's African American students, state-sanctioned attempts to impede the district's annexation efforts could be judged intentionally segregative.[65] Fear of metropolitan litigation, Virginia Prentice suggested, might make an already beleaguered state board reluctant to preserve "havens of Columbus schoolchildren who are avoiding desegregation by being in suburban school districts."[66]

On April 29, 1980, the board emerged from an hourlong closed session to announce that it had directed an administrative team led by Assistant Superintendent Howard Merriman to begin gathering data on the tax valuation, pupil density, and projected costs of the common areas.[67] "It opened up tremendous controversy," recalled Williams, "because the staff, in order to find out how much land and how many people [were in the common areas], had to ask other districts. The parents in those districts became paralyzed with fear that we came to annex them, which we did not. There was no intention to annex them. They just interpreted that."[68] Repeatedly, the board tried to reassure jittery neighbors that its intentions were innocent. Alarmed suburbanites, however, refused to believe that Merriman's "annexation feasibility study" was anything but the prelude to an imminent invasion.

Indeed, immediately after the board's announcement, the issue exploded with exceptional ferocity. Local state legislators leaped to the defense of their home-owning constituents. State Senator John Kasich, a brash, young Westerville Republican, told a gathering of area business, political, and civic leaders, "People from many parts of Franklin County are extremely upset. I've never had so many calls [in the two years] I've been in office than in the last two weeks on annexation. People choose an area to live in, work hard to purchase property and assume their children will attend certain schools. Then, when all of a sudden the rug is pulled out from under them, they are frustrated and mad." Suburban school officials helped form antiannexation groups to marshal public backing for House Bill 385, proposed state legislation that would grant residents of annexed territory veto power over school land transfers.[69] Three days before the house vote, hundreds assembled at a Statehouse gathering to express support for the proposed bill. The event, reported the *Dispatch*, had the "feel of a high school football rally," with homemade placards declaring "No Annexation Without Representation," "We Don't Want Any Part of Columbus Schools," and "It Isn't Cool to Annex My School."[70]

On June 14, the Ohio House voted overwhelmingly in favor of HB385, sending the charged legislation back to the Ohio Senate, where it had languished for over a year without action. As testimony began before the Senate Education Committee, rowdy antiannexers packed Statehouse hearing rooms, cheering their representatives and jeering Columbus administrators. Supporters of the bill asserted that an issue as personal and emotional as school territory transfer should be decided by affected voters, hardworking home owners who had intentionally settled in specific school districts and feared having "the rules changed in the middle of the game." [71] "I am arguing," declared Kasich, "for all the people who worked all their lives to send their kids to the school they want to send them to." [72] The proposed legislation, suburban officials contended, merely reaffirmed the cherished ideal of local control over public schools. Moreover, they maintained, rapidly expanding suburban districts could not securely plan for growth given the perpetual threat of a voracious urban system on their borders. Columbus representatives, on the other hand, condemned the bill as barely cloaked racism, a covert antibusing effort designed to permanently corral the city school district's black and poor population within existing boundaries. All the while, senate Republicans were exploiting the election-year issue as a tool with which to wedge control of the senate from a fragile Democratic majority.

The annexation controversy caught Columbus city leaders in a bind. With an extended campaign already in the works to pass a desperately needed operating levy, they were reluctant to oppose publicly a still-innocuous school initiative such as the annexation study. The study itself, meanwhile, by demonstrating the board's efforts to explore integrative options, could accelerate the district's escape from court control. Enactment of foreseeably segregative antiannexation legislation, on the other hand, could conceivably delay the district's escape by giving civil rights advocates grounds for a metropolitan desegregation suit. Finally, real estate interests feared that legislation democratizing territory transfer could backfire against them; in general, they preferred to keep decisions affecting development away from the public eye and out of the control of the unpredictable masses.

At the same time, however, the city's economic interests stood to benefit from the preservation of noncoterminous school district boundaries. It was the common areas, after all, that had allowed Columbus to continue growing in the face of school desegregation. Developers expecting to profit from the status quo would suffer substantially from annexation to the city schools. With buyers willing to pay 15 to 20 percent more for the same house in a suburban district, commented Harley E. Rouda, president of the area's largest residential realty company, "busing is pushing the price of homes upward. Families are moving to avoid busing because they think suburban school systems are better than Columbus."[73]

Perhaps annexation's most pressing issue, however, was the uncertainty that the controversy engendered. The prospect of a battle royal between city and suburban school districts threatened the stability needed to attract and nurture development. Consequently, as with the 1972 integration clash and the 1979 implementation of desegregation, city leaders simply wanted to see the issue resolved quietly, moderately, and with minimal public conflict, in a way conducive to the area's continued growth. The response of the *Dispatch* typified attempts to balance on annexation's public tightrope. "What is essential," the paper advised, "is that the [school board's] call is for a feasibility study, a *cool-headed* determination as to whether annexation could be considered *within reason.*"[74]

Ultimately, the appeal of quiet compromise won out. On September 18, 1980, the Ohio General Assembly approved the first of what eventually would be three two-year moratoria on the transfer of suburban school territory to urban districts.[75] Legislators claimed that the delay would allow them to reach a reasoned, responsible, unemotional solution to a complex issue. But what it really offered was a way for state politicians to avoid handling a racially loaded election-year grenade that many viewed as an exclusively central Ohio problem.

The six-year moratorium served multiple purposes for Columbus's growth consensus. By diffusing controversy, it helped stave off legislation granting suburban residents veto power over school land transfers, legislation with foreseeably segregative effects and therefore the potential to snowball into a metropolitan desegregation suit.

In the meantime, it allowed development in the common areas to intensify, facilitating Columbus's mid-1980s boom while making annexation even less likely in the future.[76] The moratorium thus ensured, at least temporarily, that issues involving the health of the city school district would remain detached from those affecting the growth of the city itself.

By examining the reaction to Columbus Public School District annexation efforts, it is possible to trace the declining status of urban education in central Ohio. In 1960, the teeming city school system was expanding at the same rate as the city. Armed with the almost automatic approval of the state board of education, the Columbus Public Schools served as a full partner in Columbus's rapid growth. By 1970, however, the district's expansion had been separated from the city's, and suburban systems were coming to be seen as safe havens from increasingly volatile urban schools. Still, pre-*Penick*, Columbus's problems were restricted to particular buildings; the bulk of its schools remained demographically similar to those in neighboring suburbs. This tension between the city's continued clout and the suburbs' escalating status can be seen in 1971's Mifflin–Golden Finger transfer: while Columbus was able to annex tax-rich suburban land, five years of legislative and legal wrangling ensued before the transfer finally took place.

The annexation moratorium of 1980 revealed that the scales of status had tipped toward suburban schools. Merely by initiating a *study* of annexation, the desegregated Columbus schools provoked a political brouhaha that proscribed even the possibility of expansion for six years. Said Davis, "The basic issue facing the people of Columbus can be stated simply—will Columbus schools be competitive with schools in the suburbs?"[77] If the moratorium exposed the city school system's lower status, however, then the Win-Win Agreement, reached shortly before the moratorium expired in 1986, officially sanctioned it. Before examining this agreement, though, it is first necessary to understand the apparent resurgence that took place in the Columbus Public School system between the beginning of desegregation in 1979 and the end of the moratorium in 1986.

"A Window of Opportunity": Jim Hyre and the Resurgence of the Columbus Public Schools

On a fall Friday a few weeks into desegregation, Robert Duncan went to see his son's Eastmoor High football game. While the parent cheered from the bleachers, the judge took note of the surprising absence of African American cheerleaders on the visiting team's squad. Preliminary statistics had shown promising systemwide biracial participation in high school extracurricular activities. Overall, 44 percent of the district's football players and varsity cheerleaders were black, well within the 20–50 percent racial balance range targeted by the court.[78] Troubled by the racial disparity he saw on the sideline, however, Duncan asked desegregation monitor Calvin Smith to investigate.

After meeting with the cheerleaders and their principal, an unsatisfied Smith assembled fifty black girls to find out why only two had tried out for the prestigious squad. "They said it was because the school used a form of cheerleading that they didn't care for," Smith recalled. The girls told the cheerleading-naive administrator they preferred the "American" style, with its emphasis on flips and dancing, to the formation-oriented "military" version their new school practiced. Before desegregation, Smith discovered, the former had been more common to black schools, the latter to white schools. Following another round of meetings, Smith convinced the current cheerleaders to fuse the two forms, and the squad was soon integrated.[79]

Acceptable racial balance, Columbus schools quickly discovered, did not equal exemplary integration. The problems of desegregation's second generation were far more intricate than numbers could indicate, as Smith's story illustrates. Unforeseen and unspoken chasms frequently proved as damaging as outright racial antagonism. In the wake of implementation, said Damon Asbury, the schools were confronted with the often "frustrating" question, "Now that we've got the kids here, what do we do?"[80]

All too frequently, this question was left unanswered by harried administrators and discontented teachers. "The biggest problem," Smith said, "was just getting people attuned to the fact that we were desegregated. You had to understand that you had children being transported to your school that lived a distance away, who hadn't come there before, and that you had to consider them." Many principals and teachers, unable to adjust to the academic, economic, and racial diversity in their classrooms, either left or were nudged out of the system. Observed OSU desegregation scholar William Wayson, "Successful desegregation comes from staff commitment. The schools lacked the 'administrative climate' to make it work."[81]

Mixing students did not necessarily mean mixing races, particularly at the higher grades. "You'd go to lunch," Principal Ed Willis said of East High School, "and what you'd see would be ten black tables, ten white tables, and four mixed tables. I'd like to tell you it was polka dot all the way, but it wasn't."[82] Student insecurity, meanwhile, combined with staff tension to produce a surge in discipline problems. The dilemma of racially disproportionate suspension, expulsion, and tracking statistics would prove particularly insoluble for the district, with whites often blaming unruly black students and blacks often faulting insensitive white teachers for the unequal numbers.[83] Frustrations were exacerbated as well by the logistical obstacles of busing: the multiple schedules and longer travel times that severed school loyalties, reduced extracurricular participation (and attendance), and further depressed already declining parental involvement.

All of these challenges were being faced on an inflation-ravaged budget by an embattled urban school system that had not passed an additional operating levy since 1968. The district was so destitute by the beginning of the 1980s that it could no longer afford to run a full list of its phone numbers in the local Yellow Pages.[84] With programming and staff slashed to state minimums, faculty morale reached its nadir. The difficulties of desegregation only heightened the hurdles created by out-of-date textbooks, deteriorating buildings, and inadequate equipment.[85]

After 1979 saw the district's fourth levy failure in as many years, school officials and chamber of commerce leaders devised a long-range campaign strategy directed at the 72 percent of the electorate who did not have children in the public schools. By luring voters without a firsthand knowledge of the system into individual buildings, administrators sought to combat commonly held assumptions about urban education. Said Superintendent Davis, "We find that public understanding of Columbus schools is based on national trends and national media coverage, rather than on actual conditions." The aim of the campaign—called "See for Yourself"—was to demonstrate that Columbus schools were more than, in the words of Northland High principal Charles Pollack, "a glorified baby-sitting service." During the yearlong effort, reported the *New York Times*, "almost 30,000 adults without children of their own in the public schools took advantage of [See for Yourself] to observe classes, go on trips with students, eat lunch with the youngsters, and participate in class discussions."[86]

See for Yourself was one of several factors that finally enabled the district in November 1981 to pass its first levy increase in thirteen years. The tax revolt of the 1970s had found its full expression in newly elected President Ronald Reagan. As a result, voters seemed to see less need to vent their anger at the convenient target of public education, particularly when presented with a convincing case of financial distress.[87] Moreover, by November 1981, desegregation had come to be accepted as the status quo in Columbus. Antibusers offered no public opposition to the levy, and many voters who had previously used the ballot to protest busing had abandoned the city schools altogether. Their absence, combined with strong voter turnout in traditionally supportive areas, swung the election in the district's favor.[88]

While school officials recognized that the 7.6-mill levy merely allowed the system to "avoid bankruptcy," its passage so soon after the beginning of desegregation further convinced local business leaders that busing's last battle had been fought. Bragged chamber of commerce president Al Dietzel, "When we talk to business people [from other cities], one of the first things we will tell them is that a very short time after we had busing and desegregation, we were able to pass a levy. I don't know any other school district in the nation that has been able to do that." Before the end of his final term in 1983, Mayor Moody cautioned that such boosterism dangerously obscured the structural weaknesses of the Columbus Public Schools: "When you think of this city, which finally made a commitment to the public school system out of its pocketbooks, it made a commitment for survival, not for excellence. . . . You have to be terrified about our going into the future . . . because the future is in the minds and not the hands." [89]

Still, even if the 1981 levy was no panacea—the board had to shut down another ten schools the following spring—it at least gave the district a sense of stability for the first time in half a decade. This stability proved fortunate, as shortly after presiding over the emotional closing of tradition-rich Central High, Superintendent Joe Davis announced his resignation. Following a nationwide search, the board tabbed Jim Hyre, the short, stocky, self-deprecating superintendent of the Canton, Ohio, schools, to run the district.

Hyre, forty-one in 1982, entered teaching in the mid-1960s as an excuse to coach football. What he saw in Columbus was a school district desperately in need of a pep talk, an urban system not overwhelmed but underconfident. Desegregation and budget cuts had taken their toll, resigning a burned-out and often bitterly divided staff to a future of instructional inferiority. "The people had been through all the emotional battles," said Hyre. "They were kind of worn out—mentally worn out—and that's what I felt was the number one thing we had to talk about. I thought Columbus was a hell of a lot better than Columbus thought it was." [90]

With characteristic candidness, the new superintendent immediately went to work on district morale. The day after his first board meeting, Hyre scolded representatives from the Columbus Council of PTAs: "You people feel like a bunch of losers and it irritates the heck out of me," he told them. "You're beaten down by your counterparts in the suburbs about how good their schools are. Don't be defensive about the school system." [91] Risking the wrath of the

Columbus Education Association, Hyre told teachers, "We are not in the business to create employment. We are here to educate children, and we have to do that. . . .[92] If you don't believe in the district, then I think you should seek someplace else where you are happier."[93]

Hyre's exuberant candor was an invigorating change from the low-key, desk-bound leadership of Joe Davis. "Jim Hyre was a presence," recalled Ed Willis. "I remember the first meeting he had [with high school principals]. He said to us, 'I might lose this damned job, but if I do, a whole lot of you are going with me!'" During his first few months as superintendent, Hyre toured every school in the district, paid unannounced visits to surprised administrators, created the monthly Good Apple Awards to recognize outstanding employee effort, and tirelessly stumped the city preaching the gospel of confidence and quality. "Speech after speech," wrote *Citizen-Journal* reporter Debra Phillips, "he nearly exhausts himself trying to pound in the message to his audience: Hey, folks, the city schools aren't as bad as you think, and they're getting better."[94]

Hyre was convinced that perception equaled reality; if people came to *believe* Columbus had quality schools, Columbus would come to *have* quality schools. Part of his strategy was to focus public attention on the advantages of urban education without downplaying its drawbacks. To accomplish this goal, Hyre knew that he needed both the media and the business community on board. The press, quickly won over by the new superintendent's sense of humor and blunt quotability, was a pushover. Securing the support of the business community, however, was a more difficult matter. Hyre recalled, "One of the shocking pieces when I got [to Columbus] was that most of the business community was kind of like, 'Everything is going all right, so just leave it alone.' . . . There was no big business presence at all. I had to do a convincing job that the city school district had an impact upon the economics of the area. They really hadn't thought about it a lot. It wasn't anything that was on the front burner."[95]

To make urban education a priority, Hyre had to combat the disengagement of businesspeople from the city schools, a phenomenon

that was both a cause and a consequence of suburbanization, desegregation, and intensifying urban poverty; he dubbed this disease
"315-itis" after Route 315, the newly completed freeway that linked
downtown to Franklin County's affluent northwest side. "Most of
the leadership in the business community," he said, "had no direct
connection to the schools. Their kids didn't go to school there. They
didn't live in Columbus anymore like they did in 1950, they lived in
Upper Arlington or Dublin or Granville or wherever. And much of
Columbus's business leadership is what I call 'new leadership.' The
Limited, Wendy's—those kind of companies came up during the
fifties, sixties, and seventies, and they didn't have the sense of community responsibility at that point in time they might have today."
Concurred Carole Williams, board president in 1981 and 1982, "At
that time, the business community didn't pay any attention what-
soever to the city school district. Most of the business leadership
were interested in the schools where their children were. It never
really clicked that the city schools were producing the workforce—
not so much the leadership in the workforce, but the workers."[96]

Hyre, however, had a unique talent for speaking the language of
businesspeople while speaking the truth to them. He could play a
round of golf with a group of city leaders one morning and then the
next afternoon tell them that "the good old days are gone forever and
are not coming back," as he did in a 1983 speech to the Columbus
Metropolitan Club. To make his case that a good urban school district was a necessity, not a luxury, Hyre had to recouple the health
of the city schools to the health of the city. "The more you talk
about how great Columbus is, the more poor people will pack up
and move to Columbus looking for a better life," he cautioned the
Rotary Club in 1984. "Since you think it's so wonderful here, help
me educate these people. If Columbus schools are strong, you'll
have a strong central Ohio area." But, he added, echoing Rowland
Brown's words almost a decade earlier, "the ostrich technique will
not work. Poor people and blacks are not going away."[97]

Hyre's arrival in Columbus coincided with two critical events: an
economic boom that fueled explosive growth in the defense, services,

and FIRE (finance, insurance, and real estate) sectors of the economy; and a spate of studies that painted a devastating picture of America's educational competitiveness.[98] While the school studies supplied the impetus for action, the economy provided the resources. Hyre's message, bolstered by an unusually compatible and cooperative school board, received an enthusiastic response from a new generation of energetic civic boosters bent on making Columbus a "world class city."[99]

The result was a series of private-public partnerships that extended business community involvement in the Columbus schools well beyond the traditional areas of levy campaign support and vocational education consultation.[100] The district's Adopt-a-School program, initiated in April 1982, quickly grew from a small, pilot project consisting of a handful of schools to a systemwide, chamber-run enterprise involving hundreds of businesses and other organizations. In 1983, the school district and the business community joined forces with Ohio State to finance and coordinate Summer-Tech, a citywide computer education summer school. SummerTech gained national recognition for throwing open public school doors to provide affordable computer classes for the whole community.[101] Also in 1983, local business leaders began the Columbus Public Schools Fund, an attempt to sidestep creativity-stifling bureaucracy by providing private grants for innovative, building-level programs. The CPS Fund blazed the trail for what would become the district's most successful business partnership, "I Know I Can," a multimillion-dollar endowment ensuring every Columbus graduate access to a college education.[102]

These programs made great public relations and represented an unprecedented level of direct private-sector involvement in the Columbus Public Schools. However, Hyre and other school officials realized that the district's momentum was not sustainable as long as those who could afford to avoid the district continued to do so. Ultimately, said *Call and Post* general manager Amos Lynch, the superintendent's goal was to make the system so good "that folks who impact on policy here and send their children to suburban and private schools" would want to get their kids back into the city district.[103] Attracting and retaining the middle class thus became the Hyre administration's oft-stated objective.

The district already possessed one powerful middle-class magnet: its lottery-based alternative schools. Started in 1975, the alternative school program had grown gradually in size (from three to ten schools) and rapidly in popularity, leading to waiting lists that numbered in the hundreds.[104] In 1983, a Hyre-appointed task force warned of the perception that "two separate and unequal school systems" were developing in Columbus, "wherein the alternative schools are viewed as superior to the conventional schools." The district was never able to erase this perception, nor did it necessarily want to. The alternative schools, with their carefully designed curricula, specially selected staffs, and actively involved parents, were widely regarded as the jewels of the system, a view reinforced by their strong test scores and higher per pupil expenses.[105] For many middle-class parents, therefore, the continued enrollment of their children in the Columbus Public Schools hinged on the results of the spring lottery.

The success of the alternative schools no doubt helped to slow the district's middle-class enrollment slide. But slots were too few and lottery luck too uncertain for alternative schools alone to arrest the trend. Hyre and his board recognized that only substantial, structural investment in the city schools by Columbus's middle class could reverse the system's gradual decay. Their target thus became the development-desegregation nexus responsible for the district's moribund single-family housing market.

Throughout his tenure, Hyre stressed that class, not race, was the key determinant of educational achievement. "Test scores," he noted, "correlate to two factors: income level of families and educational level of families." Concentrated poverty generates a host of academic obstacles: family breakdown, violence, health problems, substance abuse, constant movement from school to school, institutional distrust, hopelessness. "The social problems of the world are what urban schools wrestle with," Hyre said. "If every parent had a job and every family was middle class, most of the problems the schools have to wrestle with would go away."[106]

But children in the Columbus Public Schools were gradually becoming poorer, in spite of the prosperity surrounding them. The proportion of AFDC students in the district had tripled between 1968 and 1984, rising from 11 percent to 33 percent. From 1980 to 1985, the percentage of children in the Columbus schools who qualified for free or reduced price meals grew from 47 percent to 59 percent.[107] Seventy percent of the district's thirty thousand elementary school students received subsidized meals in 1984, and the figure reached 100 percent at seven Columbus primary schools that year.[108] Statistics from 1985–86 revealed that at all but three Columbus elementary and middle schools, one-third or more of the students received subsidized meals.[109] All too often, said Hyre, poor children "come from homes where the TV goes eighteen hours a day, but there are no written materials in the whole house. They start out behind . . . and some of them are always behind."[110] Reaching a critical mass of such disadvantaged students, he argued, would undermine learning systemwide.

Yet as long as being black remained a disproportionate determinant of poverty, race and class could not be separated, a fact that Hyre confronted forthrightly. "We fight this constant image," Hyre told Mayor Moody's Economic Development Council, that "we have an awful lot of black people and an awful lot of poor people, so, therefore, we can't be very much good. We still have a lot of latent racism. And I say that to you because you may as well deal with it because a lot of people don't want to talk about it."[111] He responded to the complaints of Clintonville residents about the uncertainties of the alternative-school lottery by admonishing them, "If you're running from blacks, it won't work. We're supposed to solve the problems you ignore. A lot of our problems are perception problems. [Columbus Public Schools have] a second-class citizen mentality. Poor people and blacks are equated with inferiority. We've got to deal with everybody."[112] The reason middle-class whites shunned the district, Hyre contended, was "just fear. They don't want their kids going to school with poor kids and black kids."[113]

Though Hyre held that desegregation helped maintain middle-class avoidance, the real villain, he believed, was the set of development assumptions that shaped residential segregation. "From day one," he said, "I've always felt this: schools did not cause desegregation. The realtors had a hell of a lot more to do with it than the school people did. . . ."[114] From firsthand experience, Hyre recognized that the presence of fair housing laws was often used as a smoke screen to shield the subtle tactics that perpetuated housing segregation. "I've talked to realtors who said they're not responsible for that," he noted, "but I know better than that. I mean, when I came to town, I had fifteen realtors either call me or write me letters. Almost to a person, they tried to sell me a house either in Upper Arlington or Worthington. Even though I was going to be the Columbus superintendent!"[115]

When companies relocated jobs to Columbus, Beverly Gifford said, employees often "were counseled before they came and were told to stay away from the Columbus city schools." "Most prospective home buyers moving into the Columbus area," Hyre wrote to one real estate agent, "have been 'pre-conditioned' to purchase a home outside the Columbus district. It's a situation that disturbs me greatly." Only by persuading real estate interests that the city schools were no longer a residential development risk could Hyre and his school board win the race to stabilize the system. "Unless a strong partnership develops between the Columbus Public Schools and Columbus area realtors," the superintendent warned, "the socioeconomic diversity, racial diversity, and intellectual diversity of our student body could change rapidly in the next few years." "We are convinced," Hyre stated in late 1984, "that realtors are the single most important group in determining the state of the Columbus school district."[116]

In a memo a few weeks later to Hyre and board president Stephen Eibling, board member Carole Williams asked, "Is 1985 the year

Columbus Public Schools gets serious about the problems we have with misperceptions about our school district among real estate agents and the buying public?"[117] Williams's query quickly devel oped into "Selling to Sellers," a long-range marketing effort designed to "convince realtors that a quality education is available in the Columbus Public Schools" and to "convince developers that they can make money building homes in Columbus." School officials would "work with realtors, developers, personnel directors, city officials, and others to attract and retain a balanced population, including middle and upper class families with school-age children, to Columbus." The district's ultimate goal was to replace the assumption of urban inferiority with a perception of suburban parity, to persuade real estate agents, developers, and home buyers that, in public relations director Laura Ecklar's words, "There are sixteen fine school districts to choose from [in Franklin County]—and we're one of them!"[118]

Three weeks after the board gave the go-ahead to "Selling to Sellers," the district's efforts to reclaim its middle-class credentials received a significant shot in the arm. On April 11, 1985, in one of his last acts before retiring from the bench, Robert Duncan released the Columbus schools from court jurisdiction. "In probability," the judge declared, "Columbus now has the most desegregated school system in the United States."[119]

Duncan's final order captured the ambiguity of desegregation's legacy in Columbus.[120] "There are no perfect remedial Court orders," it acknowledged. "All racial problems in the Columbus School District have not been eliminated by this litigation. Although the Court is satisfied that the remedy ordered in this case has substantially accomplished its objective, racial problems persist." The stubborn constancy of racially disproportionate discipline figures was particularly troubling to Duncan. Though the district was only 43.5 percent black in 1984–85, 66.8 percent of the students expelled were black, as were 56.2 percent of the students suspended.[121] "Once the door is closed and you have twenty black students and twenty whites," said school board member Gary Holland, "there's nothing to say that the teacher won't treat the blacks in an inferior way."[122] Nevertheless, wrote Duncan, "alarming as the statistics are, there is no direct evidence that the results are causally related to any unlawful, improper, or even unprofessional acts or omissions of the defendant Columbus Board or its employees." Indeed, pre-desegregation figures exhibit similar racial disproportionality. "There is no evidence," the judge noted, "that the statistics showing disparity are significantly out of line for a large urban school district, even a district not undergoing school desegregation."[123]

The disparity in discipline figures, declared the court, merely tainted "an otherwise outstanding job of responding to an obligation to desegregate." In many ways, the district was healthier in 1985 than it was when busing began. Surveys found that both student and teacher attitudes toward desegregation had grown more positive annually. Community perception of the district had also improved significantly. Asked to grade the Columbus schools, 41 percent of survey respondents in 1985 gave them an "A" or "B," compared to just 27 percent in 1981. Moreover, the percentage of those surveyed who viewed "desegregation/busing" as "the biggest problem facing the Columbus Public Schools today" dropped from 38 percent to 14.9 percent during that time.[124] Meanwhile, student attendance was creeping higher, the district's fiscal footing was far more sound, and enrollment decline, considerably less than originally projected, had virtually ceased by 1985.[125]

Most important, Duncan observed, "a comparison of April 1984 data with predesegregation shows that if desegregation has had an impact upon achievement in Columbus schools, in the long run that impact has been a positive one." Test scores for elementary and middle school students were generally on the rise, and "black student performance continued to increase at all levels," even though, Special Master Luvern Cunningham noted, "outmigrating kids were generally brighter by one grade and inmigrating kids were less bright by one grade." Between 1980 to 1985, the SAT scores of the district's high schoolers improved, while ACT results held steady. Given the commonly held perception of a "basic inconsistency or unbearable tension between school desegregation and quality education," the district's educational data demonstrated, Duncan wrote, that the "defendants have had significant success in doing what many view as impossible."[126]

A systematic study of the impact of court-ordered desegregation in Columbus is beyond the scope of this book. Given the available statistical and anecdotal evidence, however, it is clear that the district's six years under court control were neither the panacea that some sought nor the catastrophe that others predicted. The intangible virtues of integration may well have been neutralized by the practical dilemmas of desegregation, problems such as intraschool academic and social segregation, loosened community bonds, and lessened parental involvement. Likewise, any educational benefits or innovations that desegregation might have brought were threatened by the accompanying rise in discipline problems and decline in middle-class enrollment. Ultimately, court-ordered desegregation may have done little more than take advantages and disadvantages once concentrated in specific schools and disperse them throughout the system. It is perhaps best, then, to describe the district as healthier in 1985 than in 1979, yet more vulnerable.

Finally free of court control, school board members publicly responded to Duncan's action by firmly reasserting their "legal and moral obligation . . . to operate [the] district as a unitary district."[127] Privately, however, conversations about revisiting and revamping the student assignment plan had already begun. "I can't tell you that there will never be changes," board president Eibling hinted the day of court release. "If there is a chance to provide better educational opportunities for every youngster in the district, we'll do it."[128] In other words, if the board could find a politically and legally permissible way to reduce busing, it would.

By late 1985, the board had remained largely silent on the issue. "Pressures have been mounting," stated a December *Citizen-Journal* editorial, "for the school board to make some moves to lessen the burden of cross-town busing and to do more to keep middle class white students in the city system." Shortly thereafter, the board acted, unveiling a tentative elementary restructuring plan that would enhance student assignment continuity, add alternative schools, and reduce transportation for racial balance.[129] While the actual plan would not be approved and implemented until 1987, its announcement sent a carefully timed signal to Columbus's white middle class that the district was serious about curtailing busing.[130]

As 1986 began and the end of the third annexation moratorium approached, the district appeared to be experiencing a renaissance. City leaders applauded when Hyre announced, "I am proud to claim we are the best urban school system in America—and we can be better!" "They wanted to believe it," said Urban League executive director Sam Gresham, "but they knew better. People all along knew that it wasn't." For the boosterish business community that drove Columbus's growth consensus, however, the veneer of educational quality was more important than the reality beneath; while the price of fixing the district was prohibitive, the cost of fixing the district's image was minimal. Urban school districts were *supposed* to be dying—that Columbus's appeared alive and well was just an added plus for the city's already sparkling marketing portfolio. "Cities are defined, at least in part, by a *perception* of the quality of their public schools," declared a *Dispatch* editorial. "The [Columbus] school system can be a talking point, rather than a negative factor, for recruiters trying to lure young executives to Columbus. . . . The public schools are becoming another asset of a city on the grow."[131]

Amid the city's heady prosperity, meanwhile, Hyre's more sobering messages fell on deaf ears. Upon arriving in Columbus in 1982, the new superintendent had declared that "there is an opportunity on the horizon now that was not here five years ago and may not be here five years from now." By 1986, that opportunity still existed. But with youth violence starting to rise, pockets of urban poverty intensifying, and the school system serving an increasingly hard-to-educate population, it was beginning to fade; without a far-reaching commitment to the district from local business and development interests, it would soon disappear. "Can we develop something that is different than the Cleveland and St. Louis model, where all the upper- and middle-class people first bail out of the school system and then the city proper?" Hyre wondered in 1985. "I don't know." Still, he maintained in a speech to the Building Industry Association, "We have a window of opportunity. Isolation or 'moving out' will not solve anything."[132]

That window, however, was starting to slam shut. "Hyre was a real pro in terms of public relations and getting people to feel good about their [school] system," said city council president Jerry Hammond. "But it wasn't enough to move the developers to the degree they needed to be moved." In Columbus, said Development Department planning administrator Steve McClary, "You've got three types of population: you've got people that are in the Columbus school district and have no choice; you have people who choose to be in the Columbus school district; and then you have people who have chosen not to be in the Columbus school district. What Jim Hyre did was instill some pride at least to those already committed to the whole concept of the Columbus schools. But I'm not sure he did a whole lot to convince people outside the schools that they should give them a try."[133] As it turned out, neither the perception nor the reality of the Columbus schools had reached the levels needed to inspire investment. In the end, not even the self-proclaimed "best urban school system in America" could make desegregation compatible with residential development.

"The Horses Are Out of the Barn": Annexation, Win-Win, and Educational NIMBY

In February 1986, Franklin County superintendents imported Miami-based conflict resolution expert Irving Goldaber to mediate annexation negotiations. Emotions were running high on both sides of the Columbus school system's boundaries, with suburbanites shouting "Democracy!" city supporters crying "Race!" and everyone screaming "Money!" As the November 30 expiration of the third annexation moratorium drew near, the decades-old school land transfer controversy had reached a level of hostility altogether consistent with the highlights of Goldaber's résumé: urban riot control, hostage negotiations, Philadelphia's MOVE organization, the Middle East, and Northern Ireland. As Columbus City Council president Jerry Hammond put it, "The political reality [of annexation] was that you have your hands on the testicles of the world if you start playing with this."[134]

With three annexation bills pending yet no resolution in sight, exasperated state legislators urged superintendents from the twelve Franklin County school districts with territory in Columbus to solve the volatile issue themselves. "Nothing leads me to believe that the General Assembly will accomplish in the next seventy-five days what it has not accomplished in the last five years," groaned state representative Mike Stinziano, a Columbus Democrat. "With the possibility of the last of the moratoriums expiring in 1986," recalled Bob Barrow, the Columbus schools' government lobbyist, "the legislature said, 'There are not going to be any more moratoriums. And since it's a local problem mostly in Franklin County and the Columbus area, you folks figure it out. Whatever you figure out, we'll enact a law to allow you to do it.'"[135]

After reading about Goldaber's successful mediation of a teacher contract dispute in Worthington, Stinziano sent a letter to Franklin County superintendents and legislators proposing that they give the sociologist's approach a try. Goldaber's "win-win" negotiation technique, an intensive, thirty-day bargaining process premised on trust, concession, and an unwavering commitment to conciliation, had a near-perfect record for resolving school labor disagreements. Impressed by Goldaber's credentials, the superintendents concluded that win-win's finite parameters offered the best hope for resolving what Stinziano in 1987 called "the most divisive issue in central Ohio in the past twenty-five years." The sociologist was hired in early March 1986, and negotiations were scheduled to begin April 2.[136]

By the time Goldaber arrived in Columbus, months of uncer-

tainty had thoroughly agitated the hornet's nest of suburban terri-
torialism. Terrified of losing their children and their tax base to the
city district, residents in suburban school systems regarded the
Columbus board as, in the words of a *Dispatch* reporter, "seven Cy-
clopes, drooling as they cast their single, envious eyes in one direction: suburban property." "Those districts are so afraid of Columbus
it's ridiculous," said board president Loretta Heard. "They've been
afraid to even meet with us, because they think we're out to get
them." One antiannexation rally drew over twelve hundred people,
and hundreds more packed every legislative hearing on the issue.
"When I'd get up to testify," remembered Barrow, "there was booing
and hissing in the background. You'd get threatened in the eleva-
tors. It was bizarre." Said board member Pauline Radebaugh, "I
would get calls starting at six in the morning, and quite often I've
had calls, 11:30, 12:00 at night—people from suburban areas calling,
threatening. You know, 'We'll get even with you because . . . we
don't want our kids in Columbus schools. We want to stay in a good
school system.'" Westerville board member Tom Fawcett best summarized the suburban perspective when he proclaimed: "We have
everything they want, they have nothing we want."[137]

The aggressive rhetoric of Columbus school board member James
Ebright only magnified suburban anxiety. During his two years on
the board, Ebright emerged as annexation's lone crusader, insis-
tently emphasizing the racial and economic consequences of the
common areas.[138] "Nothing is going to keep the white middle class
in the district as long as we keep the current boundaries," he contended. "The net result is a resegregated school system, where the
poor and blacks go to Columbus Public Schools and the middle-
class whites go to school in the suburbs. [But] the board is unwilling
to do anything about it because it's a politically unpopular issue."[139]
Hearings he held on the issue in 1985 galvanized the support of a
small group of mostly white, liberal Columbus parents, who established an annexation advocacy group called the Apple Alliance.[140]
Ebright remained an annexation gadfly even after stepping down
from the board in mid-1985 to tend to his collapsing marriage and

failing computer software firm. At a Columbus Metropolitan Club debate in late 1985, he denounced proposed legislation giving residents the right to veto school territory transfers as "the kind of democracy you find in South Africa, where only white people vote. It's extremely bad educational policy to confine all the poor and minority students to one school district and then deprive that district of all the resources it needs," he added.[141]

Columbus board members took pains to distance themselves from Ebright. Even Gary Holland, his most ideologically compatible boardmate, complained that Ebright's crusade was "creating a certain paranoia in the Franklin County area." The bulk of the Columbus board at the time believed that annexation was either educationally unnecessary, financially undesirable, or politically unrealizable.[142] Still, said Gahanna-Jefferson superintendent Roger Viers, Ebright "created some nervousness and anxiousness on the part of suburban districts. He was a renegade. And you say, 'He's probably just a renegade.' But, then, you never know." Suburban suspicions were stoked in early February when the Columbus board approved a resolution endorsing the principle of coterminous boundaries. Though board members repeatedly emphasized that it was merely a "negotiating position," not a "basis for action," the resolution alarmed suburban residents. "We must insist that we keep the boundaries as they are, because we want to keep not only our students but also our tax base," stated Dorothy Young, chair of the Coalition for Local School Systems (CLASS), an areawide antiannexation group. With tension and mistrust escalating, the chances of a settlement seemed as remote as ever. "There was a bloodbath in the making," recalled Groveport-Madison superintendent Charles Barr. "We had people out here in this district that were ready to go down and take the Statehouse apart, brick by brick."[143]

Sitting down at the same table for the first time, however, to begin what the *Call and Post* called "the most important multilateral negotiations in Franklin County since Franklinton merged with Columbus [in 1870]," the superintendents concluded that resolving their dispute was both possible and imperative. "There was a spirit of cooperation that we haven't seen before on this issue," Hamilton Local superintendent Mark O. Stevens said after a January 30 introductory meeting. "Everyone seemed willing to compromise. The gun is to our heads."[144] A self-imposed news blackout allowed the superintendents and their staffs to negotiate in the eye of the storm surrounding them. And with so much at stake—40 percent of the city of Columbus (72 square miles), 19.6 percent of its students (16,586), 21 percent of its property tax base ($43.7 million per year), and land valued at $1.1 billion—the rhetorical winds were fierce. In the six years since the imposition of the first moratorium, residential and commercial construction in the common areas had boomed, making the territory that much more valuable and annexation that much more volatile. Suburban districts also feared losing major industrial taxpayers and potentially lucrative undeveloped land to the Columbus schools.[145] Table 1 shows what each affected district had at stake in the common areas.

Yet, even with antiannexation groups from suburban districts stepping up their six-year war, and Columbus's Apple Alliance emerging as an organized protransfer force, city leaders remained largely silent about the emotional issue. In 1986, the economy of the seven-county Columbus metropolitan area was booming: 65,000 jobs had been created in three years;[146] Franklin County's unemployment rate stood at 5.5 percent, well below the state (8.1 percent) and national (7 percent) averages;[147] and tangible personal property had grown 71 percent countywide between 1980 and 1985, a far higher rate than the 33 percent growth statewide.[148] Over $500 million worth of construction had taken place downtown since 1979, and a gleaming skyline was emerging on the banks of the Scioto.[149] Home building, meanwhile, hit its 1980s apex, as four times more residential building permits were issued in Franklin County during 1986 than during the recession year of 1982.[150]

Focused on developing the city's downtown and promoting the area's vibrant image, business leaders did not want the disruption and hostility of a racially loaded, interjurisdictional brawl.[151] While they favored the preservation of the school district status quo to

Table 1. Status of common-area school districts, 1986

Franklin County School District	Tax Base ($/year)	Tax Base (%)	Area (sq. mi.)	Students (no.)	Students (%)
Dublin	3,200,000	34.3	7.4	2,023	48.8
Gahanna-Jefferson	2,600,000	35.8	2.5	320	6.2
Groveport Madison	2,300,000	34.0	14.0	2,877	48.9
Hamilton Local	167,000	9.3	3.8	381	18.7
Hilliard	3,900,000	43.6	12.0	915	22.0
Pickerington	N/A	1.2	1.9	0	0
Plain Local	5,000	4.9	2.6	0	0
Reynoldsburg	457,000	8.2	0.6	233	5.3
South-Western	5,900,000	29.7	N/A	4,200	26.5
Westerville	4,000,000	26.1	N/A	2,779	25.9
Worthington*	9,600,000	43.4	10.0	2,856	37.3

*Worthington was protected by its 1968 boundary agreement with Columbus.

Source: Ohio Department of Education statistics compiled by the *Columbus Dispatch* (Kathy Gray Foster, "Board Expected to Support Citywide District," *CD*, February 5, 1986; *CD* chart, February 6, 1986; *CD* chart, February 23, 1986).

the animosity sure to be engendered by annexation, reaching a quick, quiet resolution was once again top priority.[152] "The business community in general did not like the controversy and the conflict between Columbus and its suburban neighbors," Barrow said. "It's very hard for people involved in economic development to get companies to come to an area where you have some of your major political entities in a state of civil war." Business leaders, agreed Hyre, "knew that it was a very volatile issue. They just wanted it solved."[153]

Initially, even those in the business community with the most at stake—home builders and residential real estate development interests—remained in the background, fearing a surge of panic selling and market flight.[154] They simply had too much invested, however, to stay silent for long. The common areas contained 80 percent of the city's new construction, including much of its industrial and commercial growth and virtually all of its new residential development.[155] Land investor Thomas Lurie reported that out of 1,826 single-family building permits issued in Columbus in 1985, only 18 were in the Columbus school district.[156] Accelerated by the completion of Route 315, runaway growth on Columbus's northwestern periphery overwhelmed existing services, creating headache-inducing traffic woes and monopolizing the attention of City Hall. As this haphazard expansion proceeded, rising property tax valuation and surging student enrollment became increasingly concentrated in the common areas.[157]

For real estate agents, the looming threat of annexation cast a shadow of uncertainty over the local market. But real estate agents only sold homes, they did not build them; concerned about controversy, not long-term capital investment, they sought only to avoid fanning the flames of the dispute. "We're basically taking a hands-off position," said George Simpson, president of the Columbus Board of Realtors and head of Ohio Equities. Debbie Briner, a reporter for the Suburban News Publications, wrote that "several real estate agents . . . refused to comment on how annexation might affect property values. Many said that it is an issue that is 'too hot' to speculate about." With several strong existing home markets within the city school system—Clintonville, German Village, Berwick, Victorian Village—real estate agents even took the time to sing the district's praises. "People are becoming more [accepting of] the so-called integrated school," realtor George Smith told Briner. "So many things have improved. We're just thankful to have a Jim Hyre. I say he's as good for Columbus as [zoo director and frequent national talk show guest] Jack Hanna, only Hanna gets more ink."[158]

Builders and developers, however, had to ensure that their investments in land and construction would fetch profitable market rates. If the common areas were suddenly transferred into the city school district, both the demand for and the value of their unsold properties would plunge.[159] "That uncertainty," said Weiler, "caused the developers to be very unhappy. You had a situation where you might start off in the Westerville schools, but we don't know if after a couple years you may be coming to Columbus. From the development side, if I want to attract a builder of homes, that builder wants to be able to tell the families purchasing the house, 'Your kid will go to such and such school and I can give you confidence that if he starts [there] in first grade, he'll stay there.'"[160] Hoping to raise $4,000 to lobby key legislators, Jim Sutliff, president of the local Building Industry Association (BIA), solicited the BIA's six hundred members for donations to its political action committee. "A few hundred dollars does attract attention," he wrote. "We certainly can't buy anybody. We can only give a small contribution to let them know we're here and get five minutes of their time. Our developers have a lot of land in those [common] areas and paid a premium price for land in a school district. If the land changes districts the value may change. The unknown is bad for everybody."[161]

As win-win negotiations wore on, builders and developers became more vocal, their rhetoric more threatening. Martin Graff, executive director of the BIA, warned that residential development in Columbus would "screech to a halt" if the city schools sought transfer of the common areas. "People in Columbus but in suburban districts are afraid they may be annexed, so they're trying to move out," Graff stated. "There is no demand among new home buyers to live in the Columbus school district." Sutliff predicted a mass exodus from sections of the city served by suburban schools: "People in those gray areas are going to be looking to get out. They may have had ideas of moving and now they'll do it. If you allow unrestricted annexation, growth in the suburbs will be astronomical."[162] Builders had already seen "a reduction in [home buying] traffic" in annexable areas, Sutliff claimed. In a comment somewhere between prediction and threat, developer Charlie Ruma, owner of Virginia Homes, said, "As we get down to [the end of the moratorium in] November and if the issue is not resolved, we will not sell a house in any district outside of the suburban school districts." Without a resolution, he warned, housing starts in Columbus would drop 80 percent in 1986 alone.[163]

Apple Alliance spokesperson Martha Crossen condemned such dire comments, calling them "sensationalistic, divisive threats" insulting to the city schools. Crossen also accused the development community of having a hidden hand in the market's shift to suburban schools: "Developers can't tell if there's a demand or not because they don't build in the Columbus district. They've created their own problems because they advertise homes based on the district they're in with the inference that other school districts are better than Columbus. They have largely contributed to the perception that you're going to lose out if you buy into the Columbus system."[164]

But with a 7.94-mill levy on the May 6 ballot, Columbus school officials were far more delicate. Administrator Tim Ilg told a fifty-member East Side Realtors association, "I do not expect you to be salespeople for the Columbus Public Schools. That's our job." A resounding levy victory, the most decisive since 1965, indicated that the district's efforts were meeting with success. At a buoyant victory party that night, Mayor Buck Rinehart hugged board president Loretta Heard and exclaimed, "We've only just begun! We're on a roll!"[165]

To underscore this enthusiasm, six "For Sale" signs prominently displaying "Columbus Schools" popped up in Clintonville the following week. District spokesperson Laura Ecklar said they were the first such signs since real estate agents began promoting specific school systems in the mid-1970s. "It's really wonderful," Ecklar glowed. "It's a nice first step." The real estate agent, Pat Kearns-Davis of ReMax, explained, "We need to let people know Columbus schools are just as good as other schools. We're not afraid to say, 'This is Columbus schools, and your kids will go here.' I get tired of people complaining about Columbus schools. I say, instead of complaining, let's promote them. Making people believe in Columbus schools can only help attract industry and business into the city. This will help the whole community." "You made my day!" an exuberant Hyre wrote Kearns-Davis. "Your willingness to support and promote the Columbus Public Schools in such a visible way marks a major milestone in your profession—and in this community."[166]

That such a "milestone" could even make headlines, however, revealed the fragility of the district's high-profile momentum. For several years, Jim Hyre had been playing a game of high-stakes poker, with the Columbus Public School District as his hand. The reward was the region's pool of middle-class students, particularly its white middle-class students. Ultimately, Hyre knew, he would have to reveal his cards, but by bluffing, stalling, and extolling the virtues of the hand he held, he hoped that just maybe he could outlast his opposition: the automatic equation of urban education with inferiority. By 1986, Hyre's hand was surprisingly strong—a financially stable city system with some excellent programs, a number of fine schools, and, fleetingly, an integrated, racially and economically diverse student body. From the beginning, however, the deck had been stacked, and the rules slanted against him. And after the Win-Win Agreement was announced on May 15, it became painfully clear that the hand Hyre held was no match for that of his powerful foe. When the cards were finally thrown down, the opponent walked off with the pot, leaving Hyre to place a final, futile bet on an uncertain future.

Win-win negotiations began on April 2, with the twelve participating superintendents seated around a circular table in a conference room at Ohio State. The multiple representatives were quickly consolidated to two negotiating parties, Columbus and the collective suburbs.[167] As the superintendents took turns rattling off their concerns, dozens of issues were compressed into a pair of fundamental dilemmas: what to do about the common areas and what to do about future annexations.[168] Administrative subcommittees were then formed and given six weeks to research relevant issues and hammer out specific compromises. At the end of the six weeks, the superintendents reconvened for three marathon bargaining sessions, during which the final form of the Win-Win Agreement was forged.[169]

The agreement that emerged contained three key elements:[170] (1) Existing school district boundaries were made permanent, (2) unincorporated land annexed to the city of Columbus in the future would be automatically transferred to the Columbus Public School District,[171] and (3) tax revenues from new commercial and industrial development in the common areas would be shared by Columbus and the suburban district involved.[172]

In short, the suburban districts got to keep their students and their tax base, while the city schools were guaranteed the territory brought into Columbus by future annexations as well as a cut from any new construction in the common areas. Under pressure from a state legislature eager to adjourn for the summer, the participating school boards ratified the agreement with minimal debate. Franklin County lawmakers then incorporated it into a pending annexation bill and quickly rammed it through the General Assembly.

Suburban residents and school officials greeted Win-Win with barely tempered glee. By solidifying existing boundaries, the agreement lifted the cloud of uncertainty that for so long had loomed over the common areas. "What the suburban districts got was stability," said Gahanna-Jefferson superintendent Roger Viers, head of the suburban delegation during the negotiating process, "and that was our concern. We had to have stability." That this stability was achieved without the sacrifice of a single pupil or existing revenue source made the agreement even sweeter for the suburbs. "We saved every dollar and every student!" exulted Hilliard board vice president Thomas Calhoon. Politicians and business leaders expressed relief that the intractable territory transfer issue had finally been resolved. The *Dispatch* called Win-Win a "workable, equitable annexation policy" that "embodie[d] the goal that all those involved kept in mind: the economic stability of the Franklin County school districts." Real estate interests were especially glad to have the controversy behind them. Said Donald Borror, chair of the Borror Corporation, a large local housing development firm, "I applaud the officials who made the effort and had the resolve to tackle a very difficult issue."[173]

Hyre, meanwhile, was thoroughly convinced that his school district had reached the best agreement available to it. From the beginning, he saw that only a long, divisive, and probably fruitless legal struggle could wrest the common areas from Columbus's suburban counterparts. Having only recently concluded more than twelve years of desegregation litigation, Columbus, he said, "wasn't willing to fight that battle." [174] "The difficulty was how you were ever going to bring about any kind of different result," said Barrow. "It was pretty clear to us that we were not going to get support from the State Board of Education to transfer all those lands to Columbus. If somebody can figure out how to get them into Columbus, I'm pleased to do it. But I can tell you, no elected state judge is going to do it and no state board of education, in my opinion, is going to take that step. I think the only way it was going to happen was through some kind of federal court intervention. And, frankly, in recent years it doesn't seem to be that the federal courts are much interested in jumping into those kinds of areas." Judging from the housing market's response to *Penick*, there was ample reason to believe that even a successful annexation effort would fail to capture the middle class. "People would just move out further," said Weiler. "It would be a bonanza for the Dublin market because everybody would be running to get into it." Agreed Rich Fahey, a Columbus attorney who worked on Win-Win and then served on the school board from 1986 to 1993, "The political reality of it is that it would probably be ten, fifteen, maybe twenty years of heated legal battles, and by the time you're done tearing everything apart, I'm not sure you wouldn't end up with a system of one of the finest sets of private schools in the United States." [175]

Essentially, said Barrow, the district was "trading the present for the future." Win-Win did not force the system to concede anything it already had, and the schools were guaranteed new revenue from any future Columbus development. "We didn't give away one darn thing," Hyre declared. [176] "The fact is, we started with absolutely 'o' and we came away with about $1 million a year in shared revenue plus an agreement that when any [territory] is annexed to Columbus, it automatically becomes part of the Columbus school district." Said Weiler, "Call it ransom, call it anything you want, but Columbus got money for allowing the kids to stay where they are. I guess it's kind of like 'the horses are out of the barn.' You're better off putting a new lock on now and letting the horses go than not having a lock at all. The point is, if you know you can't win, do you finally reach a situation where you say 'let's look forward instead of backward'?"[177]

Moreover, Hyre and his school board were riding a wave of confidence at the time, a feeling heightened by the district's convincing 1986 levy victory. Despite the hostile rhetoric of developers and builders, the superintendent truly trusted that their reluctance to invest in the Columbus school district would eventually dissolve. "I think Jim Hyre absolutely believed that," said Viers. "I think he felt that the Columbus school system was going to be a high-quality urban school district under his leadership, that he was going to be able to do certain things, and that, why not? Why wouldn't people want to buy homes in the Columbus school district if it was indeed a top notch urban school district?" "Jim believed the development would happen within the Columbus city school boundaries," concurred Columbus board member Gary Holland. But, Holland added, "he knew it was up to the developers to make it happen."[178]

It was Hyre's faith in this uncertain future that drew the ire of Columbus school supporters. "Everything that's offered to Columbus is totally speculative, everything that the suburbs wanted and primarily got is concrete," said Martha Crossen of the Apple Alliance. "[Win-Win is] a double slap in the face of Columbus. We don't get any students, [and] we don't get any land." James Ebright called the agreement "the closest thing to a complete capitulation to the suburbs that I could have possibly imagined." Outspoken board member Bill Moss derided it as "a fantastic, unmitigated sellout," "terrible," "sickening," and "foul." And the *Call and Post* wondered "how the school system can focus so hard on protecting the interests of the affluent students in Reynoldsburg, Worthington, Westerville, Dublin, Gahanna, and Upper Arlington—which have some of the highest per capita incomes in the state—while neglecting to find a dime for the education of poor Black children in Columbus."[179]

Win-Win's detractors did not share Hyre's hope that the city school district would get its fair share of future development. "Builders and developers have made it painfully and publicly clear," Crossen noted, "that there will be no residential development in the Columbus Public School District now or in the future. So we won't get any students there to speak of and for practical purposes there won't be much land annexed anyway." The agreement, critics contended, preserved the ability of suburban residents to stay "safe" in the common areas yet maintain access to city services. "What ticks me off," Columbus City Council president Jerry Hammond said, "is that they use your resources—your infrastructure, your water and your sewer, your Outerbelt and your Innerbelt, your jobs, your airport—and they beat the hell out of you." "Columbus taxpayers are subsidizing the suburban school districts," asserted State Representative Otto Beatty, a black Columbus Democrat who had played a prominent role in annexation's legislative battles.[180] "[Win-Win] takes from the poor and gives to the rich." With Win-Win, influential development attorney Harrison Smith said, school officials "permanentized the dislocation of most of the upper-middle-class population of Columbus. They created a duality in citizenship." Lacking the stomach to stand up to the suburbs, Columbus officials, critics claimed, yielded to their counterparts' lone demand, getting only empty promises and some token cash as compensation. "Hyre and six board members wanted to avoid a fight at almost any cost," wrote reporter Herb Cook Jr. "The 'compromise' almost surely ensures that the city's schools will become blacker and poorer. . . . They should have called them win-wimp negotiations for all the good they did the city schools."[181]

The hollow irony of Win-Win was that both Hyre and his detractors were right. If the district failed to gain anything from the agreement to arrest its inexorable impoverishment, it was not because of a failure to fight, but because the battle had already been lost. In all probability, Hyre got about as much out of the deal as he could have, and therein lay its relevance. For the city schools, Win-Win was nei-

ther a financial triumph nor an educational tragedy. More than anything else, it was a symbolic milestone: the formal declaration of
the Columbus Public School District's second-class status.

Win-Win embodied the catch-22 that had come to characterize
the Columbus schools. District officials knew that in order to sustain the long-term educational viability of the system, they needed
all of the resources represented by the common areas: an expanding
tax base, stable middle-class families, political clout, the children of
local civic leaders, educational and extracurricular amenities, parental involvement, access to job networks, and so on. But the lack of
these resources is precisely what made pursuing them so quixotic.
Well before Win-Win negotiations began, Jim Hyre fully understood
the obstacles arrayed against his increasingly poor, increasingly
African American, and still desegregated district. Any effort to secure the common areas would incur the wrath of suburban residents, the hostility of state legislators, the resistance of the Ohio
Board of Education, the icy opposition of local business leaders, and
the paralyzed silence of a city hall balancing divided constituencies.
Given the growth consensus that governed Columbus politics, the
emergence of a school board willing to pursue such an effort was virtually unthinkable.

These political pressures would affect any attempted legal push
as well. The district's main weapon, the threat of a metropolitan desegregation suit, offered the unappetizing prospect of another lengthy,
vitriolic court battle, one with only a limited chance of success.
Moreover, the response of the residential development community
to *Penick* had vividly demonstrated the elusiveness and flexibility
of the structures that sustained educational inequality. Without the
unlikely backing of business and political leaders, a metropolitan
remedy risked driving development out of the county and sparking a
rush to private schools.

Crucially, Hyre had no notable grassroots support to use as proan-
nexation leverage. The Apple Alliance made some noise, but its con-
stituency seemed from the start a limited one: urban white liberals

with children in the Columbus schools. Far more significant—and especially revealing—was the relative silence of the African American community throughout the annexation debate. While suburbanites noisily mobilized to protect the status quo, city blacks evinced little passion for the issue. Though that may have been a sign of quiet faith in Franklin County's black legislative delegation, it was much more likely an indication of the black community's century-old ambivalence toward integration itself.

The ideal of integration had long been tarnished by the reality of desegregation, in Columbus and nationwide. Intended to increase black access to educational resources, desegregation instead often seemed to dilute black control over them. African American children in Columbus were being disproportionately disciplined and tracked, and they were dropping out all too frequently, yet the district's public focus—its alternative-school program in particular—seemed directed predominantly at the white middle class. Instead of distributing investment around the district, desegregation largely seemed to be driving it away. Increasingly, the product of *Penick* looked to be not equal access to abundant resources, but insufficient control over inadequate resources. Given the fierce suburban resistance to any encroachment on the common areas, blacks held little faith that annexation could solve either problem. Bringing thousands of resentful families involuntarily into the city schools hardly seemed an educational panacea for the children already there.

At the same time, however, most African Americans maintained a lingering faith in integration, a faith buttressed by the reality of segregation's inevitable economic limitations. And so, while the lack of active black support for pursuing the common areas was likely the result of annexation's uncertain consequences, the vocal criticism that the Win-Win Agreement itself engendered can be read as a reaction to the racial and economic inequality it symbolically sanctioned. The pressing question of the Columbus schools thus mirrored the postdesegregation dilemma of black Columbus: Can we survive on our own, without access to the resources around us? For both, the understandable hope was "yes," while the underlying reality was "no."

With Win-Win, response to the possibility of Columbus school territory transfer once again proved the measure of the city district's relative status. The agreement left little doubt that by 1986 the scales had shifted completely in favor of suburban schools, with no sign of tilting back. The increasingly hysterical response of suburban school district residents to urban education, meanwhile, indicated that a more ominous transformation had taken place.

Between 1970 and 1980, the city school system had gone from being essential to residential development in Columbus to being incompatible with it. The furor that preceded Win-Win, however, signaled the rise of an even darker perception of the Columbus Public School system, marking the triumph of a kind of educational NIMBY in Columbus. The city school district as a whole, despite being dubbed "the best urban system in the country," had come to be seen as not just inferior but actually noxious, a threat to the sanctity of suburbs, the safety of suburban children, and the security of suburban property values. As such, it was little different from a prison, a toxic waste storage site, a paint factory, or a sewage treatment plant. As with these other development hazards, nobody questioned the need for the services a city school system provided, as long as the dangers such a system symbolized—race, poverty, violence, and irresponsibility—remained reliably self-contained and safely distant. The prospect of annexation, however, threatened to dismantle the protective walls that had been invisibly erected around the Columbus schools. Suburban response to this danger was identical to what the reaction would have been to plans being announced for a federal correctional facility in Dublin, or a trash-burning power plant in Worthington. With the tacit blessing of city leaders, angry residents formed committed grassroots groups, held well-attended protests, and pressured sympathetic public officials in a display of defensive activism as swift and furious as it was effective. The poisons they were protesting were neither chemicals nor criminals, however, but children. Given the worsening disparity in resources between Columbus and the suburban school systems, this rejection offered a somber eulogy for school desegregation and sent a chilling message about the feasibility of future attempts to ensure equal educational opportunity.

4

Epilogue: Demoralization and Decline

When Jim Hyre disclosed in April 1987 that he would be stepping down from the superintendency at the end of July, his announcement generated a hail of praise for the man many considered the catalyst of the city schools' resurgent confidence. "It's not the result of fate or happenstance the district is in the best shape ever," wrote one reporter. "Rather, it is a direct result of Hyre's leadership." "More than anyone else," proclaimed the *Dispatch*, "Hyre is responsible for turning around the image of the Columbus Public School system." *Dispatch* education writer Kathy Gray Foster called Hyre "a revered school leader," adding that because of the outgoing superintendent, "People don't look down on Columbus schools as they used to from their suburban perches. Many have realized that a good reputation for Columbus schools is important for the community as a whole."[1]

Accompanying the acclaim, however, was a more ominous undertone, an anxious murmur that the irrepressible Hyre would prove an irreplaceable superintendent. While Bill Moss praised Hyre for being "concerned about children getting an education—all children," he worried that Hyre was abandoning the ship before it entered rough waters.[2] "Maybe the guy sees storm clouds on the horizon," Moss suggested, "and he's catching his hat. He might be saying 'I'm getting the devil out of there.'"[3] Mayor Buck Rinehart was more direct, calling Hyre's departure "a tragic loss" that "could be devastating for the city of Columbus." "Jim Hyre has brought magic to this district," declared board member turned *Business First* publisher Carole Williams. But, she noted in her publication, his agenda lay unfinished. "The best tribute the city's business leadership can give to his down-to-earth greatness," she implored, "would be an increased corporate commitment to finding ways for this city's school district to fulfill Hyre's dream of it becoming the best urban school district in the nation. That will take an even greater corporate commitment and involvement of the roll-up-the-sleeves and dive in variety."[4]

Indeed, for a time, such a commitment appeared imminent. In June 1987, M/I Schottenstein Homes unveiled plans to build two small subdivisions inside the boundaries of the Columbus school district, the first since the early 1970s. Six weeks later, developer Don Epler announced his intention to annex 182 acres of Jefferson Township farmland to Columbus for a 415-home subdivision called McNeill Farms. Because municipal annexation now meant automatic school territory transfer, McNeill Farms represented what Columbus schools spokesperson Laura Ecklar called "the first direct benefit to the school district since the [Win-Win] agreement was reached." "This underscores the reality, not the perception, that people are willing to invest in the school system," said interim superintendent Damon Asbury.[5]

For over a year after Win-Win, Jim Hyre's forward-looking faith in the Columbus Public School District's competitiveness appeared as though it might be justified. From the start, however, the "House That Hyre Built" was a fragile structure, assembled on a base of slowly eroding resources and held together by both the superintendent's galvanizing leadership and the city's prosperity. Nervous school officials saw new home building as the cement that would finally fill in the foundation. "We need the middle class housing starts that are planned," insisted government affairs supervisor Bob Barrow, "and we need them now."[6]

It soon became evident, however, that the influx of investment the district so desperately required would not materialize. Within two years after Hyre's departure, the real estate market had faltered, Epler's development had stalled, and M/I's new subdivisions had proven little more than successful anomalies.[7] Meanwhile, changing economic circumstances, combined with a series of systemic traumas, arrested the district's delicate momentum. By the beginning of the 1990s, "the best urban school system in the nation" seemed like a sad memory, somewhere between willful masquerade and involuntary mirage. "The problem was that the district's PR was about a zillion times more successful than its product," said school board member Anne Hall. "We thought we could maybe bring up the system to match the PR. Instead, we let the PR come down to match the product. We knew there had to be movement. We just went the wrong way."[8]

When Win-Win was signed in 1986, the commentary that attended the agreement focused primarily on the impact it would have on the city and suburban school districts. Lost was the crucial fact that Win-Win fundamentally transformed desegregation from a development nuisance that private interests could easily avoid to a municipal growth obstacle that the city could no longer ignore.

Before *Penick*, Columbus schools were largely a locational concern to area developers: where and how quickly can we build (segregated) neighborhood schools that will serve the city's burgeoning population? With the threat and implementation of desegregation, the schools became a development redline: where in Columbus can we build without having to deal with busing? Still, through 1985, the city's growth remained detached from that of the Columbus schools. By formally linking city and school district annexation for the first time in thirty years, however, Win-Win abruptly reunited urban growth and urban education: how can Columbus continue to grow now that all new land automatically enters the (desegregated) city school system?

With little time to examine the Win-Win legislation before the General Assembly ratified it, city officials found themselves in a quandary. They could either keep quiet about their concerns and back the hard-won compromise, or they could criticize the agreement and risk reigniting the annexation controversy. They chose the former. "I'm saying [to myself], 'We have a mess on our hands,'" then city council president Jerry Hammond recalled. "But because of my reluctance to take on the school board and say, 'I think you've made a terrible mistake,' we just said, 'Okay, we understand what you're saying, fine, very good,' and never made an issue out of it." Said city council economic development aide Pete Cass, "The city got briefed on Win-Win the day before the legislature was ready to announce it. Quite frankly, city people were dumbfounded. They thought, 'This is going to stop development in the city of Columbus.'" The most prominent figure to denounce Win-Win publicly was annexation attorney Harrison Smith, who warned, "I think the plan will substantially limit the growth of the city of Columbus. There will be no annexation for single-family development."[9]

For over a year, the city-school growth conflict remained in the background, obscured by the optimism of the M/I Homes and McNeill Farms announcements. During the fall of 1987, however, the facade of compatibility was suddenly and dramatically demolished by the seismic shock of Wexley. "Wexley" was the nickname quickly affixed to an enormous luxury housing development envisioned by Leslie Wexner, billionaire founder of The Limited, and his partner Jack Kessler, a prominent developer, civic booster, and Columbus North High School graduate.[10] Using a number of innocuous front companies, Wexner and Kessler had quietly amassed over four thousand acres of gently rolling farmland in northeastern Franklin County's Plain Township. On this bucolic property, they hoped to develop a community of unrivaled status in central Ohio, a superelite village combining the tasteful, faux-rural elegance of the

equestrian set, the nouveau riche country-club lifestyle of Dublin's
Muirfield Village, and the executive convenience—courtesy of newly
completed I-670—of a ten minute drive to the airport and a fifteen-
minute commute downtown.

Before building their opulent idyll, Wexley developers first needed
to ensure the provision of unglamorous but essential water and
sewer services. In July, however, Columbus had innocently canceled
an unused service contract that would have obligated it to supply
Wexley with utilities.[11] Unless they could market septic tanks as
status symbols, the developers were left with three noisy, public,
and controversial options for obtaining services: annex Wexley to
Columbus and, consequently, to the Columbus schools; use Les
Wexner's seemingly unlimited wealth to circumvent the city's water-sewer monopoly; or use the seemingly unlimited influence that
accompanied Les Wexner's wealth to nudge the Columbus City
Council into offering a new service contract to tiny Plain Township
municipality New Albany. If the developers refused to annex to Columbus, it would represent an unambiguous rejection of the city
school district. If they convinced the council to extend services
without annexation, it would be a double snub, a rebuff of the city
schools and an intentional evasion of Win-Win; and if they built
their own water-sewer facilities or found services elsewhere, it
could signal the sealing off of Columbus's ability to expand to the
northeast.[12] What appeared to be the simplest option of the three—
annexing Wexley to the city of Columbus—was complicated by the
antiurban obstructionism of Plain Township property owners and
by the fact that the status of the city school district was irreconcil-
able with the dreams of the developers.

Involving at least nine separate governmental jurisdictions, in-
numerable political and economic interests, and, perhaps most important, the $2 billion behind Les Wexner, the efforts of Wexley
developers to secure services became an extended media explosion
that shook the entire central Ohio area. The convoluted controversy, described by reporter Herb Cook Jr. as "'Lifestyles of the Rich
and Famous' meets '60 Minutes,'" took traditional American social

fissures—black versus white, rich versus poor, rural versus urban—
and jumbled them together. By the time it was settled, the controversy had also managed to pit rich against rich,[13] rural against
rural,[14] black against black,[15] and school board and city council
members against each other. It took a year of remarkably elaborate
political and legal machinations for the Wexley forces to get what
they had wanted all along: to obtain Columbus services for the
whole development while keeping the most expensive, elite lots
out of the Columbus school district.

For all its complexity, the Wexley controversy sent two very clear
messages to the Columbus school district. The first was that, despite the gains of the Hyre years, civic leaders still viewed the city
school system as a growth liability. Summarizing Wexley's significance, Columbus school board member Rich Fahey said, "The question at the time was: 'How big of a player are we?' Are we a Triple A
team in the big league? I mean, how are we going to get treated?
What do we come out of this with? Do we have enough clout that
we can demand it all? Obviously, we didn't."[16]

An even more demoralizing message, however, was sent by the
incredible determination of normally controversy-averse developers
to keep their most valuable territory out of the Columbus schools.
Rather than a dramatic investment in the supposedly resurgent city
system, Wexley became a drawn-out saga that laid bare the rhetoric
of the area's economic elite. By seeking so doggedly to see their executive lots served by the poor, white, rural Plain Local schools, the
developers conveyed a signal to the Columbus board that seemed to
say, "We'll take anything but you."[17] In 1983, Plain Local had been
rated the worst suburban school district in Franklin County by *Columbus Monthly*. By 1988, its enrollment was less than 850, having
dropped more than 400 over the previous decade. The district had
no special education courses, no gifted program, no vocal music or
drama, no swimming pool, and no tennis courts. Only a few years
earlier, its superintendent had predicted that the cash-poor district
would have to be consolidated with another school district by the end
of the decade. "To suggest that the level of teaching in Plain Local is
superior to Columbus is a joke," said Columbus board member and

developer Robert Weiler. "But the difference is, when kids go to school in Plain Local, they're going to school with predominantly white children. There's that deep-rooted prejudice that still exists today, that 'I as a white family want my kids to go to school with white kids.' I can't be any more blunt about it, or, hopefully, honest about it."[18] While the controversy was as much about control as anything else—the public-education equivalent of a corporate take-over—the racial implications of Wexley were indeed inescapable: post-Hyre, post-Win-Win, the integrated Columbus Public School District was still considered an unacceptable risk for developers and an unsuitable education for the children of city leaders.

The Wexley battle placed the city-school growth conflict in painfully stark relief. For the first time, city leaders began viewing the Columbus school district as a malignant cancer rather than a benign blemish, a worsening urban disease that could be fatal in the long run if left untreated. Civic boosters already preparing for Columbus's 1992 coming-out party—the quincentennial anniversary of Christopher Columbus's voyage—feared that a sickly school system could prove contagious, spoiling the image of the city itself. An added degree of urgency was injected by the gradually growing proportion of black students in the district: 46.3 percent in 1988–89.[19] For a business community long devoted to the *perception* of a quality urban school system, a majority black enrollment symbolized educational unsalvageability, a "tipping point" beyond which urban chaos lurked. "There's the perception," said James Kunde, an urban leadership consultant who had worked closely with Columbus's business elite, "that if [the school district] gets over 50 percent black, you've lost it. Rather than 'we can still do high quality with a mostly black school' . . . it falls off the edge of a cliff." "Once it gets past 50, 51 percent," concurred Urban League executive director Sam Gresham, the business community believes "the whole school system has tipped and it's going to hell."[20]

The Wexley controversy thus stepped up the intensity with which school board members, city officials, and business leaders sought to lure middle-class whites back to the district. The agenda that emerged went beyond the end of busing to embrace a wholesale, corporate-style restructuring of the school system: find a strong "CEO" and resolute board willing to make difficult changes, downsize bloated middle management in order to enhance organizational responsiveness and redirect resources to the building level, and inspire educational innovation by granting teachers and principals more instructional independence. In snowballing sequence, however, each item on the agenda went drastically awry.

The school board election of 1987 was a model of Columbus growth consensus politics. The campaign promised to be wide open and unpredictable, with thirteen candidates running for five seats. It was, city leaders concluded, an uncertain situation that warranted unprecedented intervention. The result was "The Coalition for an Effective School Board," a singular alliance consisting of the Columbus Area Chamber of Commerce, Columbus Education Association, and the Franklin County Democratic and Republican parties. Given the resources and clout that these groups represented, the election was decided the day the coalition endorsed its five-candidate slate: incumbents Rich Fahey, Robert Weiler, and Pauline Radebaugh, and newcomers Anne Hall and Sharlene Morgan.

Critically, however, the coalition's slate consisted not of specifically handpicked individuals but of previously declared candidates. As a result, after the election, the stabilizing, moderate consensus the coalition's endorsements were designed to create never materialized. What quickly emerged instead was a balkanized, squabbling, ineffective board, "a three-ring circus," as Weiler called it. Absent the strong hand of a James Hyre, the fractious, meddlesome board became a political laughingstock. "My favorite story," quipped Harrison Smith, "was the vote on a major issue which the Columbus school board opposed one to one to one to one to one to one to one."[21]

The board's first major undertaking—the hiring of a new superintendent—proved a fiasco. After a failed initial search, it ran a secret CEO headhunt, eventually settling on Savannah, Georgia, superintendent Ron Etheridge, who had not even made the original list of finalists and received only a bare majority of votes in the board's private caucus. Before the surprise press conference that sprang the new superintendent on the city, one reporter commented, "Whoever this turns out to be, he could be Jesus Christ and he'd be walking into a bad situation."[22] By his resignation in late 1990, some indeed viewed Etheridge as a martyred messiah; to too many others, however, he had become the most demonized figure in the recent history of the Columbus schools.

The board gave Etheridge two charges: reorganize and reduce the district's central office administration, and reform and strengthen its educational program. Aloof, abrasive, and blunt, he proved temperamentally unsuited to the delicate politics of cutting high-level staff. By bringing an ax rather than a scalpel to the process, Etheridge decimated both central office and building-level morale. His leadership, employees came to believe, rested on henchmen, hitmen, and spies. Administrative trust subsequently plummeted, stifling rather than unleashing educational innovation and infusing even the most basic district operations with suspicion.

Moreover, Etheridge made the mistake of targeting several of the system's highest-ranking black administrators for termination. Columbus African Americans, already innately suspicious of a white southerner brought in to "reform" the city school system, exploded when Etheridge's first victims included community pillars such as assistant superintendent Evelyn Luckey. The furor that ensued became Columbus's most extended and intense African American protest in a generation, producing a successful black-led campaign to defeat the district's 1990 levy effort.

Black opposition also undermined Etheridge's ambitious but untested educational reform initiatives. Under James Hyre, the district's efforts to increase business community involvement and attract middle-class white homeowners had received the tacit support of the black community because they were constrained by two tethers: a sufficient degree of trust in the straightforward superintendent and the sense of security provided by the watchful eye of district court judge Robert Duncan. Neither qualification existed under Etheridge, however. As a result, the hostility provoked by his administrative moves spilled over onto his educational reforms. Attacking Etheridge's ideas as a covert effort to resegregate the schools, African American leaders criticized the superintendent for being more concerned with attracting suburban whites than educating urban blacks. Many blacks viewed the business community's enthusiastic support of Etheridge as further proof that the Norfolk, Virginia, native had been brought in to weaken African American influence over the school system, eliminate busing, and return the district to a pre-*Penick* state of internal educational disparity.

In November 1990, following a divisive levy loss, Etheridge announced that he would be leaving Columbus to become superintendent of the Santa Barbara, California, school system. His acrimonious tenure had ensured the indefinite postponement of needed educational and administrative reforms, leaving "ending busing" as the only remaining miracle cure for the district's ills. In early 1990, the board had retained Robert Duncan, then in private practice with the firm of Jones, Day, Reavis, and Pogue, to advise the district on the legal ramifications of altering its student assignment plan. The former judge recommended that a citizens' committee be set up as a buffer against accusations of intentional resegregation. Former board president Carole Williams and departed city council president Jerry Hammond, an integrated team of influential local decision makers, accepted the board's invitations to head the potentially incendiary committee. The timing for such an effort appeared especially fortuitous, as an increasing number of local black leaders had begun expressing disenchantment with the school district's voluntary commitment to court-ordered desegregation mandates. During that fall's mayoral campaign, black Democratic city councilman Ben Espy had called repeatedly for "an end to busing," outflanking and nearly upsetting his heavily favored white Republican opponent, Greg Lashutka. "Over time, crosstown busing has only fostered the very alienation and segregation it was designed to eliminate," Espy declared.[23] "We're busing for racial balance, but in cities like Philadelphia and Cleveland, Detroit and Chicago, one day they looked up and found out there were no more races to balance. So if [we] don't want to get to that point, we must be candid about what busing is doing to our economic base."[24] Had Espy won, he would have joined a growing number of black, big city mayors committed to ending busing in order to reinvigorate urban development and re-channel educational resources.[25]

On December 10, 1991, after a year of research, meetings, and debate, the Citizens' Committee for Improved Student Assignment unveiled its recommendations. Decreasing the time and distance of bus rides and maintaining racial diversity were incompatible goals, Hammond and Williams told the board. If the district wanted to reduce busing, they advised, it should do so carefully, avoiding the politically loaded and demographically outdated phrase "neighborhood schools" and expanding integrative options to counter increased racial isolation. Most important, the committee's report forewarned, "The mere assignment of students does not create an excellent school system. Improved image, increased enrollment, and return of the middle class to the Columbus Public Schools cannot be generated simply by a student assignment plan, unless the board of education, at the same time, addresses all relevant issues of quality and equity."[26]

The committee's cautious counsel was not what the school board wanted to hear. After thanking Hammond and Williams for a year of hard work, the board unceremoniously jettisoned their recommendations. Rearranging the committee's proposed guidelines, the board directed a team of administrators to construct a new assignment plan using "choice" and—despite the committee's warnings—"neighborhood schools" as its top two priorities. Over the next several months, planners repeatedly tried to impress upon board members the controversy that such massive change and substantial resegregation would engender. But because so little trust remained between frustrated administrators and a micromanaging board, their message fell on deaf ears. Goaded by business leaders hoping that a return to neighborhood schools would bring residential development back to the district, the board ordered its planning team to press ahead with formulating a proposal.

Finally released on September 8, 1992, the long-awaited student re-assignment plan accomplished exactly what the board had demanded, opening up more alternative-school slots and allowing 8,300 more students to walk to school. In doing so, however, the proposal reassigned 45 percent of the district's 64,000 students, reduced the number of racially balanced schools from 113 to 60, and chucked at least one particularly explosive change into practically every section of the city.[27] Predictably, opponents appeared en masse at a series of public meetings designed to gauge reaction to the plan, while satisfied supporters stayed home. Parents and students who may otherwise have backed its goals demanded that they be exempt from its dislocations. Black parents and community leaders in particular rejected the plan as precisely the kind of "reassignment for the sake of reassignment" gambit against which Hammond and Williams had warned, a developer-driven effort to end busing first and address education later, if at all. An unspecified "educational component" added belatedly to the plan did little to dispel criticisms of its inequitability. "When you have $3 for books, you *know* who's going to get the $2 part," explained *Call and Post* business editor and Hammond-Williams committee member Paul Anderson.[28]

Public backlash brought a hasty retreat from the weak and fractious board, despite *Columbus Dispatch* calls not to "drop [the plan] over the side of the ship as soon as some big waves appear."[29] Finally, on November 16, interim superintendent Larry Mixon—the district's fifth new leader in five years—drew a thirty-second ovation from a packed board meeting by "strongly recommend[ing] that a halt be called to the continued development of the student reassignment plan." The board's 5–2 vote to declare the plan "unacceptable" marked the ignominious defeat of the district's most concerted attempt to abandon its voluntary commitment to the principles of *Penick.*

The student reassignment disaster vividly illustrated the quandary the school district had come to face. City leaders, both black and white, recognized that the implications of "busing" had to be erased before residential development—and, consequently, the resources of the middle class—could be lured back to the Columbus schools. Yet the emphasis on dismantling desegregation obscured the fact that a generation of students had passed since 1979. To most of the district's constituents, systemwide change was more intrusive than a transportation plan that had become the status quo. Consequently, any attempt to tinker with student assignments in a way significant enough to attract parents from outside the system inevitably would generate angry resistance from parents inside the system. Moreover, "busing for racial balance" could not be eliminated without producing substantial resegregation. The city schools thus faced an apparently intractable dilemma: get rid of busing and immediately create marked *intra*district educational disparities, or maintain the status quo and allow *inter*district educational disparities inexorably to worsen.

Political and policy-making debacles were not the only waves to rock the Columbus schools in the years after Jim Hyre's departure. Social and economic forces combined to accelerate the deterioration of the school system, further complicating efforts to reinvigorate urban education in Columbus.

Long defined by its stable, balanced economy, Ohio's capital has always remained relatively insulated from the cyclical downturns that plague most other cities. The recession of the late 1980s and early 1990s, however, revealed that not even Columbus could escape the wrenching structural changes occurring in the nation's economy. Disappearing was the backbone of America's postwar prosperity—low-tech, high-wage, high-security manufacturing jobs—the victim of improved transportation technology, globalized labor markets, computerization, and borderless capital. Emerging in its place was a service-based economy characterized by an increasingly bifurcated wage structure, a labor market in which the capacity to produce or process information was becoming the most significant determinant of an individual's prospects. Thus, while blue-collar labor declined as an available outlet for the uneducated, the economic significance of learning grew.

Though central Ohio has never been dependent on industry for its prosperity, manufacturing jobs have always made up a prominent portion of the area's labor base. Over the past two decades, however, the relative significance of manufacturing has steadily declined. While total employment in the seven-county Columbus Metropolitan Statistical Area rose 59 percent from 1970 to 1989, manufacturing employment fell 10 percent. The goods-producing jobs that supplied 31.4 percent of the area's employment in 1970 provided only 19.2 percent of its jobs in 1989. This decline is particularly important because the average annual wage of a goods-producing job in the Columbus area was, as of 1989, 38 percent higher than that of the typical service-sector position.[30]

The negative effects of these changes fell first on unskilled, poor and minority central-city residents. As a result, the giddy mid-1980s boom that seemed to be symbolized by the sparkling skyscrapers rising downtown was actually better captured by the division of labor hidden within: the disparity between those who worked in the spacious offices during the day and those who cleaned them at night. In 1990, for instance, the Columbus school district contained 70 percent of the city's residents, but 91.4 percent of those living in poverty. While the 1990 poverty rate for those living within the city school boundaries stood at 19.9 percent, the poverty rate for the common areas was only 5.7 percent. Other statistics provide a similar picture of economic divergence along racial and geographical lines: the unemployment rate within the city school district was 6.9 percent in 1990, but only 3.1 percent in the common areas;[31] in 1988, the average household income in older, central-city Columbus was $22,432, compared to $35,336 in the rest of the county;[32] and the per capita income of whites in Franklin County in 1990 was 42.6 percent higher than that of African Americans.[33]

In *American Apartheid: Segregation and the Making of the Underclass,* Douglas Massey and Nancy Denton convincingly demonstrate that "black poverty is exacerbated, reinforced, and perpetuated by racial segregation."[34] Though tempered by central Ohio's relative prosperity, their assessment is certainly applicable to Columbus, and the process they describe was intensified during the past decade by economic dislocation, crack cocaine, and violent crime. These dynamics have affected the entire region to some degree, but they have hit black youth—and, in turn, the Columbus Public Schools—with disproportionate force. The result: a combination of multiplying out-of-school risk factors and declining in-school discipline that throws barrier after barrier in the way of academic progress. "Most poverty-family children, regardless of race," an in-house chamber of commerce report observed, "enter the educational system with severe disadvantages—poor diets, little home encouragement to learn, exposure to crime and drugs, often from single-parent homes, peer pressures. Those who succeed in the face of these odds are truly exceptional."[35]

Though the Columbus Public Schools contained pockets of excellence, the cycle of poverty and violence that existed reinforced the continuing exodus of middle-class resources from the district. According to a Columbus Development Department report, the value of residential real property in the common areas grew 330 percent during the 1980s, compared to just 73 percent in the city district; between 1980 and 1989, the Columbus schools' share of the city's residential property value declined from 84.4 percent to 68.5 percent.[36] Indeed, by the beginning of the 1990s, it had become all too apparent that the new residential development that James Hyre hoped would follow the Win-Win Agreement was not going to materialize. In 1989, for example, only 2 percent of the single-family building permits issued in Franklin County were for homes in the city school district; the city itself, on the other hand, captured 51 percent of these permits.[37] Of 185 housing developments under construction in the county that year, just three were served by the Columbus district.[38] Through 1991, the spoils of Win-Win included only 23 students and 2,865 acres.[39]

Business investment, meanwhile, followed residential growth beyond the Columbus school system's borders. From 1980 to 1989, the taxable value of personal property in the city school district declined 16.2 percent in real terms. During that time, the proportion

of personal property value located in the common areas nearly doubled, growing from 16.6 percent of the city's total to 31.9 percent.
Businesses were drawn to the common areas despite the higher tax
rates of suburban school systems. "The attractions," explained a
Columbus Development Department report, "include growing and
relatively affluent populations, well educated labor forces, more
abundant and lower priced land for development, and the various
amenities typically perceived as suburban."[40]

While the Columbus schools are in adequate shape physically
and fiscally compared to some other urban systems, the gradual hemorrhaging of resources from the district will eventually take its
toll. If current conditions continue, the school district can, at best,
struggle to tread water. At worst, it will slowly sink.

Columbus's business leadership has come to view the declining
health of the city school district with growing alarm.[41] Ever since
the Win-Win Agreement reconnected municipal annexation and
school territory transfer, the city's growth has suffered. In 1984, 68
percent of all land annexed to Columbus was for single-family homes;
from 1986 to 1990, the figure dropped to 3 percent.[42] An equally
pressing worry has become the effect of the district's educational
standards on the quality of the area's workforce. "An increasing
share of Columbus's young people do not graduate from high school
and a growing share of those who do graduate lack the reading, writing, computing, and communicating skills to qualify even for an
entry level office or factory job," asserted a recent chamber of commerce report. With city leaders seeking to position Columbus as a
new kind of high-tech, inland information hub, improving the pro-
ductivity and employability of city school graduates has emerged
as an economic imperative. "Columbus is not only competing with
San Diego, Indianapolis and other cities," wrote Midland Mutual
CEO and 1990 chamber chair Gerald Mayo, one of the business
community's most respected school advocates, "but with cities in
other countries with educated labor forces. If our workers are not as
skilled, then we cannot compete. The economic growth of this community is dependent on the education of our children, because good

schools attract new companies, new jobs, and provide us with skilled workers to fill those jobs." An ailing city school system, on the other hand, produces not just an uncompetitive labor force, but a host of expensive social ills that mar the city's image and damage its quality of life. Where preserving the perception of a good urban district once seemed such a luxury, creating the reality of such a system has now come to be viewed as a necessity by many Columbus business leaders. "Failure to correct current [educational] deficiencies, especially in the Columbus City Schools," warned the chamber's economic development strategy report, "will cripple the Columbus area economy within the next ten years." While the report noted that "the problems are still solvable," it added, "To mobilize support for a massive effort to address this full range of problems, the education challenge must be viewed as more than a social issue. It is, in fact, a problem that can bring the Columbus area's economic growth to a standstill, eventually producing the kind of stagnation now found in larger urban areas (e.g. New York and Detroit). Because it is also a 'survival' issue for Columbus's business community, it merits the same level of attention and commitment that business leaders give to other challenges that threaten their profitability."[43]

But just what form could such a "massive effort" take? Who would provide the leadership? And where would the resources come from? Unable to assume a satisfactory degree of predictability and control, skittish Columbus business leaders have shied away from any high-visibility investment in the city school district. For despite the chamber's dire warnings, no immediate civic catastrophe looms, no economic emergency seems imminent. Absent some sudden and dramatic disaster, no easy symbolism exists to spark a crusade to revitalize the city schools. Moreover, given the school system's fragmented constituencies, trip-wire political sensitivity, and countless competing interest groups, there is little evidence of an emerging reform consensus in Columbus. Old approaches have failed to ensure equal educational opportunity, and compelling new ones have not yet arisen to replace them. As a result of the unbridgeable chasm between what is necessary and what is possible, a sense of policy-making paralysis has come to surround the Columbus schools. With this bleak picture in mind, and as a way of revisiting some of the main themes of this book, I conclude with a hypothetical policy proposal whose centerpiece is at once elementary and revolutionary: the abolition of the Columbus Public School District.

Conclusion

In the four decades since *Brown v. Board of Education*, the law of the land has been neutralized by the law of unintended consequences. As the moral clarity of that decision has been blurred by the messy reality of its application, the prospect of fulfilling *Brown*'s promise has become increasingly remote, intimidating, and perhaps even hopeless. That we have failed to give full meaning to *Brown*, however, does not mean that we should cease to try. Inequality of opportunity remains the distinguishing characteristic of America's public education system, and Chief Justice Earl Warren's 1954 words are echoed in the rhetoric of end-of-the-century school reformers of all political stripes: "In these days, it is doubtful that any child may reasonably be expected to succeed in life if he is denied the opportunity of an education. Such an opportunity, where the state has undertaken to provide it, is a right which must be made available to all on equal terms."[44] To reassert *Brown*'s aims, we must reassess its failures. The story of school desegregation in Columbus, Ohio, with all its complexity, controversy, drama, and banality, offers an instructive look at the barriers to and boundaries of efforts to ensure educational opportunity.

In telling this story, I chose to focus not on the courtroom or the classroom, but on the city itself and those who shape it. From the beginning, school desegregation was about the relationship between where children lived and where they went to school. In Columbus, as in most northern urban areas, public and private discrimination worked symbiotically to concentrate almost all of the area's African American population in a small section of the central city served by a handful of all black schools. When years of frustration and protest failed to shatter segregative practices, blacks were forced to seek redress in the courts and, eventually, remedy in busing. Columbus's powerful business community worked aggressively to ensure that the implementation of Judge Robert Duncan's desegregation order in the *Penick* case proceeded peacefully, without the kind of headline-grabbing violence that could have hindered the city's promising economic prospects. All the while, however, private- and public-sector actions were combining to decouple the state of the city from the status of its school system; the business-led "growth consensus" that governs civic affairs in Columbus both knowingly permitted and actively encouraged a jurisdictional peculiarity that allows 40 percent of Columbus to be situated in suburban school districts. These "common areas" have acted as a middle-class safety valve, enabling the city to prosper even as the city schools have come to serve a rising proportion of poor white and black students.

Busing as a constitutional remedy was designed to render irrelevant the relationship between housing and school attendance patterns. While the courts could control pupil assignments, however, they had no jurisdiction over the local residential development market. Those in Columbus most responsible for shaping the city's living patterns—politicians, bankers, builders, developers, real estate agents, and others—were complicit in but not accountable for the creation and perpetuation of segregated schools. Far more fluid and adaptable than the race-conscious judicial system's halting, unwieldy remedy process, the equally race-conscious private market was quickly able to anticipate, evade, and ultimately profit from *Penick*'s outcome. By the time desegregation was implemented, the border of the Columbus Public School District had been tacitly designated a residential development redline, within which virtually no single-family home building would take place.

As with all affirmative action remedies, planned obsolescence was essential to busing's legitimacy. Its advocates believed that because segregated schools helped produce and solidify segregated residential patterns, therefore desegregated schools would eventually spur integrated housing, in turn making desegregation unnecessary. But busing had two unforeseen effects: it exacerbated rather than reduced the impact of race and racial fear as housing market variables, and it severed rather than transformed the relationship between city schools and single-family home building. Since new houses for central Ohio's growing population were available only in suburban school systems, the city school district slowly lost the critical mass of middle-class families necessary to desegregation's success. Perhaps even more important than the property tax revenues and extracurricular funds that followed these families was the hemorrhaging of social capital, the less quantifiable resources— employment opportunities, access to stores and services, new infrastructure, political energy, social stability—that generally accompany middle-class residential development and ensure a community environment more conducive to the education of children. It was access to these resources that school desegregation sought ultimately to equalize. Overcoming their inequitable distribution seemed feasible as long as they were concentrated within the same jurisdiction. By driving the single-family housing market beyond the boundaries of the city school district, however, busing inadvertently fragmented these resources and thereby made gaining access to them even more complicated and elusive than before.

While desegregation in Columbus has by no means been the disaster its opponents predicted, it has plainly failed to ensure equal educational opportunity for all children. Inequities that existed between individual schools a generation ago persist, only now they are defined on a broader scale by urban-suburban school district borders. Meanwhile, the backlash against busing has largely chilled any discussion about the interaction of race, class, residential patterns, and educational opportunity. Whites and blacks alike have grown weary of the sacrifices demanded by integration and dubious of its presumed benefits. With government-supported desegregation efforts in retreat, current attempts to reinvigorate urban education simply assume the inevitability of economic and racial isolation.

Critics of public education often argue that its problems start in the home, yet most categories of reform—funding, administration, choice—focus solely on the schools. While new approaches to these areas are necessary, they are also insufficient. The development of most children is shaped by the interplay of home, school, and neighborhood environments. The more unsafe, unpredictable, or impoverished any of these elements is, the more complicated the path from infancy to productive citizenship becomes. Efforts to address the particular problems of urban education (in short, the difficulty of educating large concentrations of poor, often minority children) must therefore do more than increase access to good schools; they must also strengthen what writer Richard Weissbourd calls the "scaffolding" that shapes healthy development.[45]

In practical terms, such efforts demand policies that seek to reduce economic isolation while increasing access to educational opportunities. Combining these considerations with the lessons learned from the history of Columbus school desegregation, I have come up with a hypothetical proposal that usefully illustrates the complexity of the issues involved and the creativity needed to address them. While the specifics of this plan apply solely to Columbus, the dilemmas that shape it are familiar to urban school districts around the country: the complicated interplay of economic growth, housing development, and educational opportunity; the ambivalent attitudes of whites and blacks toward integration; the impact of the private market on public education and the often conflicting role of business leaders in addressing public education's problems; and the need to reduce concentrations of poverty in order to expand access to educational resources.

The three elements of the plan are as follows:

1. Eliminate the Columbus Public School District and extend the boundaries of Franklin County's suburban systems to cover the territory currently served by Columbus.

The Columbus Public School District is neither the best nor the worst urban system in America. It contains some fine schools, numerous innovative programs, and many superb, devoted educators. Yet the district is trapped in a catch-22 that makes it less and less able to keep pace with the accelerating demands of a rapidly changing, knowledge- and information-based society: called on to educate a growing proportion of poor or near-poor children, the district itself has become a barrier to the resources demanded by the task. The consequence of these mutually reinforcing conditions is, if not inexorable decline, at least increased educational inadequacy. What follows is therefore not a repudiation of the city school system itself, but a condemnation of the structures that have allowed the current situation to develop.

The first step of this proposal is the elimination of the Columbus Public School District. As the expansion of the common areas over the past three decades demonstrates, it is the city school system, not the city itself, that the middle class has come to reject. If urban school boundaries have become such powerful walls, why not tear them down? It would be the opposite of both annexation and metropolitanization: instead of extending the city district's borders, the boundaries of Franklin County's fifteen suburban systems would be redrawn to cover the territory currently served by Columbus schools, a geographically feasible process given the county's unusual combination of suburbs and inburbs. City students would then be distributed among suburban systems in such a way as to ensure that no district becomes identifiable as predominantly poor or minority.

By erasing the status distinction that city-suburban school boundaries symbolize, abolishing the Columbus schools would eliminate the barrier to urban development that the district now represents. Middle-class families would have no central city school system to avoid or escape, public education would no longer stand as an obstacle to Columbus's annexation efforts, and the economic fruits of metropolitan growth would be more broadly accessible. At the same time, the preservation of existing suburban districts and the absence of "forced busing" would mute suburban fears, speak to the suburbs' powerful sense of jurisdictional defensiveness, and address the residential development-education nexus more effectively than either metropolitanization or a Columbus school territory grab.

2. Create an "experimental education district" within the old boundaries of the Columbus Public School System.

Though simply doing away with the Columbus school district would break down the existing urban-suburban educational dichotomy, it would do little to make the central city more attractive to middle-class families and much to exacerbate African American concerns about cultural preservation and white educational indifference. The second part of this policy proposal would tackle these issues while rallying business community support for urban education.

The aim of creating an "experimental education district" would be to establish a concentrated hub of educational innovation within the old borders of the city school system. A half-elected, half–mayorally appointed board would oversee the establishment of choice-driven charter schools developed by a variety of sources: local community groups, enterprising parents and teachers, private educational consultants, area corporations, universities, and others. To provide an incentive for urban development, access would be restricted to students living within the old Columbus school boundaries; middle-class families would thus have to settle in the central city to avail themselves of particularly successful experiments. For Columbus's business elite, meanwhile, the idea of an "experimental education zone" would be attractive not only because it would appeal to the private sector's growing involvement in public education, but also because it would hold the potential to transform central Ohio into a national showcase of educational reform, exactly the kind of investment-attracting publicity city leaders covet.

Just as important, such a setup could accommodate the complexities of the black community much more effectively than mandatory desegregation did. For over a century, African Americans in Columbus have viewed integrated education with ambivalence, seeing it as the sacrifice of instructional control to indifferent, often hostile whites in return for access to the greater resources of the dominant majority. *Penick* represented the faith of many that this trade-off would be both favorable and temporary. A generation later, this faith seems tarnished, if not altogether discredited. At the same time, however, a significant black middle class has emerged, further complicating the integration debate by magnifying the significance of economic status and introducing the issue of "black flight."

The result is a diverse, sometimes contradictory set of interests that demands more options and more autonomy than desegregation allowed. This proposal would provide both, offering black parents greater freedom to tailor the educational environments of their children. Through existing choice programs, students could either remain in their current schools or transfer to other schools in their newly drawn districts. The opportunities for central-city students would be further multiplied by the alternatives available in the experimental education zone. A lab school developed and run by Ohio State, an Africentric school, a high-tech trade school supported by a consortium of local companies, an all-male academy emphasizing discipline and basics—these are just some of the possibilities. By vastly expanding African American educational options while neither abandoning nor demanding integration, this plan would de-emphasize the dilemma that desegregation has so long stressed, reducing racial balance to just one in a series of factors to be weighed and prioritized by black parents.

3. Use Columbus's water and sewer service monopoly to encourage the development of mixed-income housing.

The first two elements of this policy proposal were designed primarily to reduce economic isolation and increase educational opportunity in the central city. Most new development in Franklin County, however, will continue to spread outward from the fringes of Columbus and its suburbs. The construction of mixed-income housing is thus necessary to begin to disrupt the patterns of isolation that these areas have traditionally reinforced. Unless such construction is encouraged, Columbus will continue to bear the growing burden of providing services and shelter to the overwhelming majority of the region's poor population.

Municipal fragmentation multiplies both the difficulty and the importance of promoting mixed-income housing. Suburban jurisdictions ensure desirability through zoning restrictions over which Columbus has no control. Unilateral attempts by Columbus to alter its own housing patterns, meanwhile, are likely futile: economic incentives for developers are costly and controversial; additional regulations would only serve to drive new development out of the city. Absent the creation of some sort of metropolitan governing body with authority over development decisions, Columbus is left with only one lever of any consequence: its near-countywide monopoly over water and sewer services.

For four decades, Columbus has used its water and sewer monopoly to control suburban sprawl and preserve its ability to expand. It is to this powerful tool, then, that the city must turn to foster not just orderly growth, but equitable growth as well. Columbus should take a "carrot and stick" approach to renegotiating service contracts with surrounding suburbs, insisting on "fair share" housing agreements—targeted percentages of low- and moderate-income housing construction—in return for the expansion of service areas. Tap-in fees would be tied to each suburb's willingness to encourage more diverse residential patterns. Lower costs would thus provide an incentive for more mixed-income development, while higher costs would serve as a disincentive to economically exclusive development. Either way, the suburbs would be required to assume more responsibility for the social welfare of the whole region, whether by absorbing a larger share of the Columbus area's low-income population or by paying more for the consequences of concentrating poverty in the city.

There are, of course, many problems with this proposal, not the least of which is its political inconceivability. Its purpose, however, has not been to provide a practical blueprint for the reconstruction of urban education in Columbus. Rather, it has been to illustrate how the politics of place continues to affect educational opportunity, and to highlight the need to develop postdesegregation policies

to fulfill *Brown*'s sagging but still-vital spirit. The aims of the plan—
to reduce economic isolation while increasing educational options—
are not themselves enough to cure the ills of urban education, in
Columbus or elsewhere; at the same time, prescriptions that ignore
these ingredients are doomed to fail.

On January 31, 1996, the Columbus Board of Education adopted a
sweeping new student assignment scheme. Hailed as "an end to
forced busing," the board's plan combined neighborhood schools
with districtwide choice, terminating more than ten years of voluntary adherence to district court desegregation criteria. "This is not
an end but a beginning," declared Rhonda Whitlow, president of the
Columbus chapter of the NAACP, which supported the plan.[46] By
finally banishing the bogeyman busing had become, the board swept
aside what was at once one of the school system's most entrenched
distractions and one of its most convenient scapegoats. Columbus,
the country, and the world have all changed dramatically in the
twenty years since Robert Duncan's *Penick* ruling; if the death of desegregation allows for a more clearheaded conversation about the
forces shaping city schools, then it may prove a sort of educational
euthanasia. More likely than not, however, desegregation's end, like
the sudden collapse of the cold war, will only serve to expose the more
complex, elusive, and intractable dilemmas that have developed in
its shadows. Though *Penick*'s premise may no longer resonate, its
promise does. And unless bold, boundary-breaking initiatives are
undertaken to address the persistence of educational inequality in
Columbus, the city school district will enter the twenty-first century without busing, simply spinning its wheels.

Notes

Introduction

1. J. Harvie Wilkinson, *From Brown to Bakke*, 39.
2. National School Boards Association, "The Growth of Segregation in American Public Schools: Changing Patterns of Separation and Poverty Since 1968," 1993.
3. Educating poor children, particularly poor minorities, has thus become, along with such undesirable public functions as sewage treatment and waste disposal, a necessary civic responsibility to which communities respond by declaring, "Not in my backyard!"
4. There are no comprehensive historical studies of Columbus school desegregation. NAACP attorney Paul Dimond provides a useful look at the legal machinations of *Penick* in *Beyond Busing: Inside the Challenge to Urban Segregation*. The only other published work on Columbus is an anti-busing polemic by black Columbus Board of Education member Bill Moss called *School Desegregation: Enough Is Enough*.
5. See Lukas, *Common Ground*; Ronald P. Formisano, *Boston against Busing* (Chapel Hill: University of North Carolina Press, 1991); and Ione Malloy, *Southie Won't Go: A Teacher's Diary of the Desegregation of South Boston High School* (Urbana: University of Illinois Press, 1986). Also see chapters in Wilkinson, *From Brown to Bakke*, and Metcalf, *From Little Rock to Boston*. For the images of Boston busing, see Part II of the television documentary series *Eyes on the Prize*.

Chapter 1

1. Mark Ellis, "Snow Worries Close Schools," *Columbus Dispatch* [hereafter cited as *CD*], January 7, 1977; "Bad Weather Slaps Freeze On

205

Schooling," *Columbus Citizen-Journal* [hereafter cited as *CJ*], January 11, 1977; "Snow, Snow, Snow!" *CJ*, January 15, 1977.

2. Betty Daft, "4-day Weeks Suggested to Save Schools," *CD*, January 7, 1977; "February 1 Gas Freeze to Hit Business, Industry, Schools," *CD*, January 21, 1977.

3. By "mothballing" buildings—closing schools and shutting off the gas—the district would save enough fuel to reopen after spring break. But leaving the buildings unheated jeopardized everything from water mains and gym floors to musical instruments and lab fish. Robert Albrecht, "Goldfish, Drums among Woes If School System's Gas Cut Off," *CD*, January 27, 1977.

4. "Columbus, Its Schools Shut, Turns to Teaching over TV," *New York Times*, February 7, 1977.

5. John Ellis interview, January 26, 1994; see also Cynthia Robins, "How TV Taught CMH, OH, a Lesson or Two," *TV Guide*, April 16, 1977, 16–18. The Wolfe family's media empire included WBNS, the area's dominant television station, along with AM and FM radio outlets and the *Columbus Dispatch*, the city's influential evening newspaper.

6. Ellis quoted in Reginald Stuart, "Columbus School Closings Prompt Community Help," *New York Times*, February 20, 1977; School Management Institute, *Educational Management Letter* 2, no. 10, February 21, 1977; Albert E. Holliday, "Columbus Tries School without Schools," *Journal of Educational Communication* 3, no. 1 (1977): 4–5.

7. John Ellis interview. See articles in *Columbus Dispatch, Citizen-Journal*, and *Call and Post* throughout February 1977 for more. The city's 16,000-student parochial school system also took part in School without Schools. Holliday, "School without Schools," 4–5. See also Charles Fenton, "Schools Closed February 7 to March 7," *CJ*, February 1, 1977; "Education Flows Better than Gas with School Plan," *CD*, February 1, 1977.

8. In November 1976, the district had failed to pass a 6.2-mill levy that would have provided it with its first additional operating money since 1968 and helped offset rapidly rising inflation. The defeat forced $7.7 million in cuts in January 1977. Merriman quoted in "Kitchen Class Thanks Hostess," *CJ*, February 26, 1977; Ellis quoted in Fred M. Hechinger, "School without Schools," *Saturday Review*, April 30, 1977.

9. Charles Fenton, "Ellis Gives High Marks to 'School without Schools,'" *CJ*, February 9, 1977; Micki Seltzer, "Busing Comes to Columbus: Here Comes the Bus, Without a Fuss!" *Call and Post* [hereafter cited as *CP*] February 12, 1977; "John E Ain't Ready, Jimmy . . . (And He's a Republican to Boot)," *CP* editorial, February 26, 1977.

10. John Ellis, letter to the community, printed in the *Booster*, March 2, 1977.

11. *Gary L. Penick et al. v. Columbus Board of Education et al.*, 429 F. Supp. 229 (1977) [hereafter cited as *Penick I*].

12. Curtina Moreland, "The Black Community of Columbus: A Study of the Structure and Pattern of Power in a Midwestern City," 57–58; Felix James, "The American Addition: The History of a Black Community," 5–6; James H. Rodabaugh, "The Negro in Ohio," *Journal of Negro History*, 31 (January 1946): 15–16.

13. According to the United States Census, 543 (9.5%) of Columbus's 6,048 residents were black, while only around 1% of the state's population was black. Mary Louise Mark, *Negroes in Columbus*, 7–8; Rodabaugh, "Negro in Ohio," 18. Other historical information: Richard Minor, "The Negro in Columbus," 191; Anne Gregory, "A History of Progress: Much Has Changed Since Arthur Brook's Arrival," *Northwest News*, August 7, 1985; James, "American Addition," 3; Mike Curtin, "Step by Step," *CD*, January 29, 1993.

14. *Ohio Statesman*, October 21, 1865, quoted in Moreland, "Black Community," 61; Rodabaugh, "Negro in Ohio," 18–20; Moreland, "Black Community," 63–64, 67.

15. Himes, "Forty Years of Negro Life in Columbus, Ohio," 136, 137.

16. Mark, *Negroes in Columbus*, 8, 16–22; Hayes, "Negro No. 3," *CJ*, February 22, 1967; James, "American Addition," 23.

17. From Frank U. Quillen, *The Color Line in Ohio*, University of Michigan Historical Series (Ann Arbor: University of Michigan Press, 1913), 145. Quoted in Himes, "Forty Years," 135–36.

18. Vinnie Vanessa Bryant, "Columbus, Ohio, and the Great Migration," 5–6.

19. Rodabaugh, "Negro in Ohio," 22–25.

20. Mark, *Negroes in Columbus*, 8–9. From 1910 to 1920, Columbus's black population grew from 12,739 to 22,181, while the city's total population increased from 181,511 to 237,031.

21. Himes, "Forty Years," 150.

22. See Patricia Burgess, *Planning for the Private Interest: Land Use Controls and Residential Patterns in Columbus, Ohio, 1900–1970*, esp. 31, 45.

23. Mark, *Negroes in Columbus*, 17; Burgess, *Planning*, 58.

24. Mark, *Negroes in Columbus*, 16–19. Blacks continued to live in pockets in every quadrant of the city, however.

25. Bryant, "Great Migration," 15–19; Himes, "Forty Years," 142.

26. Lovell Beaulieu, "For Some, Black History Is a Way of Life," *CD*, February 22, 1989; Curtin, "Step by Step"; Himes, "Forty Years," 145–46.

27. Bryant, "Great Migration," 18; Himes, "Forty Years," 151; Starita Smith, "Woman's Life Could Be Chapter in the History of Black Americans," *CD*, February 3, 1988.

28. Melvin L. Murphy,. "The Columbus Urban League: A History, 1917–1967," 53–56.

29. James, "American Addition," 67; Murphy, "Urban League," 56.

30. John B. Combs, "Capital City Blacks Slowly Winning Political Struggle in Bicentennial," *CP*, July 3, 1976; Curtin, "Step by Step"; "Local Black History Spans Two Centuries," *CD*, February 18, 1987; Moreland, "Black Community," 76–78.

31. From the time of Columbus's first recorded annexation in 1834 to 1954, the city grew from .92 square miles to 41.73 square miles. From 1954 to 1959 alone, it grew 47.29 square miles. The city's annexation and water-sewer policies will be discussed in more detail in chapter 3. For descriptions of the establishment of postwar city-suburban segregation, see Arnold Hirsch, "With or Without Jim Crow: Black Residential Segregation in the United States," in *Urban Policy in Twentieth-Century America*, ed. Hirsh and Raymond A. Mohl, 65–99; Jackson, *Crabgrass Frontier: The Suburbanization of the United States*; Douglas S. Massey and Nancy A. Denton, *American Apartheid: Segregation and the Making of the Underclass*; and George Metcalf, *Fair Housing Comes of Age*.

32. Curtin, "Step by Step." To minimize protest, the construction of Interstate 71 north spared two of Columbus's oldest and most powerful black churches, knifing in between Shiloh Baptist Church on Mt. Vernon Avenue and St. Paul A.M.E. on Long Street. Adolphus Andrews, "Urban Redevelopment and the Structure of Power: The Impact of Private Interests on the Policy-Making Process in Columbus, Ohio," 639–641.

33. "Columbus '76" Chamber of Commerce Economic Symposium, October 19, 1966. Clusters of small, single-family Hanford Village homes still remain, beneath the shadow of Interstate 70's Alum Creek curve, about two miles east of downtown Columbus. Betty Daft, "There Stands Hanford Village, Decimated but Undaunted," *CD Magazine*, July 22, 1979, 30–31.

34. Census figures from City of Columbus Development Department, Planning Division; Andrew Hacker, *Two Nations: Black and White, Separate, Hostile, Unequal*, 229; Richard M. Bernard, ed., *Snowbelt Cities: Metropolitan Politics in the Northeast and Midwest Since World War II*, 268–73.

35. Alan D. Miller and Jonathan Riskind, "Areas in City Sinking," *CD*, February 23, 1992; Ray Paprocki, "The Struggle to Save South Linden," *Columbus Monthly* [hereafter cited as *CM*] 8, no. 4 (April 1982): 80, 88; John B. Williams, "South Linden: From Grandeur To Ghetto!" *CP*, April 11, 1991.

36. Harold Lloyd Carter, "Domestic Colonialism and Problems of Black Education with Special Reference to Columbus, Ohio," 148, 149; R. W. Stevenson, *Superintendent's Report: 1874–1875*, Columbus Public School District files, 142; Myron Seifert, Columbus Public School District files; Micki Seltzer, "The Segregation of Schools in Columbus—How It All Happened," *CP*, October 18, 1975.

37. Seltzer, "Segregation of Schools"; Sylvia Brooks, "Racial Struggle Goes Back to 1869," *CJ*, July 14, 1975; Carolyn Focht, "Schools' Historian Traces Integration Effort to 1880," *CD*, May 1, 1976.

38. Carter, "Domestic Colonialism," 150.

39. Himes, "Forty Years," 140; Hayes, "Negro—No. 7," *CJ*, February 28, 1967. Though Loving was the leading school board advocate for a new building for blacks, he voted against the school that bore his name because he believed it was being situated in an undesirable part of town. Seltzer, "Segregation of Schools."

40. *Board of Education v. State*, 45 Ohio St. 555, 16 N.E. 373 (1888); Sylvia Brooks, "Fight Moves into City's Back Yard," *CJ*, July 18, 1975.

41. Seltzer, "Segregation of Schools"; Minor, "Negro in Columbus," 196.

42. Carter, "Domestic Colonialism," 153–54, 156–157. In addition to the public protests, a legal challenge—the city's first desegregation suit—was mounted to oppose the opening of Champion. In 1909, a black parent filed suit in Franklin County Common Pleas Court claiming that the establishment of an all-black school was illegal under state law. The court dismissed the case, however, and efforts to appeal were exhausted by the end of 1912. *Penick* I, 235; Seltzer, "Segregation of Schools."

43. *Penick* I, 236; Carter, "Domestic Colonialism," 159. Segregative boundary changes in 1932 even drew the threat of a lawsuit from national NAACP officials, who called them "cruel and unjust." Micki Seltzer, "Novice Fawcett Is First School Board Witness," *CP*, June 5, 1976.

44. Seltzer, "Segregation Of Schools."

45. The most glaring examples of race-based teacher assignments were the 100 percent white-to-black faculty transfers that occurred at Garfield, Felton, and Mt. Vernon in the early 1940s. By the time of *Brown v. Board of Education* in 1954, there were no black high school principals in the district and no black administrators in predominantly white schools. Also,

black student teachers could do their practice teaching only at black schools, where the only job openings offered black teachers were available. Interview with Barbee and Anna Mae Durham, October 2, 1991; Dimond, *Beyond Busing: Inside the Challenge to Urban Segregation,* 241; *Penick I,* 236.

46. According to the Columbus City Health Department, there were 4,830 babies born in Columbus in 1940, 7,827 in 1946, and 12,830 in 1957. "The Story of the Columbus Public Schools" (Columbus Public School District 1958 Annual Report), 25.

47. *Penick* I, 236; HEW enrollment figures, Columbus Public School District files; Harold Eibling, "Dateline 2000" (paper presented at Chamber of Commerce "Columbus '76" symposium, Columbus, October 19, 1966), 38; Nancy McVicar, "Rudy Discusses Building, Growth of City's Schools," *CJ,* June 8, 1976; Sylvia Brooks, "Enrollment Figures Spark Major Issue," *CJ,* July 15, 1975.

48. Carter, "Domestic Colonialism," 185–87; Carolyn Focht, "School Principals Assigned by Race, Analyst Testifies," *CD,* May 21, 1976; Nancy McVicar, "Principal Determination Linked to Segregation," *CJ,* May 21, 1976; Lori Noernberg, "Segregation Intentional, Expert Says," *Lantern,* May 21, 1976; 429 *Penick* I, 241–43; Don Pierce interview, April 21, 1994.

49. Moreland, "Black Community," 77; Murphy, "Urban League," 79; Anna Mae Durham, Anna Mae and Barbee Durham interview, October 2, 1991.

50. Robert Duncan interview, April 22, 1994; Ed Willis interview, October 4, 1991.

51. Willis interview.

52. Columbus Public School District files; Willis interview; Amos Lynch interview, October 17, 1991; Will Anderson interview, February 27, 1994.

53. Frank Lomax interview, May 10, 1994.

54. Turner quoted in Gilbert Price, "Busing Fails to Solve City's Education Ills," *CP,* October 6, 1983. Walker background in Raymond Smith, "Medical Pioneer, Educator Dies," *CP,* May 31, 1990.

55. Micki Seltzer, "Walker Recalls Early Battles, Highs, Lows of Board Career," *CP,* January 7, 1978.

56. Ohio Council on Civil Rights, *Racial Imbalance in the Public Schools: A Survey of Legal Developments* (April 1965).

57. President Johnson, commencement address at Howard University, June 4, 1965, quoted in Thomas Byrne Edsall with Mary D. Edsall, *Chain Reaction: The Impact of Race, Rights, and Taxes on American Politics,* 53.

58. President Johnson, commencement address at Howard University, June 4, 1965, quoted in Godfrey Hodgson, *America in Our Time: From World War II to Nixon, What Happened and Why,* 181. Carmichael first publicly used the phrase "Black Power" at a June 1966 civil rights demonstration in Greenwood, Mississippi. Edsall and Edsall, *Chain Reaction,* 58–59.

59. Education Committee, Columbus Urban League, "Historical Fact Sheet of Racial Integration Commitments and Plans by Columbus Public Schools, 1964–1975," Columbus Public School District files, 1; Micki Seltzer, "Expert Cites School Board Role in Black Containment," *CP,* May 29, 1976.

60. Education Committee, Columbus NAACP, "Racial Segregation in the Columbus Public Schools," position paper presented August 10, 1966, quoted in Carter, "Domestic Colonialism," 177–79.

61. Columbus Urban League, "Quality-Integrated Schools for Columbus, Ohio," April 1967.

62. "A Report to the Columbus Board of Education," Ohio State University Advisory Commission on Problems Facing the Columbus Public Schools," June 15, 1968 [hereafter cited as OSU Advisory Commission Report], 24–29, 269, 300, 18, 19–22. The Columbus Public Schools used a "priority" ranking system to channel Title I funds from the Elementary and Secondary Education Act to the district's most needy schools. The sixty-six priority schools were ranked from I (most needy) to V (least needy). There were ninety-four nonpriority schools in 1968. The commission's recommendations illustrate the debate over the federal Office of Education's *Equality of Educational Opportunity* study, better known as the Coleman Report. That massive 1966 survey challenged liberals' belief that funneling more resources to poorer schools would improve pupil achievement, instead concluding that family background was a far more significant factor than educational facilities and funds in determining student success. Neoconservatives used the Coleman Report as ammunition in their argument that black educational problems stemmed from a "culture of poverty," not from racism in the public schools. Liberals, meanwhile, seized on the study's conclusion that black achievement levels rose when poor blacks were educated with middle-class whites as evidence of the advantages of desegregation.

63. For case studies of the tension between desegregation and school district organization, see Daniel J. Monti, *A Semblance of Justice: St. Louis Desegregation and Order in Urban America;* and Doris Fine, *When Leadership Fails: Desegregation and Demoralization in the San Francisco Schools.*

64. OSU Advisory Commission Report, 154–56, 163–64; Ellis interview; Pierce interview. The board of education consisted of seven unsalaried, nominally nonpartisan members, elected to unlimited four-year terms in staggered, biannual, at-large elections.

65. John Ellis interview; "Historical Fact Sheet," Columbus Urban League; "Plans for Developing Better Ethnic Understandings," Columbus Public Schools Policy Statement, July 18, 1967; OSU Advisory Commission Report, 159.

66. "Historical Fact Sheet," Columbus Urban League, 5–6; Nancy McVicar, "Boundary Changes Explained," *CJ*, April 24, 1976. Craig quoted in Carter, "Domestic Colonialism," 204.

67. Black students in the higher grades of Columbus Public Schools were also influenced by radical student and faculty activism at Ohio State, where black protests led to the creation of the university's Black Studies Department. See Martha Brian and Mary Carran Webster, "The Campus Radicals: Where Are They Now?" *CM*, February 1977; Michael Norman, "The Struggle for Control of Black Studies at OSU," *CM*, March 1985; "Timeline, 1968—Here and Elsewhere," *CM*, June 1988.

68. "Proposal—By Marion Franklin High School Black Parents," March 18, 1969, and administrative responses, March 21, 1969, Columbus Public School District files; Anderson interview; Damon Asbury interview, February 15, 1994.

69. "Administrative Guidelines for the Program of Voluntary Registration," July 17, 1967, Columbus Public School District files; "Historical Fact Sheet," Columbus Urban League, 8; "Proposal—By Marion Franklin High School Black Parents"; Carter, "Domestic Colonialism," 209–13.

70. Linden-McKinley shifted from 60 percent white in 1967 to 90 percent black in 1973. "Administrative Guidelines for the Program of Voluntary Registration"; "Transfer Denied Youth Who Claims Beating," *CD*, October 25, 1973; "Ellis Transfers Linden Student," *CD*, November 21, 1973; *CD*, *CJ*, and *CP* newspaper reports, January through May 1971; Asbury interview, February 15, 1994; Anderson interview.

71. From 1945 to 1968, all twenty-two Columbus Public School District ballot issues passed. (This success rate was due in part to the fact that until the late 1960s, levies only lasted a certain number of years and had to be renewed by the voters. A change in state law, however, made all school tax increases permanent except emergency levies and bond issues.) A 1968 levy increase, passed by the smallest margin of any postwar school ballot measure to that time (51 to 49 percent), was followed by a resounding 1969

bond issue defeat (71 to 29 percent). In May 1971, voters rejected another bond issue try (66 to 34 percent) as well as a 9.7-mill levy increase (69 to 31 percent). Kathy Gray Foster, "School Levies Once Sailed Past Voters," *CD*, April 29, 1986.

72. Before coming to Columbus, Ellis had been superintendent of the affluent Lakewood (Ohio) School District outside of Cleveland.

73. In 1970, black enrollment in the Columbus Public Schools was 29 percent; the city's overall black population was 18.5 percent. *Penick I*, 237.

74. Edsall and Edsall, *Chain Reaction*, 78.

75. Wilkinson, *From Brown to Bakke*, 103–6. The act also allowed the Justice Department to file, intervene in, and provide financial support for desegregation cases.

76. See, for example, Constance Curry, *Silver Rights: A True Story from the Front Lines of the Civil Rights Struggle*.

77. *Green v. County School Board of New Kent County*, 391 U.S. 436 (1968), emphasis in original. Supreme Court opinions collected in Derrick A. Bell Jr., *Civil Rights: Leading Cases* (Boston: Little, Brown, and Company, 1980).

78. *Alexander v. Holmes County Board of Education*, 396 U.S. 19 (1969), quoted in Bell, *Race, Racism and American Law*, 388; United States Commission on Civil Rights, *Twenty Years After Brown*, 48–49.

79. In 1970, for example, bombs exploded in Chattanooga, Tennessee; Columbus, Georgia; and Kannapolis, North Carolina. In Lamar, South Carolina, state troopers needed tear gas to control a mob of ax-handle-wielding whites who had attacked a busload of black children. Nevertheless, the thousands of southern school districts that desegregated did so with comparatively little conflict. Judith Buncher, ed., *School Busing Controversy, 1970–75*, 207–9; Wilkinson, *From Brown to Bakke*, 122–23.

80. Georgia parent quoted in Metcalf, *From Little Rock to Boston*, 55. Charleston *Gazette*, September 9, 1971; Buncher, *School Busing Controversy*, 225. McNair quoted in Metcalf, *From Little Rock to Boston*, 57.

81. Buncher, *School Busing Controversy*, 99.

82. On desegregation and the "Southern Strategy," see Stephen E. Ambrose, *Nixon: The Triumph of a Politician, 1962–1972* (New York: W. W. Norton, 1992); Edsall and Edsall, *Chain Reaction*; and James Reichley, *Conservatives in an Age of Change*, esp. 179.

83. Utilizing the Title VI fund cutoff provision and the force of the federal courts, HEW had succeeded in desegregating all but a few hundred of the 4,476 southern and border state school systems by 1970. By transferring

enforcement to the understaffed Department of Justice, however, the Nixon administration ensured that desegregation would proceed on a far more gradual, case-by-case basis. As a result, after 1970, pressure to dismantle dual school districts would come primarily from privately initiated litigation. To protest the administration's tactics, the assistant solicitor general refused to argue the case. Orfield, *Must We Bus?* 286–88, 325–27.

84. Buncher, *School Busing Controversy,* 101.

85. Polls generally showed that between 75 and 85 percent of the public opposed busing, even though the same polls indicated that strong majorities also approved of desegregation.

86. Wilkinson, *From Brown to Bakke,* 210–11.

87. For a case study exploring this idea, see Richard A. Pride and J. David Woodward, *The Burden of Busing: The Politics of Desegregation in Nashville, Tennessee.*

88. A 1971 Gallup poll found that 47 percent of African Americans nationwide opposed busing, while 45 percent favored it; Edsall and Edsall, *Chain Reaction,* 298. This split was magnified the following year when the NAACP withdrew its support of the National Black Political Convention's fifty-eight-page "black agenda," citing the document's opposition to busing as a "particularly outrageous" example of the convention's "separatist and nationalist" ideological slant (Buncher, *School Busing Controversy,* 112).

89. Buncher, *School Busing Controversy,* 101; Bob Woodward and Scott Armstrong, *The Brethren: Inside the Supreme Court,* 96.

90. *Swann v. Charlotte-Mecklenburg Board of Education,* 402 U.S. 1, (1971), 13, 26, 28.

91. Orfield, *Must We Bus?* 332.

92. See Woodward and Armstrong, *Brethren,* 97–112; Wilkinson, *From Brown to Bakke,* 147; Diane Ravitch, "The Evolution of School Desegregation Policy, 1964–1979," in Adam Yarmolinsky, Lance Liebman, and Corinne S. Schelling, eds., *Race and Schooling in the City,* 13–14; Thurgood Marshall Papers, Box 71, Folder 6, Library of Congress.

93. Memo from Justice Brennan to the Court, March 8, 1971, and memo from Justice Black to the Court, March 25, 1971, Marshall Papers.

94. Memo from Chief Justice Burger to the Court, April 8, 1971, Marshall Papers; *Swann v. Charlotte-Mecklenburg Board of Education,* 21; Wilkinson, *From Brown to Bakke,* 126.

95. Metcalf, *From Little Rock to Boston,* 112.

96. Reichley, *Conservatives,* 174; Orfield, *Must We Bus?,* 335.

97. For a favorable view of Roth's ruling, see Dimond, *Beyond Busing,* 21–118; for a critique of Roth's handling of the case, see Eleanor P. Wolf,

Trial and Error: The Detroit School Segregation Case. For the Richmond order, see Robert A. Pratt, *The Color of Their Skin: Education and Race in Richmond, Virginia 1954–89*

98. Prentice took the top spot in all three of her school board races—1969, 1973, and 1977.

99. Sylvia Brooks, "Racial Disputes Flare within Board," *CJ*, July 16, 1975; Sylvia Brooks, "Meanwhile, the School Board Tables 'Law and Peace,'" *CM*, April 1976, 30; "Residents Question School Board Member," *Spectator*, July 7, 1972.

100. Langdon would eventually step down in 1983, the longest-serving board member in the history of the Columbus Public School District.

101. George Sweda, "Board Refuses Desegregation Plan," *CJ*, May 2, 1973; Gerald Tebben, "Integration Plan Kept by School Board," *CD*, May 2, 1973; Sandy Smith, "Modified Integration Plan Favored by School Board," *CJ*, August 28, 1974; "School Segregation Decision Forced by Dr. David Hamlar," *CP*, August 31, 1974.

102. Sandy Smith, "Hot Lunch Meets Opposition," *CJ*, October 16, 1974.

103. Michael Salster, "School Board Candidates Are Attacked by Langdon," *CD*, October 29, 1975.

104. Brooks, "Racial Disputes Flare."

105. Marilyn Redden interview, October 14, 1991.

106. Sweda, "Board Refuses Desegregation Plan"; Tebben, "Integrational Plan Kept"; Jane Robinson, "Board Unifies to Okay Bond," *Spectator*, July 19, 1972.

107. "Integration Plan Receives 'Racial' OK," *CD*, September 4, 1974; Sandy Smith, "Board Asks Integration Action," *CJ*, September 4, 1974; Micki Seltzer, "Desegregation Measure Turned Down in Black-White School Board Split," *CP*, September 7, 1974; "Spokesperson," *CD*, December 2, 1973.

108. Graydon Hambrick, "Ellis Berated on Appointee," *CD*, September 6, 1972; George Sweda, "Human Relations Staffing Divides City School Board," *CJ*, September 6, 1972.

109. Graydon Hambrick, "School Desegregation Urged," *CD*, June 29, 1973; Micki Seltzer, "School Board Spurns Chance to Avoid Court Action," *CP*, May 5, 1973.

110. "Reaction Varied to School Board's Tabling of Bond Issue Question," *Linden News*, July 6, 1972.

111. As testament to the respect Moyer received from both board factions, he was voted board president in 1972 and 1973, the first consecutive-term president since 1955.

112. Eric Rozenman, "Moyer Sees Integration Suit," *Northland News,* May 24, 1973.

113. Jack Wittenmeier, "Court-Ordered Integration Urged for Columbus Public Schools," *Spectator,* December 1, 1971; "Rights Council Reiterates Strong School Busing Stand," *CP,* September 30, 1972.

114. The earliest indication of the black-white split over school desegregation actually occurred at the March 21, 1972 meeting, when the board rejected, 4–3, Hamlar's resolution opposing antibusing sections in the Emergency School Assistance Act pending in Congress. Hamlar called "busing for racial balance" a "smoke screen" meant to obscure the idea of busing for quality education. Prentice answered by saying that the district had integrated schools and arguing that most integration should take place via open housing. *CP,* April 1, 1972; Graydon Hambrick, *CD,* 22 March 1972; George Sweda, "Board Rejects Busing Resolution," *CJ,* March 22, 1972.

115. Columbus Public Schools, "Promises Made—The 1972 Bond Issue," Columbus Public School District files; bond issue campaign ad, *CD,* September 26, 1972. The real estate implications of the 1972 bond issue will be explored in more detail in chapter 3.

116. "Overcrowding Hits Schools," *Booster,* August 31, 1972.

117. Columbus Public Schools, "Promises Made"; Mary McGarey, "Old Schools Tie Educators' Hands," *CD,* October 12, 1972.

118. Columbus Public Schools, "Promises Made."

119. Already on the November 7, 1972, ballot was a measure seeking repeal of the state's first income tax, passed only the year before. While voters ultimately rejected the measure, 60 percent to 40 percent, its presence on the ballot signaled the first stirrings of an antitax backlash that would have a devastating effect on the Columbus Public Schools by the end of the decade. Had the measure passed, Ohio voters would have become the first state in the country to repeal an income tax via the ballot.

120. "Sweet Compromise," *Spectator* editorial, July 5, 1972; Graydon Hambrick, "Board Splits over Policy," *CD,* July 2, 1972.

121. George Sweda, "School Pack Put on Ballot," *CJ,* July 19, 1972; Graydon Hambrick, "School Board Agrees on Bond Issue Need," *CD,* July 19, 1972.

122. Columbus Board of Education Statement on Integration, July 18, 1972.

123. Jane Robinson, "Board Unifies to Okay Bond," *Spectator,* July 19, 1972; "Residents Question School Board Member," *Eastern Spectator,* July 7, 1972; Graydon Hambrick, "Moody Appeal in Vain," *CD,* July 12, 1972. In

1970, the black unemployment rate in Columbus was 50 percent higher than that of the city as a whole (5.7 percent to 3.8 percent); unemployment in Franklin County was 65 percent higher for blacks than it was for the county overall (5.6 percent to 3.4 percent). The national unemployment rate averaged 8.2 percent for blacks in 1970 and 4.9 percent overall. "Overall Economic Development Plan," City of Columbus Department of Development (October 1976), 288–90.

124. The compromise also included a $180,000 staff development and human relations program sponsored by Ellis to sweeten the deal.

125. George Sweda, "School Bond Issue Given Big Boost," *CJ*, October 5, 1972; "We Support the Bond Issue, But . . . ," *CP* editorial, October 21, 1972.

126. By gobbling up large tracts of farmland, Columbus had more than doubled its municipal boundaries since World War II. New schools were thus often constructed in fields, with the expectation that neighborhoods would quickly emerge around them. The relationship between the Columbus Public Schools and the city's annexation-driven expansion will be explored in detail in chapter 3.

127. Thomas B. Connery, "Racism Board Issue," *Spectator*, December 13, 1972.

128. Columbus Public Schools, "Promises Made"; George Sweda, "School Board Studies Priorities," *CJ*, November 9, 1972.

129. Graydon Hambrick, "School Board Rejects Committee Proposal," *CD*, November 29, 1972; John Meekins, "School Proposal Rejected," *CJ*, November 29, 1972; Connery, "Racism Board Issue."

130. Prentice quoted in Connery, "Racism Board Issue." Moyer quoted in ibid. and Hambrick, "School Board Rejects." Castleman quoted in Meekins, "School Proposal Rejected." "Betraying Our Confidence," *CP* editorial, December 16, 1972.

131. *Keyes v. Denver School District No. 1*, 413 U.S. 189 (1973).

132. Complaint quoted in "Suit Charges Bias in School Plans, *CD*, June 22, 1973; Charles Fenton, "Parents Suit Alleges Race Imbalance in City Schools," *CJ*, June 22, 1973. Davis quoted in Eric Rozenman, "No Vacation for School Officials," *Linden News*, July 12, 1973. Plaintiffs were eight Columbus families; defendants included the Columbus Board of Education, Columbus Public Schools Superintendent John Ellis, the State Board of Education of Ohio, State Superintendent Martin Essex, Attorney General William Brown, and Governor John Gilligan.

133. Micki Seltzer, "Pamphlet Answers Questions on School Bond Issue Suit," *CP*, October 13, 1973. Other high-priority projects included

96 percent black Franklin Junior High, 99 percent white Alpine Elementary, 100 percent white Cedarwood Elementary, and 100 percent white Parkmoor Elementary. Sandy Smith, "Court Halt Asked on School Building," *CJ*, October 9, 1973; Charles Fenton, "Suit Filed to Stop City School Building," *CJ*, October 10, 1973; "Lawyers Seek Halt in School Building," *CD*, October 10, 1973; John B. Combs, "Suit to Halt School Construction Filed," *CP*, October 13, 1973.

134. Sandy Smith, "Racial Suit Looms in City Schools," *CJ*, March 6, 1974; "Expanded School Suit Eyed," *CP*, March 9, 1974; "School Executives Play Games," *CP* editorial, March 16, 1974.

135. Jack Willey, "Court Action Halt a School Reprieve," *CD*, April 18, 1974; Sandy Smith, "School Building Suit Ends," *CJ*, April 18, 1974.

136. "Desegregation Here within Two Years, OSU Prof Expects Full-Scale School Suit," *CP*, April 27, 1974.

137. David Hamlar interview, March 11, 1994; Pauline Radebaugh interview, February 17, 1994.

138. Ellis interview; "Plans for Developing Better Ethnic Understandings," Columbus Board of Education Policy Statement, July 18, 1967, Columbus Public School District files.

139. In a comment that vividly illustrated the gulf between her conception of integration and that of the black board members, Prentice added, "To say a school is not integrated is not true. Just look at East High or Whetstone." In 1974, East was 99 percent black, Whetstone was 96 percent white. George Sweda, "Columbus Plan Opposed," *CJ*, March 14, 1973. See also "Board Splits on Transit Plan," *CD*, March 14, 1973, and "Busing Plan Is Center of Conflict," *CJ*, March 15, 1973.

140. Micki Seltzer, "Voluntary Integration Proposal Ripped by Integration Proponents," *CP*, March 17, 1973; *CP*, April 7, 1973.

141. Beverly Gifford interview, October 4, 1991; Seltzer, "Walker Recalls Career"; Ellis interview.

142. Ellis interview.

143. District statistics would eventually show a rise in Columbus Plan applicants from several dozen to several thousand. However, officials never released an accurate count of how many students actually attended the schools to which they applied.

144. The OCRC's original complaint, issued on October 16, 1972, accused the Columbus Public Schools of racial discrimination in the assignment of teachers. It noted that 47 of 174 schools had no black teachers in 1972, and 80 percent of all black teachers in the district taught at just four

schools. Ellis's compromise called for every school to have around 17 percent black faculty, plus or minus 7.5 percent, by 1975–76.

145. All three were elementary schools: Indianola, Linden Park, and Stewart.

146. Ellis's authority was enhanced by the January 1975 retirement of veteran Deputy Superintendent Cleo L. Dumaree, whom many within the district considered more powerful than the superintendent.

147. Micki Seltzer, "Board Votes to Transport Students in Voluntary Racial Balance Plan," *CP*, December 21, 1974; Sandy Smith, "School Board OK's Voluntary Bus Plan," *CJ*, December 18, 1974; Graydon Hambrick, "No Major Effect Seen from Busing Plan," *CD*, December 18, 1974. The impact of Boston on Columbus business leaders will be explored in greater depth in chapter 2.

148. Ellis interview. In January 1975, Tom Moyer had stepped down to become Governor Rhodes's chief aide. With the board deadlocked on a replacement, the decision was turned over to Republican Franklin County Probate Court Judge Richard Metcalf, who selected Capital University law professor M. Steven Boley. Boley, the fifth-place finisher in the 1973 board elections, proved to be much more conservative than Moyer, freezing the antibusing bloc's four-person majority.

149. Micki Seltzer, "Board Desegregation Airing Leaves Questions Unresolved," *CP*, October 11, 1975; "Four Dangerous Whites," *CP* editorial, October 11, 1975.

150. Seltzer, "Questions Unresolved"; Ellis interview.

151. This idea will be explored extensively in chapter 2.

152. Ellis interview.

153. Orfield, *Must We Bus?* 277. The NAACP focused its post-*Keyes* efforts on Ohio because the state had several major cities that were relatively close together and contained large, significantly segregated black populations. In addition, NAACP general counsel Nate Jones was a Youngstown native with an extensive network of connections throughout the state. During the 1970s, the NAACP filed desegregation suits against Cincinnati, Cleveland, Columbus, Dayton, and Youngstown. Akron, Cleveland Heights–University Heights, Lima, Lorain, Toledo, and Warren were also involved in desegregation litigation during the 1970s. "Desegregation in Ohio: Background for Current Litigation," Citizens' Council for Ohio Schools, January 1976; "Desegregation Update," Citizens' Council for Ohio Schools, August 1979, 9–11; Joe McKnight, "Desegregation Affects 10 School Systems," *CD*, August 26, 1979.

154. Strategic and personal disputes almost kept the NAACP out of Columbus. The local NAACP chapter, already wracked by internal divisions, wanted to maintain control of both the litigation and the research it had already done. "Wild Bill" Davis also opposed the choice of white attorney Lou Lucas as head of the *Penick* legal team. Finally, a compromise was reached: the national NAACP would intervene in the case, taking control of all completed research, and local NAACP attorney Leo Ross would be added to the legal team.

155. Ellis interview.

156. Duncan interview, April 22, 1994; "Court Urges Settlement of Desegregation Suit," *CJ*, September 30, 1975; "Desegregation Suit Agreement Unlikely," *CD*, September 30, 1975. Duncan inherited the *Penick* case from Judge Rubin in July 1974, shortly after Duncan's appointment to the United States District Court for the Southern District of Ohio. Rubin was already busy with Dayton's acrimonious desegregation suit.

157. Lower-class whites in Boston, for example, found an extra source of enmity in the Wellesley residence of district court judge Arthur Garrity, Jr.

158. Robert Duncan interview, December 27, 1990.

159. Duncan interview, April 22, 1994.

160. Ibid.

161. Ibid.

162. Ibid. Bowen would go on to become Franklin County's first black state senator.

163. Duncan interview, April 22, 1994.

164. Gilbert Price, "Judge Duncan Looks Back over 30-Year Career," *CP*, December 13, 1984; Adrienne Bosworth, "Robert Duncan: The Federal Court Loses a Star," *CM*, April 1985, 46.

165. In 1970, running unopposed at the request of black Democrats, Duncan became the first African American to win a statewide election in Ohio.

166. The first was Judge Damon Keith in Pontiac, Michigan. Micki Seltzer, "Decision Not 'Emotional' One for Duncan," *CP*, March 12, 1977. The politicians primarily responsible for Duncan's ascent were Saxbe and Ohio governor James Rhodes. Seltzer, "Decision Not 'Emotional'"; "Judge Robert M. Duncan: A Biographic Sketch," Columbus Public School District files.

167. Duncan interview, December 27, 1990.

168. Ibid.; "Placid Judge Duncan Sees 'Just Another Trial' Ahead," *CD*, April 18, 1976; Carolyn Focht, "Pupils Segregated Since Civil War, Blacks' Lawyer Tells School Court," *CD*, April 19, 1976.

169. *Penick* I, 234; Nancy McVicar, "Judge Nears End of School Case Study," *CJ*, January 21, 1977. For a detailed description of the trial itself, see Dimond, *Beyond Busing*, 229–48.

170. Nancy McVicar, "Decision on Schools Months Away," *CJ*, June 18, 1976; Focht, "Desegregation Ruling Is Unlikely until November," *CD*, June 18, 1976.

171. Duncan interviews, December 27, 1990, and April 22, 1994.

172. *Penick* I, 232.

173. Robert Duncan interview, April 22, 1994.

174. Ibid.; Robert Albrecht, "Duncan Raps Objections to Federal Judges," *CD*, May 27, 1981.

175. *Penick* I, 233, 263; "School Trial Focuses on State Board," *CD*, June 14, 1976; Nancy McVicar, "State Board Not Sure of Powers, Judge Told," *CJ*, June 15, 1976; Micki Seltzer, "Black State Official Defends Policies, but Judge Duncan Tells Hearing He Has 'Difficulty with Board's Position,'" *CP*, June 19, 1976.

176. See James Coleman, Sara D. Kelly, and John A. Moore, *Trends in School Segregation, 1968–73*.

177. Plaintiffs in *Penick* noted that in 1975–76, only 14 of 592 students transferring for racial balance under the Columbus Plan were white. Nancy McVicar, "Columbus Plan Defended by Ellis," *CJ*, June 11, 1976; Carolyn Focht, "Ellis: Schools Can't Carry Integration Burden Alone," *CD*, June 11, 1976.

178. Micki Seltzer, "Report Cites 'Negative Effects' of Teacher Integration Plan," *CP*, September 13, 1975; "Principals Outline Objections to Plan," *CP*, June 15, 1974.

179. Moss ran unsuccessfully for the U.S. House of Representatives as an antibusing independent in 1976, siphoning enough votes from Democrat Fran Ryan to throw the election to Republican Samuel Devine. He won a seat on the school board the following fall.

180. Robert Albrecht, "'We Were Scrooge,' Says Ellis of Recommended Cuts," *CD*, December 30, 1976. The cuts approved by the board in January 1977 totaled $7.7 million. In April 1976, the board had slashed $5.8 million from the budget, and reductions in state aid that year had cost the district $1.5 million. The Columbus Public Schools' general fund in 1976 totaled $114.4 million.

181. Katherine Hamilton, "Defeated Levies," *Northland News*, November 10, 1976.

182. *Penick* I, 264, 266.

183. Ibid.

184. Duncan interview, December 27, 1990.

185. Jennifer L. Hochshild, *The New American Dilemma*, 159; *Penick* I, 266.

186. Duncan interview, April 22, 1994; *Penick* I, 235, 264.

187. "During the 1975–76 school year . . . 70.4 percent of all the students in the Columbus Public Schools attended schools which were 80–100 percent populated by either black or white students; 73.3 percent of the black administrators were assigned to schools with 70–100 percent black student bodies; and 95.7 percent of the 92 schools which were 80–100 percent white had no black administrators assigned to them." *Penick* I, 240.

188. Plaintiffs must "prove not only that segregated schooling exists but also that it was brought about or maintained by intentional state action." *Keyes v. Denver School District No. 1*, 198.

189. Duncan interview, April 22, 1994; *Penick* I, 260. The *Keyes* precedent, Duncan said, "provided for a shift in the burden of proof when plaintiffs' proofs reach a certain standard." Once this standard was reached, the defendants had to demonstrate the absence of a causal link between past and present segregation, a nearly impossible task.

190. *Penick* I, 260.

191. Ibid., 240.

192. Ibid., 259.

193. Ibid., 232.

Chapter 2

1. Eric Rozenman, " 'We're Going to East and We'll Share Respect,' " *CJ*, September 7, 1979; Roger Snell and Steve Wilson, "Columbus's Big Busing Day Goes Off Without a Hitch," Cincinnati *Enquirer*, September 7, 1979; Willis interview.

2. Rozenman, "Going to East."

3. Carol Stevens, "Columbus's Forced Busing Ran Relatively Smoothly, Despite Tough Moments," Buffalo *Courier-Express*, June 30, 1981; Willis interview.

4. Calvin Smith interview, January 7, 1991; "School Openings Quiet, Orderly," *CD*, September 6, 1979; "Buses Roll in Peaceful First Day," *CJ*, September 7, 1979; "Real Test for Schools to be Friday—Davis," *CJ*, September 7, 1979.

5. See William Chafe, *Civilities and Civil Rights*, an examination of the civil rights movement in Greensboro, North Carolina. Chafe concludes that Greensboro's business community sought to maintain peace and safeguard the city's reputation for relatively progressive race relations by conceding enough to civil rights protestors to silence them but not enough to meet their demands. Chafe's concept of "civility" encompassed not just civic peace, but also the preservation of a treasured sense of southern gentility that had historically characterized the political dealings of Greensboro's elite. Because the latter notion of "civility" was not a part of Columbus's political milieu, I have altered Chafe's phrase to fit the concerns of Columbus's business community: civic order.

6. Henry L. Hunker, *Industrial Evolution of Columbus, Ohio*, 1–2.

7. In 1824, Columbus became the county seat of Franklin County. When it reached a population of 3,500 in 1834, it was incorporated as a municipality.

8. Hunker, *Industrial Evolution*, 32–33; Andrew Jonas, "Local Interests and State Territorial Structures: Integration and Fragmentation in Metropolitan Columbus in the Post-War Period," 103; Andrew Mair, "Private Planning for Economic Development: Local Business Coalitions in Columbus, Ohio, 1858–1986," 94.

9. Columbus's population grew from 31,274 in 1870 to 125,560 in 1900; manufacturing employment rose from 5,150 to 17,000. Hunker, 40–41.

10. Jonas, "Local Interests," 103.

11. Columbus was—and still is—within five hundred miles of the majority of the nation's population.

12. City of Columbus, *An Overall Economic Plan* (Columbus Department of Development, 1976), 8; Jonas, "Local Interests," 104.

13. Ninety percent of the city's 1900 population was native-born. Hunker, *Industrial Evolution*, 41.

14. *Overall Economic Plan*, 14–15.

15. The Columbus Chamber of Commerce was founded in 1884, the fourth effort to organize a board of trade in Columbus since 1858. Quotation from *Addresses to Columbus Board of Trade at its 2nd Annual Meeting*, Columbus Board of Trade, 1874. See Mair, "Private Planning," 92–101, quotation at 99.

16. *Overall Economic Plan*, 14.

17. Ray Paprocki, "Inside The Wolfe Empire," *CM*, April 1986, 39–48, 133–34. The Wolfes controlled Columbus's largest bank, BancOhio, from the early 1900s through the late 1970s; they owned Wolfe Brothers Shoe

Company and Wolfe Wear-U-Well, a chain of footwear retailers, through the late 1950s; the Wolfe-controlled Ohio Company is currently the city's largest brokerage and investment firm; the family owns thousands of acres of rural, industrial, and commercial real estate, as well as Ohio Equities, Inc., one of Columbus's largest commercial real estate companies; and Wolfe representatives have sat on countless corporate, philanthropic, and civic boards.

18. Ibid. The daily *Columbus Dispatch* has been, since 1903, the most prominent arm of the Wolfes' media empire. The family consolidated its command of the local print media in 1959 when it merged its morning *Ohio Journal* with the rival Columbus *Citizen;* the *Citizen-Journal* ran for the next twenty-five years as "the weaker partner in a joint operating agreement" with the *Dispatch.* In 1949, the Wolfes established WBNS-TV (WBNS = Wolfe Banks, News, and Shoes), which thoroughly dominated the local television market until the mid-1980s; they also own two local radio stations, an Indianapolis NBC affiliate, and the monthly *Ohio Magazine.*

19. The Lazarus family, owners of Columbus's dominant department store chain, served as something of a liberal counterweight to the Wolfes. Also powerful were the heads of Buckeye Steel and Jeffrey Manufacturing, the city's two largest (and two of its oldest) manufacturers. These four business interests dominated the chamber of commerce until the late 1930s. According to Delmar Starkey, chamber president from 1937 to 1963, they actively discouraged industrial development in Columbus, fearing that new industries would drain workers, raise labor costs, and spur unionization. Others dispute this theory, however, arguing that Columbus "chased smokestacks" as hard as any city, just with less success. Mair, "Private Planning," 183–86; Jerry Hammond interview, November 18, 1992. For a history of the Lazarus family, see Herb Cook Jr., "Lazarus, the Family: The End of a Dynasty," *CM,* May 1990, 46–54.

20. Eighty-one percent of Franklin County residents lived in Columbus in 1930. From U.S. Population Censuses, cited in Jonas, "Local Interests," 105.

21. Burgess, "Planning," 35; Jackson, *Crabgrass Frontier,* 139; Jonas, "Local Interests," 104, 117. From 1930 to 1980, Cleveland grew only 14 percent, expanding from 71 to 81 square miles from 1930 to 1950 and not at all from 1950 to 1980. Columbus, on the other hand, grew 472 percent during the same fifty years, from 39 to 184 square miles. The only other northern city with a comparable growth rate is Indianapolis (689 percent), although much of its expansion is attributable to city-county consolidation. Other northern urban growth rates from 1930 to 1980: Boston, 12 percent; Pitts-

burgh, 8 percent; Chicago, 10 percent; New York City, 2 percent; St. Louis, 0 percent; Baltimore 0 percent; Washington, D.C., −1 percent; Philadelphia, −2 percent. Jackson, *Crabgrass Frontier*, 139–40.

22. U.S. Population Censuses, cited in Jonas, "Local Interests," 105, 108; Hunker, *Industrial Evolution*, 105.

23. Jonas, "Local Interests," 186–88; Hunker, *Industrial Evolution*, 59–62.

24. Mair, "Private Planning," 188–92; Jonas, "Local Interests," 108; Hunker, *Industrial Evolution*, 59.

25. The business leaders called in by Rhodes were Edgar T. Wolfe, *Dispatch* publisher and head of Wolfe Industries; Simon Lazarus, president of Lazarus Department Store; Herbert Lape Sr., Columbus Area Chamber of Commerce president and head of a local shoe manufacturing firm; Edwin Tharp, vice president of Ohio Fuel Gas Co.; Paul Gingher, lawyer and former two-term state senator; Roy Brentholts, past president of the Columbus Board of Realtors; and Paul McCarthy, a local labor leader. For the history of the Metropolitan Committee, see Mair, "Private Planning," 115–30; Jonas, "Local Interests," 134–36; Adrienne Bosworth, "Out of Hibernation: The Reawakening of the Metropolitan Committee," *CM*, November 1979; Chris Eversole, "Metropolitan Committee May Resurface to Aid Schools," *CJ*, January 10, 1979.

26. In 1945, the nascent organization called two or three meetings to explain issues to assembled businesspeople. That enabled its leaders to claim they were merely the "executive committee" for a broad-based citizens' group called the "Metropolitan Committee of 100 Organizations." Mair, "Private Planning," 122–24.

27. The Development Committee for Greater Columbus (DCGC) was formed in 1956 to facilitate infrastructure planning and to ensure that capital improvements were not delayed by governmental inefficiency or jurisdictional squabbling. It had between one hundred and two hundred members and was run by a steering committee that included most of the individuals on the Metropolitan Committee. Between 1956 and the early 1970s, DCGC's planners were largely responsible for plotting the specifics of Columbus's infrastructural growth. Mair, "Private Planning," 144–55, quotation at 120.

28. By the mid-1950s, all three local newspapers, the two most prominent downtown department stores, two of the three largest banks, and the area's biggest investment securities firm were represented on the Metropolitan Committee. Ibid., 118–19.

29. Bosworth, "Out of Hibernation," 74.

30. Jonas, "Local Interests," 108; Eversole, "Committee May Resurface"; Bosworth, "Out of Hibernation," 74.

31. Land area figure from City of Columbus Planning Division Annexation Log; population figure from U.S. Population Census, cited in Jonas, "Local Interests," 105. Shrugged off as the cost of progress was the consequence that African Americans had to pay higher taxes for public projects that funneled resources away from their neighborhoods and literally paved the way for whites to abandon the central city. Ironically, while the majority of Metropolitan Committee–endorsed ballot issues were approved by over 70 percent of the electorate, most of the handful that failed were urban renewal levies. Columbus voters rejected such levies in 1954, 1964, and 1965, largely out of fear of the spillover from black residential displacement. Mair, "Private Planning," 122–23; Amos Lynch, "Amos Lynch Asks: 'How Many of You Have Ever Had to Move a Home or Business because of Some Government Plan,'" *Columbus Business Forum*, March 1977.

32. The chamber, with the support of small firms seeking manufacturing's high economic "multiplier," managed to land a few major factories, most notably General Motors, Westinghouse, and North American Aviation plants. However, other business leaders continued to object to the expensive drain on services, wage pressures, and unionization that new industries brought to Columbus. Moreover, they argued, branch plants lacked loyalty to the city; their managers did not take an active role in the community, and the transient, up-and-down nature of manufacturing injected a potentially destabilizing unpredictability into the local economy. Chamber of Commerce Annual Reports, 1949–1963; Mair, "Private Planning," 193–202; Hunker, *Industrial Evolution*, 87; David Lore, "Selective Growth Shaping Future for Columbus," *CD*, February 10, 1977.

33. Mair, "Private Planning," 170–82, 250–59; "Today's Urban Renewal Efforts Benefit Tomorrow's City," *Columbus Business Forum*, September 1965.

34. Bosworth, "Out of Hibernation," 74.

35. Eversole, "Committee May Resurface."

36. Although Columbus's manufacturing sector grew significantly between 1940 and 1970, its importance to the area's overall economy remained relatively minor. Even at its postwar peak, manufacturing accounted for only around 30 percent of the jobs in the Columbus Metropolitan Statistical Area. In 1964, for example, 26.1 percent of the jobs in Columbus were in manufacturing, compared to 47 percent in Youngstown, 38.3 percent in Cleveland, and 39 percent in Ohio overall. By contrast, Columbus led the state in the percent of jobs in government, services, finance, and construc-

tion (Columbus Area Chamber of Commerce Annual Report, 1966). By the mid-1970s, manufacturing made up a mere 19.4 percent of the SMSA's jobs, and the city's top four employers were Ohio State University, the State of Ohio, the federal government, and the Columbus Public Schools. Moreland, "Black Community," 40; Thomas M. Stanback Jr. and Thierry J. Noyelle, *Cities in Transition*, 91. See also Robert Tenenbaum, "The Economy: We've Suffered, but Not as Bad as Everybody Else," *CM*, August 1975, 22–27.

37. In fact, by the early 1970s, Columbus had engulfed its first ring of suburbs, turning Bexley, Whitehall, Upper Arlington, and Grandview Heights into "inburbs."

38. In 1966, 1976, and 1986, Columbus received Moody's Investor Service's second-highest municipal bond rating (Aa), a uniquely confident assessment for a Frostbelt city. See chart in Jonas, "Local Interests," 127.

39. Ibid., 124.

40. *CM*, January 1981, 54. Moody's mayoral motto was "Quietly Effective."

41. "Hello Columbus: Thriving Ohio City Seeks to Shed its Image as a Country Bumpkin," *Wall Street Journal*, December 8, 1980. See also Reginald Stuart, "Columbus: The Largest Small Town in America," *New York Times*, reprinted in the November 27, 1978, *CJ*. Trillin quotation from *Business Week*, quoted in *CM*, January 1979, 43. Carson quotation in *CM*, January 1982, 51. *CJ* reporter Betty Garrett statement from 1972, quoted in Fred M. Hechinger, "Why Columbus?" *Saturday Review*, April 30, 1977. An article in the *Iowa Law Review* echoes this assessment, a generation later: "One of the dangers of growing up in Columbus, Ohio is that banality and reality are so indistinguishable, perhaps even co-extensive, that I am never sure when I am in the presence of either, or both." Louise Harmon, *Iowa Law Review* 79 (1994): 385.

42. For analyses of Columbus's power structure during the 1970s, see Moreland, "Black Community," 98–104; Andrews, "Urban Redevelopment," 618–59; Max Brown, "Power in Columbus," *CM*, March 1976, 24–30; Julia Osborne, "The Kid$," *CM*, February 1977, 34–41; Max Brown, "Power: The More Things Change," *CM*, March 1980, 51–59. For examinations of the city's African American elite in the 1970s, see Moreland, "Black Community," 109–34; Martha Brian, "Columbus's Black Community: Who Has the Clout?" *CM*, October 1975, 35–39; Herb Cook Jr., "Goodbye to the Token Blacks," *CM*, June 1980, 54–61; Brown, "More Things Change," 58.

43. Emblematic of the city's dilemma was the much-trumpeted transfer of Borden, Inc.'s administrative headquarters from New York City to Columbus in the early 1970s. While the Fortune 500 food company moved

hundreds of employees into a new downtown office building, its chair and top executives remained in New York. David Lore, "Grades Stamp Columbus City of Exciting Potential," *CD*, October 12, 1977.

44. David Lore, "Boredom, Apathy Haunt Outlook for Columbus," *CD*, October 9, 1977. Battelle had only a few years earlier been forced by a court order to become actively involved in community affairs. Breaking a half century of civic seclusion, Battelle in the early 1970s offered over $35 million to build a new convention center, thrusting itself dramatically into the controversial battleground of downtown redevelopment.

45. See Michael Curtin, "Columbus Not Sure of Own Image," *CD*, January 25, 1976; David Lore, "Does Columbus Have What It Takes to Outshine Sunbelt?" *CD*, February 16, 1977; "Columbus's Inferiority Complex: Are We as Weak as We Think We Are?" *CM*, March 1978, 45–59.

46. Tipton quoted in Michael Curtin, "Columbus Growing Rapidly, But Direction Unknown," *CD*, January 11, 1976. Guided by 1974's "Action Program for Downtown Columbus," the product of a yearlong chamber of commerce–sponsored study by planner Vincent Ponte, the business community's development efforts focused primarily on revitalizing the city's moribund core. From 1961 to 1970, $144 million in public and private capital investments were made in downtown; between 1971 and 1978, that figure leaped to $584 million and would grow even higher over the next decade. Andrews, "Urban Redevelopment," 38–43.

47. Lore, "Boredom, Apathy." For the development battles of the 1970s, see Herb Cook Jr., "The Race to Revitalize Downtown," *CM*, March 1977, 36–43; David Lore, "Columbus Lacking Venture Capital, Some Claim," *CD*, October 11, 1977; and especially Andrews, "Urban Redevelopment."

48. Harvey Molotoch, "Strategies and Constraints of Growth Elites," in *Business Elites and Urban Development: Case Studies and Critical Perspectives*, ed. Scott Cummings, 25.

49. Duncan interview, April 22, 1994; Lynch interview.

50. In 1963, attorney and former speaker of the Ohio House of Representatives Kline Roberts took over for Delmar Starkey as chamber president. With Roberts at the helm, the chamber for the first time began addressing social issues such as education, poverty, and racial inequality, framing them as economic development problems. Wrote Roberts in the chamber's 1972–73 annual report, "Gone forever is the belief that a chamber of commerce should concern itself entirely with matters of 'business development' alone. . . . You cannot have a good business in a bad community."

51. POTIC did chalk up a few minor accomplishments, such as helping to establish the Police Athletic League in the early 1970s. However, said

John Henle, then the chamber's metropolitan affairs director, the chamber's conservative rank and file stifled POTIC's more ambitious aims. The real estate and development community in particular wanted nothing to do with the committee's efforts to ensure open housing. Chamber of Commerce Annual Reports; John Henle interview, March 3, 1994.

52. Willis interview; Ellis interview.

53. Bill Vance interview, December 4, 1991.

54. Metcalf, "From Little Rock to Boston," 207; *Boston Globe* editorial, October 9, 1974, in Buncher, *School Busing Controversy*, 253; Wilkinson, *From Brown to Bakke*, 207.

55. Florence Levinsohn, "TV's Deadly Inadvertent Bias," in Levinsohn and Benjamin D. Wright, *School Desegregation: Shadow and Substance* (Chicago: University of Chicago Press, 1976), 88; United States Commission on Civil Rights, *Fulfilling the Letter and Spirit of the Law: Desegregation of the Nation's Public Schools*, 39, i.

56. *Call and Post* editorial, "Germany Urges Caution When Addressing School Incidents," October 26, 1974.

57. See Chafe, *Civilities and Civil Rights*; also, Elizabeth Jacoway and David R. Colburn, *Southern Businessmen and Desegregation*. Brown quoted in "Preparing for Whatever Decision Comes in the School Desegregation Suit," *Columbus Business Forum*, May 1976, 9.

58. Carolyn Focht, "Desegregation Edict Predicted for City," *CD*, June 11, 1975; "City Warned to Prepare for Order on Desegregation," *CJ*, June 11, 1975.

59. Tom Moody interview, January 9, 1991; Rowland Brown interview, January 6, 1991. Although race was not allowed to become a major factor in the fall campaign, Rosemond's upset victory in the June Democratic primary was attributed to black anger over a police brutality incident at the Kahiki restaurant that occurred the Saturday before the vote. Stan Wyman, "A Surprise for the Democratic Pros," *CM*, August 1975, 46–47.

60. "Pledge of Peace Support Sought," *CD*, October 8, 1975. CORC circulated a "peace pledge" for religious congregations to endorse. When David Hamlar offered a school board resolution supporting CORC's efforts, the white majority twice rejected it. Marilyn Redden contended that CORC's parent organization, the Metropolitan Area Church Board (MACB), was packed with "avid desegregationists" who were "using the issue to make a climate conducive to desegregation and mass busing. The court would then get the feeling that Columbus was ready for it and would get on with it. . . . They could be accused of starting brushfires." Others, however, viewed the board's rejection of the resolution's "basic moral commitment

to law and peace" as an ominous sign of conflicts to come. Rich Brooks, "A Pledge for 'Peace' and a Course of 'Non-Support,'" *Booster*, January 14, 1976; Sylvia Brooks, "Meanwhile, the School Board Tables 'Law and Peace,'" *CM*, April 1976, 31.

61. Emphasis in original. "Report and Recommendations of the School Issues Committee on the Role of the Chamber of Commerce in the School Desegregation Issue," September 10, 1975, Columbus Public School District files.

62. Emphasis in original. George Rosinger, Battelle Laboratories Center for Improved Education, "The Role of the Community in Preparing for Desegregation" (paper presented at a public forum on desegregation in the schools, Upper Arlington, Ohio, March 14, 1976), Columbus Public School District files. Umbrella organizations studied by Columbus included the Dallas Alliance; IMPACT—Involved Memphis Parents Assisting Children and Teachers; Concerned Citizens for Omaha; the Committee of 100 in Milwaukee; PRO-Detroit; and Boston's Citywide Coordinating Council.

63. John Henle, to HEW representative at October 31, 1979, MCSC staff meeting, Metropolitan Columbus Schools Committee (Ohio) Records, MSS 747, Ohio Historical Society [hereafter cited as MCSC Records]; Sam Gresham interview, March 1, 1994. The Committee of Ten consisted of representatives from the Columbus Area Chamber of Commerce, AFL-CIO, Columbus Area Civil Rights Council, Columbus NAACP, Columbus Education Association, Ohio Education Association, Urban League, League of Women Voters, Metropolitan Area Church Board (including CORC), and Project Red Apple.

64. The Citizens' Council for Ohio Schools was already actively researching desegregation-related citizens' groups around the country. See Rachel B. Tompkins, "Community Education and Planning—The Lessons from Other Cities," Citizens Council for Ohio Schools, 1977, MCSC Records; Lila M. Carol, "Court Mandated Citizen Participation in School Desegregation Monitoring Commissions," Citizens' Council for Ohio Schools, 1977, MCSC Records.

65. Nor was desegregation a personally emotional issue for the city's elite. While some graduated from Columbus Public Schools, few sent their children to them, opting instead for private, suburban, or parochial schools. "They were worried about [desegregation] as sort of an intellectual exercise," said Robert Duncan, "but their kids weren't going to school here." Duncan interview, April 22, 1994.

66. Gresham interview; Ellis interview.

67. Brown interview; letter from Rowland Brown to Mel Schottenstein, September 11, 1978, MCSC Records.

68. Letter from Rowland Brown to "members of the steering committee concerned with quality education in greater Columbus," July 12, 1976, MCSC Records. See also minutes from Convenors Steering Group, June 23, 1976, MCSC Records.

69. John Elam interview, February 4, 1994.

70. The key passage read, "The Metropolitan Columbus Schools Committee is formed, consisting of a broad-based voluntary association of citizens concerned with maintaining quality education in metropolitan Columbus and in assisting the community to achieve peaceful and lawful responses to any Federal Court rulings respecting the Columbus School Desegregation Suit." Significantly, the statement of purpose only mentioned "quality education," not "quality integrated education." MCSC Records.

71. Representatives from MCSC's more than sixty endorsing organizations made up its governing General Assembly. A smaller Steering Committee ran MCSC's day-to-day operations and implemented its policies and programs. The Steering Committee at the time of Duncan's decision consisted of: Rowland Brown, chair; Urban League executive director Frank Lomax, vice-chair; Don Pierce, executive director; Columbus and Franklin County AFL-CIO president John Hodges, treasurer; retired Major General Hugh Higgins, secretary; chamber of commerce Quality Education Committee chair John Elam; chamber of commerce vice president John Henle; Jerry Gafford, executive assistant to Mayor Moody (Ron Poole later took Gafford's place as Moody's representative, but Gafford remained on the Steering Committee as Lazarus's vice president of community affairs); OSU president Harold Enarson; *Call and Post* general manager Amos Lynch; Fraternal Order of Police president Ross Rader; Rev. Leon Troy, pastor, Second Baptist Church; Columbus Council of PTAs president Liz Wolfe (later replaced by Loretta Heard); Columbus Education Association (CEA) president John Grossman; Bishop Edward Herrman of the Catholic diocese; Capital University president Dr. Thomas Langevin; Anti-Defamation League regional director Carol Lister; attorney Thomas Palmer; Columbus Youth Services Bureau administrator Cliff Tyree; former YWCA president Grayce Williams; Metropolitan Columbus League of Women Voters president Gloria Davis (later replaced by Sue Phillips); Ohio Farm Bureau Federation, Inc., executive vice president C. William Swank; former CEA vice president Polly Fugate; and Metropolitan Area Church Board executive director Rev. John T. Frazer. Powerful Nationwide Insurance CEO Dean Jeffers was originally a

Steering Committee member, but he quietly resigned six weeks before Duncan's ruling.

72. On March 15, the State Board of Education also voted (19–3) to appeal Duncan's decision.

73. Robert Albrecht, "Board to Fight School Decision," *CD*, March 16, 1977; Micki Seltzer, "Black Board Members Oppose Appeal; Charge 'Outright Discrimination,'" *CP*, March 19, 1977.

74. Joe Davis interview, January 3, 1991; Robert Sohovich, "Public Helps Shape Plan," *CD*, April 24, 1977.

75. Smith interview, January 7, 1991; Davis quoted in Charles Fenton, "Desegregation Plan Strives for '3 Points,'" *CJ*, March 23, 1977; Robert Albrecht, "Public Aid Asked for Schools Plan," *CD*, March 23, 1977. The CIPs ran from late March to April 25. A team of teachers, administrators, and PTA members would meet with requesting organizations anywhere in the city to answer questions about the *Penick* decision and hear suggestions on how the district should proceed. In addition, Davis sent letters soliciting input from 675 community organizations.

76. Criteria from an interim report on desegregation compiled by Davis and submitted to the Columbus Board of Education, Columbus Public School District files; Sohovich, "40,000 Pupils in Columbus Would Be Uprooted by Plan," *CD*, June 1, 1977; also Fenton, "3-Phase School Plans Outlined," *CJ*, June 1, 1977.

77. Three days later, the State Board approved (20–3) a three-phase, $20 million plan that desegregated all but five all-white schools to within 15 percent of a 33.6 percent black average.

78. Charles Fenton, "School Board Plan Sent to Judge," *CJ*, June 11, 1977; Robert Sohovich, "4–3 Vote Advances City School Plan," *CD*, June 11, 1977.

79. The administrative planning team had offered several options that were rejected by the board majority as too immediate or too integrative. Asbury interview, February 15, 1994; C. Smith interview, January 7, 1991; and Charles Newman interview, March 2, 1994.

80. Ross quoted in "Plan Won't Desegregate Schools, NAACP Claims," *CJ*, June 11, 1977; "Black Group Opposed Phased-In School Plan," *CD*, June 15, 1977; "Education Consortium Raps Majority Board Plan," *CP*, June 18, 1977; "All Schools Must Be Included in any Busing Plan," *CP* editorial, June 4, 1977. Hamlar quoted in Micki Seltzer, "Black-White Differences May Result in 'Hung Board,'" *CP*, May 21, 1977; "Minority Panelists to Ask Refinement of Other Plan," *CD*, June 11, 1977.

81. The 15 percent range was a commonly used remedial standard that originated during the 1960s as part of a California administrative code used to define segregated schools. Christine Rossell, *The Carrot or the Stick for School Desegregation*, 30; Micki Seltzer, "Minority Plan Involves All White Schools," *CP*, June 18, 1977.

82. David Hamlar interview, January 3, 1991.

83. As special master, Cunningham had broad powers to advise Duncan on educational issues and monitor the district's compliance with the court's orders.

84. White board members quoted in Micki Seltzer, "Board to Change Remedy Plan; Objects to Court Appointment," *CP*, July 2, 1977. Cunningham, OSU's Novice Fawcett Professor of Educational Administration, had also worked on urban school issues in Louisville, Chicago, St. Louis, Detroit, and San Francisco. See Fine, *When Leadership Fails*, 151–161; Luvern Cunningham Papers, Ohio State University Archives. NAACP memorandum to the court quoted in Micki Seltzer, "Court to Require New Remedy Plans From City, State," *CP*, July 23, 1977; *Dayton Board of Education v. Brinkman*, 433 U.S. 406 (1977), 420, 418 [hereafter cited as *Dayton I*].

85. The revised plan involved 26 schools, bused 4,074 students, and cost $729,311 the first year. Robert Sohovich, "Little Busing Required with Revised Proposal," *CD*, July 5, 1977; Charles Fenton, "Revised School Plan Ratified," *CJ*, July 6, 1977; Robert Sohovich, "Board Votes 4–0 on Plan Slashing Busing Schedule," *CD*, July 6, 1977; Micki Seltzer, "Revised Plan Gets 4–0 Vote," *CP*, July 9, 1977; "Board Was Grasping At Straws," *CJ* editorial, July 9, 1977; Charles Fenton, "Debate on School Proposals Begins Monday," *CJ*, July 9, 1977.

86. "Approval and Disapproval of the Duncan Court Order of March 1977: An Attitude Survey of Registered Voters," prepared by Hugh M. Clark of Decision Research Corporation, 75–76, 55, MCSC Records.

87. MCSC Steering Committee minutes, April 27, 1977 and May 11, 1977, MCSC Records. Lister's impatience was shared by several other Steering Committee members.

88. Halley quoted in Mark Ellis, "Citizens Organize on Busing," *CD*, May 4, 1977. Cook quoted in Rodger Jones, "Citizens against Busing Canvas Door-to-Door," *CJ*, May 11, 1977; "Support, Funds Sought in Antibusing Effort," *CD*, May 11, 1977; Karen Foster, "Citizens Speak Out Against Forced Busing," *Booster*, May 25, 1977.

89. Tom Fennessy, "Organizer Keeping Secret a 'Plan' to Block Busing," *CD*, July 14, 1977; "No Quarter," letter from Kaye Cook to *Dispatch*,

June 15, 1977; Joe Gillette, "Divisive Perils Cited in School Issue Here," *CJ*, June 23, 1977.

90. MCSC Steering Committee minutes, May 25, 1977 and June 7, 1977, MCSC Records.

91. Moody's comment echoed similar warnings by Dallas mayor Earle Cabell sixteen years earlier, as the Texas city prepared to desegregate. In many ways, the response of Columbus business leaders to the implementation of busing mirrored the reaction of southern elites to school desegregation in their cities, with Boston replacing Little Rock as the emblem of disastrous disorder. For instance, in Dallas, wrote historian William Brophy, "civic leaders . . . decided that the issue should be presented to the people as one of law and order versus civil disorder and violence" (143). As a result, a group of over two hundred business leaders formed the Dallas Citizens' Council (DCC). DCC produced a short film promoting peaceful implementation called "Dallas at the Crossroads" and showed it to small civic and neighborhood groups. It also marginalized and monitored extremists, portraying them as dangerous to the community, the city's image, and the children. Dallas's peaceful implementation took place in 1961. William Brophy, "Active Acceptance, Active Containment: The Dallas Story," in *Southern Businessmen and Desegregation,* ed. Jacoway and Colburn, 137–50. For Moody quotations, see "Moody to Stay Neutral, Won't Back Antibusing Groups," *CD*, June 23, 1977.

92. John Combs and C.A. Bryce Jr., "Klan Rally on Capital Steps Ends in Riot," *CP*, July 9, 1977; "Center Sets Workshops on Schools," *CD*, July 6, 1977; "Speak Out Against Violence," *CJ* editorial, July 6, 1977.

93. MCSC ad, July 27, 1977.

94. Lister quoted in Mark Ellis, "Busing Plan Blitz Set," *CD*, August 4, 1977. See letters to the editor in August 3, 1977 and August 4, 1977 *CD* and *CJ* for antibusing responses. Letter from Brown to Gene D'Angelo, WBNS-TV general manager, August 15, 1977, MCSC Records.

95. MCSC ad, August 4, 1977; Rowland Brown interview; Moody interview.

96. Hamlar interview, January 3, 1991; Pierce interview.

97. Quoted in "Up Front," MCSC/CORC newsletter, no. 7, August 8, 1977, Cunningham Papers.

98. Duncan quoted in Dimond, *Beyond Busing,* 255; Davis interview.

99. From text of Duncan's October 4, 1977 ruling, reprinted in October 5, 1977 *CD*.

100. Edwards quoted in Dimond, *Beyond Busing,* 271. The three-judge panel consisted of Gilbert Merritt, Pierce Lively, and Edwards. Robert Sohovich, "3-Judge Appellate Panel Hears City's School Case," *CD,* February 16, 1978; Charles Fenton, "Court Weighs Columbus Desegregation Appeal," *CJ,* February 16, 1978; Sam Porter interview, January 4, 1991.

101. *Penick et al. v. Columbus Board of Education et al.,* 583 F.2d 787 [hereafter cited as *Penick* II], at 845–47.

102. Lomax quoted in Tom Fennessy, "Ruling Removes Most Uncertainty," *CD,* July 15, 1978. Moody quoted in Tom Fennessy, "Moody: City Prepared For Busing," *CJ,* August 1, 1978. Full text of peace pledge printed in *Linden News,* August 8, 1978. *CD* editorial, July 18, 1978.

103. Robert Sohovich, "City Schools Open amidst Legal, Financial Problems," *CD,* September 7, 1978. Davis quoted in Charles Fenton, "Schools Plan to 'Make Go' of Desegregation," *CJ,* August 8, 1978.

104. The "incremental segregative effect" test would force judges to undertake the virtually impossible task of calculating the specific impact of every intentionally segregative act and precisely tailoring a remedy to fit the result. Criticized Columbus civil rights activist Barbee Durham, "It would require a staff of sociologists, psychologists, mathematicians, investigators, projectionists, computer analysts, etc. constantly at work for years. . . . It's like a paper I was asked to write when I was a fraternity pledge. The subject of that paper was, 'Why Is Water Wet?'" Letter from Durham to *CD,* August 24, 1978.

105. 439 U.S. 1348 (1978); Rehnquist's order, printed in August 13, 1978 *CD.* Memo from Rehnquist to Chief Justice Warren Burger, August 15, 1978, Marshall Papers.

106. Memo from Burger to William Brennan, August 17, 1978, Marshall papers. Even with the United States Attorney General's Office filing an amicus curiae brief urging the Court to vacate Rehnquist's stay, the chances of a special session being convened were extremely slim. According to Porter, only ten had occurred in the previous 160 years. "Lawyers Unsure of Court Reaction," *CD,* August 13, 1978.

107. S. Porter interview; Michael Cull and Brian Usher, "'Stop-Desegregation' Order Jolts Schools in Columbus," *Akron Beacon-Journal,* August 20, 1978.

108. On May 1, the board had authorized the administration to prepare contingency plans in case the district won its appeal.

109. "Variety of Remarks Accompany Ruling," *CD,* August 13, 1978.

110. Charles Briggs, "'Columbus Plan' Damned as 'Black Brain Drain,'" *CP*, August 19, 1978; Don Baird, "City Blacks Feel Cornered," *CJ*, August 14, 1978; Statement of NAACP president Tom Fullove in response to Rehnquist's stay, August 15, 1978, MCSC Records.

111. The Youth Task Force (YTF), run by Cliff Tyree and Sue Phillips, coordinated activities for high school students with leadership potential. The goal of the YTF was to use the influence of student leaders to cultivate a constructive atmosphere in newly desegregated schools. The Cooperating Neighborhoods Program, coordinated by Frank Lomax, Carol Lister, and Metropolitan Human Services administrator Khari Enaharo, brought together parents and concerned citizens from areas of the city linked by the school board's remedy plan. The junior high schools involved were selected largely based on their potential for disruption.

112. MCSC Steering Committee minutes, August 16, 1978, MCSC Records.

113. Ibid.; "Remarks by Rowland C. W. Brown/MCSC Regarding Judge Rehnquist's Stay," MCSC Records.

114. MCSC Steering Committee minutes, August 16, 1978, MCSC Records; MCSC Statement of Purpose, MCSC Records.

115. Herb Cook Jr., "MCSC's Dilemma: What Do We Do for an Encore?" *CM*, November 1979, 58–59.

116. Kaye Cook interview, February 15, 1994. NANS never revealed an official membership count, though Cook acknowledged that "there were always many more people at rallies than were actual members." Membership estimates generally ranged from one hundred to five hundred. Still, while other antibusing groups emerged in Columbus (Citizens Against Forced Busing, Neighborhood Schools Coordinating Committee, Concerned Citizens of the Centennial Area), only NANS had the backing of a national organization (NANS, Inc.) and the overt support of school board members. Langdon and Redden even became national NANS, Inc. board members.

117. This vacuum was lamented as early as August 1977, when David Milenthal, the advertising executive in charge of MCSC's public relations program, observed that unless a countervailing force emerged on the left, MCSC would come to be identified as probusing, not propeace. MCSC Steering Committee minutes, August 24, 1977, MCSC Records.

118. The closest Columbus got to a "probusing" group was the two-person letter-writing factory of Barbee and Anna Mae Durham. The Durhams

evidently did try to solicit broader support, but with no success. In MCSC's files, for example, is a copy of a letter from Barbee Durham to Muhammed Ali seeking $250,000 from the heavyweight champion for "an organization [in Columbus] that would be committed to desegregation so that it might then be able to develop a program designed to counteract the propaganda of the antibusing groups." The files contain no response from Ali. Letter from Barbee Durham to Muhammed Ali, September 1977, MCSC Records.

119. MCSC's March 1977 poll found that 59.7 percent of whites "strongly support keeping children in neighborhood schools if busing is the alternative." Only 15.6 percent of blacks answered the same way. Overall, however, "black opinion was divided, though a plurality supported busing for integration . . . 43.8 percent support busing, 16.7 percent are neutral, and 35.4 percent prefer neighborhood schools." Attitude Survey of Registered Voters, March 1977, MCSC Records.

120. Briggs, "Columbus Plan Damned." CMACAO administered Head Start and other social programs in the Columbus area.

121. Duncan interview, April 22, 1994.

122. Anderson interview; Frank Garner, "Desegregation Debate Answers Some Questions, Ends Some Confusion, and Gives Blacks 'Sounding-Off' Forum," *CP*, August 11, 1979.

123. MCSC's March 1977 survey found that 56.3 percent of black respondents accepted the statement "Integration will improve the quality of the schools," versus 29.9 percent of whites. Of blacks, 36.5 percent agreed with the statement "Better to let black and white children go to school in their own neighborhoods," versus 76.2 percent of whites. And blacks overwhelmingly rejected the statement "Schools are pretty well racially mixed" (69.8 percent to 21.9 percent), while a plurality of whites accepted it (47.9 percent to 44.1 percent). Attitude Survey of Registered Voters, March 1977, MCSC Records.

124. John Henle to HEW representatives at October 31, 1979 MCSC staff meeting, MCSC Records; letter from Joe Davis to Don Pierce, March 13, 1978, MCSC Records.

125. Revealingly, MCSC's local money-raising requests emphasized peaceful implementation, while its applications for federal funds and national foundation grants stressed "quality integrated education." MCSC Records.

126. MCSC Steering Committee minutes, January 10, 1979, MCSC Records.

127. MCSC Steering Committee minutes, November 22, 1978, MCSC Records; Report on Cooperating Neighborhoods and Youth Impact Programs, November 4, 1978, MCSC Records.

128. Report on Cooperating Neighborhoods; MCSC application for ESAA funds, December 4, 1978, 171–72, MCSC Records.

129. The Supreme Court announced on January 8, 1979, that it would hear Columbus's appeal. The case was consolidated with *Dayton Board of Education v. Brinkman* [hereafter cited as *Dayton II*]. Oral arguments for both cases would be heard the same day. The Court's decision to hear the Columbus and Dayton cases was viewed as a signal of its determination to clarify increasingly cloudy desegregation law.

130. S. Porter interview; audio tape recording of oral arguments provided by Drew Days III; Dimond, *Beyond Busing*, 364. Tom Atkins argued for the NAACP. Drew Days III, U.S. assistant attorney general for civil rights, followed, putting the weight of the Carter administration behind *Penick*'s original plaintiffs.

131. Nina Totenberg, National Public Radio's well-connected Supreme Court reporter, predicted in May that the Court would try to extricate itself from the controversial issue of school desegregation by overturning the lower court decisions. Dimond, *Beyond Busing*, 375.

132. Lister quoted in MCSC Steering Committee minutes, May 16, 1979, MCSC Records. Henle quoted in MCSC Steering Committee minutes, June 5, 1979, MCSC Records. While maintaining their faith that desegregation would take place that fall, MCSC officials began setting out contingency plans in case the Supreme Court ordered otherwise. If the Court ordered a limited remedy—"in effect, no remedy"—MCSC would alter its PR program and press for a more equitable plan. If the Court reversed *Penick*, MCSC would either "change its purpose and by-laws and adopt a goal of working for voluntary quality integrated education in Columbus" or disband and reemerge under a different name to pursue this aim. Such an organization, MCSC officials acknowledged, would have a difficult time attracting local funding. Options for MCSC's response to the Supreme Court decision, June 8, 1979, MCSC Records.

133. 1979 letter from Don Pierce to Bruce Evans of the Battelle Foundation, MCSC Records.

134. The court discussed *Penick* I and *Dayton* II at conference on April 27. White's opinion went through at least four drafts, and final versions were being circulated as late as June 28. Marshall Papers.

135. Dimond, *Beyond Busing*, 377.

136. *Columbus Board of Education et al. v. Penick et al.*, 443 U.S. 449 (1979), 455, 464. A seven-justice majority affirmed *Penick* I. Justices Blackmun, Brennan, Marshall, and Stevens joined White's opinion. Burger and Stewart filed separate concurring opinions. Powell dissented and also joined Rehnquist's dissent.

137. In *Dayton* II, the Court ruled 5–4 that the segregative actions of the Dayton school board justified the imposition of a systemwide remedy. Legal scholars generally viewed the Columbus and Dayton cases together as a crucial, if not decisive, victory for desegregation. Burger's qualified concurrence in *Columbus* indicated that the Court majority's deference to stare decisis outweighed the mounting ambivalence of some justices toward busing: "It is becoming increasingly doubtful that massive public transportation really accomplishes the desirable objectives sought. Nonetheless our prior decisions have sanctioned its use when a constitutional violation of sufficient magnitude has been found." *Columbus Board of Education v. Penick*, 469. For a sampling of the legal commentary that followed the Court's decision in *Columbus*, see Edmund W. Kitch, "The Return of Color-Consciousness to the Constitution: Weber, Dayton, and Columbus," *Supreme Court Review* (Chicago: University of Chicago Press, 1979), 1–15; *Harvard Law Review*, November 1979, 119–30; *Emory Law Journal*, spring 1980, 481–515; *North Carolina Central Law Journal*, fall 1980, 219–33; *Hastings Constitutional Law Quarterly*, winter 1980, 505–22; *Baylor Law Review*, winter 1980, 154–63.

138. "When the Court Was at its Best," *New York Times* editorial, July 7, 1979; "The Law of the Land," *CJ* editorial, July 3, 1979.

139. Tom Sheehan and Robert Sohovich, "Duncan: Fall Busing Order Is 'Unavoidable,'" *CD*, July 13, 1979; Jerry Condo and Marilyn Greenwald, "Busing in Fall Unavoidable, Board Is Told," *CJ*, July 13, 1979. Text of Duncan's August 2 order reprinted in August 3, 1979 *CD*. The week before Duncan's order, another avenue of avoidance long pursued by antibusers nationally had been sealed off. After being bottled up for two years, an antibusing constitutional amendment was discharged from the House Judiciary Committee and scheduled for a floor vote. The proposed amendment, which the Columbus school board endorsed 5–2 on July 11, guaranteed the "right to neighborhood schools," stating that "no student shall be compelled to attend a public school other than the one nearest his residence." Advocates of desegregation argued that a "right to walk" amendment would trivialize the Constitution and undercut efforts to integrate public schools. On July 24, after an emotional debate, the House voted 216–209 to reject

the proposal. Dimond, *Beyond Busing,* 376, 385; Whitt Flora, "Antibusing Campaign Close to Showdown," *CD,* June 2, 1979; "Foes of Antibusing Proposal Escalate Effort to Kill Measure," *CJ,* July 13, 1979; "Losers on Busing Say Price Heavy," *CD,* July 25, 1979.

140. Text of Duncan's August 2 order, *CD,* August 3, 1979.

141. MCSC Steering Committee minutes, July 2, 1979; Columbus Board of Education resolution, July 11, 1979, Columbus School District files.

142. Redden interview.

143. Because of her dramatic declaration at the August 6 MCSC forum, Prentice generally has been given credit for this phrase. However, several interviewees credited the superintendent with "feeding" Prentice the line, which he then displayed on a banner hung at administrative headquarters. School officials may well have lifted the line from another desegregated district. A 1976 *Call and Post* article, for example, quotes the Hoke County, North Carolina, superintendent saying, "It shall be done—and done well." "Varied Plans Available to Desegregate Schools," *CP,* December 4, 1976.

144. Marilyn Greenwald, "Callers Swamp School FACTline," *CJ,* August 20, 1979.

145. See diagram, Columbus Public School District files.

146. Moody interview. Changing an officer's demeanor did not mean changing his view of desegregation, of course. NANS's Kaye Cook contended that she received police intelligence from sympathetic officers who were also clandestine NANS members. "Some of them," she said, "would escort me to the rallies." Cook interview.

147. Also, police intelligence units collaborated with the FBI to infiltrate and monitor antibusing organizations ranging from NANS to the American White Nationalist Party, which may at least partially explain the cozy relationship Kaye Cook describes in n. 146.

148. For example, said Desegregation Task Force chief James Rutter, the department was prepping officers to deal with citizens who had never before broken the law. In Louisville, they had learned, police were "not prepared to meet their wives, neighbors, and relatives" on the other side of the barricades. Jim Smith, "City Police Intend to Be 'Ready for Any School Problem,'" *CJ,* August 27, 1979; Billy House, "Desegregation Security 'Ready' as School Opening Nears," *Northland News,* August 15, 1979.

149. House, "Desegregation Security"; Jerry Lovett, "Desegregation Task Force Hopes to Sit Out Busing," *CD,* August 28, 1979.

150. Robert Sohovich, "Massive School Bus Fleet Is Ready to Roll," *CD,* August 26, 1979. Seniors, kindergartners, and special education students were exempted from the plan.

151. Because ESAA Title VII funds could only be granted to districts where good-faith desegregation plans were in place, the Supreme Court decision and Duncan's ensuing order also resuscitated MCSC's grassroots programs.

152. Lyrics of MCSC radio/TV jingle, written by Joe Ashley. Reprinted from David Drake, "Kids Talk to Adults in TV Ad," *CJ*, September 5, 1979. Advertising statistics from MCSC ESAA Title VII Proposal, May 28, 1980, 25–28. The campaign also included 3,000 radio and 180 television public service announcements donated by local electronic media outlets.

153. Henle to HEW representatives, MCSC October 31, 1979 meeting, MCSC Records.

154. The figure given in MCSC's 1980 ESAA application was $300,000, though the specific breakdown of funding sources is unclear. According to audits of MCSC's finances, money for the Community Awareness Program came primarily from these local private donors: the Battelle Foundation, the Columbus Foundation, the Yassenoff Foundation, and the Columbus Area Chamber of Commerce's Forward Columbus Fund. By far the biggest contributors to MCSC were the chamber ($143,000) and the Battelle Foundation ($141,000). MCSC ESAA application, May 28, 1980; audited financial statements, June 30, 1978 (Ernst and Ernst) and June 30, 1980 (Ernst and Whitney), MCSC Records.

155. Michael Taylor, "Sportsmanship as Guide, Woody Advises City Students," *CJ*, August 31, 1979; Brown interview.

156. Letter to the *Dispatch* from Mrs. Joy Lee of Columbus; Tom Fennessy, "Budding Columbus Actress Really Is Thinking of 'Us'," *CD*, September 7, 1979; "Effective Campaign," *CJ*, September 19, 1979.

157. City National Bank, BancOhio, and Huntington Bank donated $5,484 for the ad. Letter from Rowland Brown to Robert Farrington, executive director of Columbus Building and Trades Council, September 6, 1979, MCSC Records.

158. Marilyn Greenwald, "Davis Is Sure CMH Will Pass the Busing Test," *CJ*, September 6, 1979; "Davis Says U.S. Watching as Columbus Takes Test," *CD*, September 6, 1979; Damon Asbury interview, January 7, 1991; Moody interview.

159. Davis quoted in Robert Sohovich, "Columbus Schools Focus of National News Media," *CD*, August 29, 1979. Pierce quoted in Bud Wilkinson, "Local Desegregation Coverage a Tricky Business," *CD*, August 29, 1979. Metz quoted in "School Openings Quiet, Orderly." Buckeye was one of several "barometer" schools on which reporters focused. Located in the middle of a blue-collar, white Appalachian neighborhood on the city's

South Side, Buckeye had an enrollment that shifted from 4 percent black to 43 percent black with desegregation. The remedy plan paired Buckeye with Beery Junior High School, situated in a mostly black working-class area across the Conrail tracks from Buckeye's attendance area. Desegregation changed Beery's racial ratio from 65 percent black to 65 percent white.

160. "What Principals Are Saying to Joseph L. Davis," Columbus Public School District files.

161. Radebaugh interview.

162. Brown interview.

163. Ibid. Zeller quoted in Carol Stevens, "How Two Cities Won and Lost on School Busing," *Buffalo Courier-Express*, June 28, 1981. Radebaugh interview. See also Robert Sohovich, "Desegregation's 'War Room' Was a Most Peaceful Place," *CD*, September 9, 1979. Boley quoted in Snell and Wilson, "Without a Hitch."

164. Willis quoted in Eric Rozenman, "Going to East"; "Buses Roll." Snell and Wilson, "Without a Hitch." Tyree quoted in Scott Powers, "Black and White: Crossing Paths, But Seldom Walking Together," *Northwest Columbus News*, August 7, 1985. The number of volunteers in the schools was estimated by Columbus administrators to be over 4,000. The official number of school district volunteers the previous year was 3,173. "An Open Letter to CMH PTA Members," Joe Davis, *Linden News*, September 19, 1979; "Choices for the 80's: Superintendent's Status Report on the Columbus Public Schools," November 1, 1978, 2, Columbus Public School District files.

165. Brown interview; Moody interview. The only significant scare occurred on Wednesday, October 10, when police and FBI agents arrested John and Edward Gerhardt for conspiring to bomb Olde Orchard Elementary, where Robert Duncan's daughter Tracey was a fifth grader. The Gerhardt brothers, leaders of the American White Nationalist Party, had an extensive and sporadically violent history of right-wing extremism. Their activities were so well monitored by the Columbus Police Department and the FBI, however, that Edward unknowingly assigned an informant to buy the ingredients needed to make the bomb. On February 2, 1980, Sixth District Court judge Joseph P. Kinneary sentenced the brothers to six years in prison for conspiring to violate the rights of schoolchildren, six years for attempting to damage an institution receiving federal funds, and one year for attempting to interfere with a court order.

166. *CD*, September 6, 1979. To ease the shock of systemwide desegregation, the district had staggered the start of the school year. Grades 1–7

and 10 began September 6, with the rest of the students arriving the following day.

167. Robert Smith interview, December 6, 1991; "Columbus Sets an Example for All," *Akron Beacon-Journal* editorial, September 9, 1979; "Columbus Did It Well," *Cleveland Plain-Dealer* editorial, September 7, 1979; Moody interview.

168. Letter to Rowland Brown from John Hamill, President of First Trust Company, the trust management company for First Banc Group of Ohio, September 7, 1979, MCSC Records. Moody to Kiwanis Club quoted in Michael Curtin, "City Is Praised for Peaceful Day," *CD*, September 7, 1979. Robert Sohovich, "Dietzel Predicts Passage of School Levy Next Year," *CD*, November 11, 1979; Robert Sohovich, "City Gets Smooth Ride with Busing," *CD*, June 22, 1980; Moody interview; Brown interview.

169. Among them: an absence of territorial ethnic enclaves; a sympathetic and sensitive judge; a low-key superintendent who quietly developed the trust of both pro- and antidesegregation forces; a relatively tranquil racial climate not dangerously strained by resistance to black advancement from the city's comparatively small population of blue-collar whites; and, ironically, Justice Rehnquist's stay, which permitted more extensive logistical preparation, provided the angriest parents more time to exit the school system, and allowed the volatility that surrounded desegregation earlier in the decade to recede an extra year.

170. Days quoted in "Columbus Busing Is Commended," *CJ*, September 11, 1979. Reporter quoted in article reprinted from unknown source, "Columbus Gets A+ in Peaceful Desegregation," *CJ*, January 1, 1980, and *CD*, January 5, 1980. Columbus Area Chamber of Commerce Annual Report, 1979.

171. MCSC Steering Committee minutes, September 17, 1979, MCSC Records. "Needs assessment" for MCSC's 1980–81 ESAA Application, MCSC Records. Judge Duncan allowed Columbus to establish a unique internal desegregation monitoring system, headed by Asbury the first year and Calvin Smith from then on. The monitoring office submitted regular reports (initially monthly, eventually semiannually) to Duncan containing detailed data requested by the judge and his special master. These reports can be found at the main branch of the Columbus Public Library.

172. "Summary of Comments" in Cooperating Neighborhood Program's November 1979 report, MCSC Records.

173. MCSC Steering Committee minutes, October 17, 1979, MCSC Records; MCSC ESAA Advisory Committee minutes, February 14, 1980, MCSC Records.

174. David Lore, "Will Chamber of Commerce Reorganization Help?" *CD*, October 14, 1977. "A Becalmed Chamber Gets a New Boss," *CM*, January 1979, 10; Max Brown, "Dietzel: The Axe Fell Fast," *CM*, August 1979, 19.

175. Dietzel quoted in Don Mader, "Chamber to Regroup to Court New Industry," *CJ*, March 10, 1979; Columbus Area Chamber of Commerce Annual Report, 1979. For details of the campaign, see Andrews, "Urban Redevelopment," 89–92.

176. John Henle's chamber contract expired in May 1979 and was not renewed. He had worked there since 1969 and was MCSC's main advocate and behind-the-scenes broker. Rowland Brown, though hailed for his leadership of MCSC, lost much of his clout as a business leader when the faltering Buckeye International merged with Worthington Industries. In late 1980, Brown became CEO of Online Computer Library Center, Inc. in Dublin. As for John Elam, see n. 177.

177. Cook, "MCSC's Dilemma," 59. A Democrat and social liberal, Elam had long been a supporter of increased integration. For the better part of a decade, he had also played a prominent role in the Roberts-led chamber. By 1979, however, his name appeared nowhere on the chamber's list of officers and directors, and the Quality Education Committee that he headed had become increasingly insignificant. His sudden and rather stark call for ending MCSC seemed more to reflect his position as the delegate of an uninterested business leadership than his personal attitude toward MCSC's aims. MCSC's September 17, 1979 minutes specifically note that "Elam spoke as a representative for the business community" when he "made the recommendation that . . . MCSC should disband." See also MCSC Steering Committee minutes, September 17, 1979, MCSC Records.

178. Among those whose endorsements did accompany the 1980 application were Mayor Moody, Superintendent Davis, teachers' union president John Grossman, and *Penick* special master Luvern Cunningham (joined by Judge Duncan). By contrast, MCSC's 1978 ESAA application contained enthusiastic endorsements from both Elam and the chamber. "Continuation of MCSC's community programs are essential to maintaining and enhancing the health of the Greater Columbus community," the chamber said. See MCSC staff meeting notes, December 17, 1979; MCSC ESAA application, November 28, 1977; MCSC ESAA application, May 28, 1980, all in MCSC Records.

179. Lomax quoted in Cooperating Neighborhoods Program minutes, April 25, 1980, MCSC Records. Henle quoted in MCSC staff meeting notes,

April 24, 1980, MCSC Records. Diehards quoted in Cooperating Neighborhoods Program minutes. Brown quoted in Cook, "MCSC's Dilemma," 59.

180. Moody interview.

181. In 1978 and 1979, MCSC received one-year ESAA grants totalling $163,000 to fund the Cooperating Neighborhoods and Youth Task Force programs. Unexpected cuts, however, nullified MCSC's 1980 ESAA application.

Chapter 3

1. Until the late 1960s, only "resident freeholders"—landowners who lived on their land—could sign annexation petitions. Pressure from pro-development forces, however, led to a change in the law that permitted "non-resident freeholders" to sign petitions. This change gave absentee landlords and businesses with large real estate holdings much more leverage to influence the annexation process.

2. "Annexation in Franklin County," *Columbus Business Forum*, March 1968; Jonas, "Local Interests," 204–7; Kathy Gray Foster, "Hot Topic of Annexation Returns to Front Burner," *CD*, March 9, 1986.

3. Ohio voters approved the constitutional amendment establishing a state board of education in November 1953. The first board was elected two years later. Ohio Department of Education, *Milestones: A History of the State Board of Education of Ohio 1956–1989*, 1–8.

4. From 1956 to 1966, the number of separate school districts in Ohio fell from 1,234 to 650 . Over the next twenty three years, the number fell by only 37 to 613. Ibid., 36–42. Territory transfer statistics compiled by Dr. George Saribalas, Ohio Department of Education.

5. The ability to expand via annexation has come to be seen by many as essential to sustaining the overall health of an urban area. Older, decaying northeastern cities have generally been surrounded by suburbs since before World War II, while newer, sprawling Sunbelt cities have had the freedom to enlarge. See Jackson, *Crabgrass Frontier*, 138–56; David Rusk, *Cities without Suburbs*.

6. Jonas, "Local Interests," 141–44. There were several far-reaching advantages to building out instead of up. Economies of scale enabled the city to service new residential and industrial development more efficiently and cheaply than surrounding municipalities could. A larger city meant a

larger tax base, and a larger tax base meant a lower tax burden on individuals and businesses. Annexation allowed housing developers to bring substantial tracts of land into Columbus that would not be subject to the stringent, exclusionary zoning restrictions of most residential suburbs; new subdivisions could thus receive services quickly and efficiently, on cheaper land, with more homes to the acre. Finally, annexation enabled the city to avoid being surrounded by suburbs often hostile to additional growth and development (particularly the industrial development sought by the chamber of commerce at the time).

At the same time, however, rapid expansion also funneled new construction, infrastructure, and resources away from the central city, leaving older, increasingly poor areas to deteriorate. As tax-funded infrastructural improvements facilitated the abandonment of the central city, discrimination concentrated African Americans within this area. Thus, while geographic expansion softened the impact of urban decay on Columbus, its benefits were by no means equitably distributed.

7. To finance infrastructure for the newly annexed areas without depending on federal funds, the Sensenbrenner administration created a capital improvements fund out of 25 percent of the receipts from the city's income tax. The fund was used to finance bonds approved by the electorate. Ibid., 194; M. D. Portman, "City Should Look Inward for Growth," *CD*, March 15, 1992.

8. Columbus's area was over ninety square miles by 1960. "Progress, Growth and Annexation," City of Columbus Department of Development, 1968; Columbus Area Chamber of Commerce Annual Report, 1956–57.

9. The city annexed only a little over five square miles of territory under Westlake. "Progress, Growth, and Annexation."

10. "Lifestyle, Columbus," *Columbus Business Forum*, August 1970, 8, 22.

11. The contracts Cremean entered into during the 1960s generally allowed suburbs to double or triple in size. Jonas, "Local Interests," 113–15; Harrison Smith Jr., "Columbus's Annexation Policy Pays Off," *CD*, June 21, 1979; Mary Yost, "Changes Described in Annexing Game," *CD*, November 22, 1987.

12. Harold Eibling, "Dateline 2000" (paper presented at Columbus Area Chamber of Commerce "Columbus '76" symposium, October 19, 1966), 63; OSU Advisory Commission report, 43.

13. *Clemons v. the Board of Education of Hillsboro, Ohio*, 228 F2d 853 (6th Cir. 1956); *Deal v. Cincinnati Board of Education*, 369 F2d 55 (6th Cir.

1966). See Ohio Council on Civil Rights, *Racial Imbalance in the Public Schools: A Survey of Legal Developments*, April 1965.

14. Overall, between 1955 and 1985, the State Board of Education received 297 territory transfer requests, approving 76.4 percent of them. The state board approved 76.7 percent of Columbus's 60 requests during that thirty-year period, with virtually all of the approvals occurring before 1965. Foster, "Hot Topic." Annexation statistics compiled by Dr. George Saribalas, Ohio Department of Education.

15. Eibling, "Dateline 2000," 64; Cremean quoted in Yost, "Annexing Game." "Annexation in Franklin County," *Columbus Business Forum*, March 1968, 11–12; Foster, "Hot Topic." In 1968, Worthington ceded 2,400 acres and 1,100 students to the Columbus schools. In return, Columbus agreed not to seek transfer of territory that had been annexed to the city of Columbus but remained in the Worthington School District. The land that Worthington retained included an Anheuser-Busch brewery that had opened the year before. The biggest industrial branch plant to locate in Columbus during the past twenty-five years, the brewery continues to be the city of Columbus's largest sewer and water consumer, yet the Worthington School District's largest tax base contributor. Kathy Gray Foster, "School Annexation: It's More Than a Land and Money Issue," *CD*, October 7, 1984; Michael Curtin, "Annexation by Choice," *CD*, March 10, 1985; Debbie Briner, "Columbus Won't Challenge '68 Agreement, Official Says," *Northland News*, March 12, 1986.

16. In 1968, Columbus voters approved an 8.2-mill levy after the board promised to spend the additional money on "supplementary" items such as art, music, and physical education teachers. Rising inflation ate away at the new funds, however, and bitter negotiations with the nascent Columbus Education Association resulted in much of the rest of the money being channeled into teacher salaries. This situation seriously damaged the district's fiscal credibility and contributed to disastrous bond issue and levy defeats in 1969 and 1971.

17. "Segregation Increase Feared if Voters Pass School Annex Bill," *CJ*, May 2, 1975; "Columbus Opposes Transfer Bill," *Northland News*, May 7, 1975. In 1971, the Golden Finger had a tax valuation worth $17,857,862, approximately one quarter of the Grandview Heights school district's entire tax base. The Columbus school system also received territory in the 1971 deal from the Madison Local, Reynoldsburg, South-Western, Upper Arlington, Washington Local, and Westerville school districts. Figures from George Saribalas, Ohio Department of Education; also Foster, "Hot Topic."

18. While suburban officials sought to delay the portion of the deal that affected them, the Mifflin transfer itself proceeded without obstruction, formally occurring on July 15, 1971. In the transfer deal, Columbus received a portion of the Westerville City School District municipally served by Columbus since 1956. It included approximately 2,800 students, almost all of them white, and 20 to 25 percent of the district's tax base. Norris's second attempt to enact territory transfer legislation passed the Ohio House but died in the Ohio Senate. Gerald Tebben, "Bill Supported in Suburbs," *CD*, March 23, 1975; Robert Ruth, "School District Annexation Faces House," *CD*, July 6, 1975; "School Transfer Appeal Defeated," *CJ*, July 10, 1975.

19. "School Lands Transfer OK, Court Rules," *CD*, February 11, 1976; Ted Vertrostko, "Transfer of Areas Upheld," *CJ*, February 12, 1976.

20. "Segregation Increase Feared"; "Columbus Opposes Transfer Bill."

21. Joseph Wagner, "City Council Backs School Bond Issue," *CD*, October 17, 1972; Graydon Hambrick, "Columbus OK's Bond Proposal," *CD*, November 8, 1972; George Sweda, "City School Bond Wins Voter Okay," *CJ*, November 8, 1972.

22. Andrew Jonas comes to a similar conclusion in his 1989 OSU geography dissertation, citing 1973 as the point when development interests in Columbus became aligned with increasingly powerful and vocal coalitions of suburban parents and officials, at the expense of the Columbus Public School District. Jonas, "Local Interests."

23. The initial development decline is in part attributable to the OPEC-driven recession of 1973–74. The complete absence of a postrecession homebuilding revival, however, can only be ascribed to looming desegregation. Interview with Carl Klein and Steve McClary, City of Columbus Development Department administrators, November 12, 1992.

24. Dan Page and Michael Taylor, "Columbus Schools Facing 'Resegregation,'" *CJ*, October 1, 1984; Klein and McClary interview.

25. Coleman, Kelly, and Moore, *Trends in School Segregation*, 79–80. By the late 1970s, researchers had reached a rough consensus that school desegregation contributed less than most people thought and more than some scholars contended to America's post–World War II middle-class suburban migration, and that whatever "white flight" desegregation spurred occurred primarily during the years immediately surrounding implementation. For the past fifteen years, the sociological debate over desegregation generally has assumed the reality of resegregation and focused instead on which desegregation plans most effectively foster integration without furthering segregation.

26. "They Came, They Saw, They Liked and Disliked," *CM*, March 1978, 48. Other factors at the time that facilitated Columbus's suburban-like sprawl included the completion of the Interstate-270 "Outerbelt," which opened previously isolated outlying areas to industrial and residential development; the opening of Muirfield Village, a high-end housing development in Dublin that pulled growth toward the county's northwest fringe; and the signing of new water-sewer service contracts between Columbus and its outer-tier suburbs that solidified development boundaries for twenty years.

27. *Milliken v. Bradley*, 418 U.S. 717 (1974). The Court's 5–4 decision disallowed Sixth District judge Stephen Roth's controversial Detroit desegregation order, which incorporated the Detroit public schools and 53 surrounding suburban districts into a sweeping, regionwide remedy. *Milliken* made it virtually impossible for plaintiffs to prove the existence of intentional, metropolitan segregation, thus largely confining desegregation remedies to central city districts. Warned Thurgood Marshall, in one of his most prescient and passionate dissents, "In the short run, it may seem to be the easier course to allow our great metropolitan areas to be divided up each into two cities—one white, the other black—but it is a course, I predict, our people will ultimately regret" (815).

28. "Redlining" was the practice, institutionalized by the federal Home Owners' Loan Corporation in the 1930s and consequently adopted by banks nationwide, of specifically delineating older, often predominantly black areas of a city and withholding investment from them. As part of a four-tiered lending-industry color code, these areas were outlined in red on "residential security maps" to indicate their lowest-priority status. Jackson, *Crabgrass Frontier*, 196–203; Massey and Denton, *American Apartheid*, 51–52.

29. Smith interview, November 18, 1992.

30. Smith interview, January 7, 1992; Jim Hyre interview, October 30, 1991. North High School was located in the virtually all-white neighborhood of Clintonville, just north of Ohio State University. Though one of the city's most prestigious and tradition-rich high schools, budget cuts and declining enrollment made it a casualty of school closings in 1978.

31. In 1977, the U.S. Department of Housing and Urban Development audited Columbus as part of a multiple-city study of housing discrimination. Using testers, HUD found that whites in Columbus received favorable treatment in 52 percent of the 29 audits involving rental units and 63 percent of the 40 involving sales units. Nationwide averages were 39 percent and 48 percent, respectively. According to Massey and Denton, "White

favoritism [is] defined to occur when white auditor receives favorable treatment on at least one of the following items and black auditors receive favorable treatment on none: housing availability, courtesy to client, terms and condition of sale or rental, information requested of client, information supplied to client" (*American Apartheid,* 100–101). Cited from Ronald Wienk et al., *Measuring Racial Discrimination in American Housing Markets: The Housing Market Practices Survey* (Washington, D.C.: U.S. Department of Housing and Urban Development, 1979).

32. Century 21 Northcountry Realty ad, *CD,* April 10, 1977; Joe Gillette, "Four Area Firms Cited in Ad Complaint," *CJ,* July 2, 1977; Gifford interview, October 4, 1991. The billboard fiasco earned HER an end-of-year citation from *Columbus Monthly:* "The White Flight Trophy (And One Free Pass to the Next Meeting of the Ohio Civil Rights Council)," *CM,* January 1978, 48.

33. At the same time, suburban officials shunned even minimal, voluntary attempts to foster interdistrict, integrative contact. After the Ellis administration wrote letters to every Franklin County school district proposing integrated student exchanges and field trips, only one such effort occurred, involving twenty-four East, Northland, and Westerville North students. Grandview Heights board member Ralph Antolino proposed matching Grandview and Columbus sixth graders for educational field trips. "Presently," his motion read, "the only integrated experience offered by R.L.S. [Grandview's Robert Louis Stevenson Elementary] is the relationship the students have with one black custodian." The proposal died when Antolino's motion was not seconded. Though these incidents involve superficial proposals, they do illustrate the depth of suburban resistance to even a hint of integration. "'Mini-Exchange' Stimulates Students," *CD,* April 3, 1976; Betty Daft, "Integrated Trip Proposal Killed," *CJ,* May 12, 1976.

34. From December 1968 to December 1976, 46.3 percent of all non-Columbus levy attempts in Franklin County passed; in 1977 and 1978, however, the rate rose to 92.3 percent. Statewide, on the other hand, well under half of all school levies passed. Eric Rozenman, "Odds Grow Longer against School Funds," *CJ,* September 6, 1979.

35. "Focus: Spring Levy Formula Certainty for Repeat," *CD,* September 15, 1977. Five districts passed levies in the spring of 1977 greater than or equal to ones that had failed the previous fall. Three others had first-try levies pass during that election, which took place shortly after Judge Duncan released his desegregation decision. Columbus board members specifically accused Groveport-Madison, South-Western, Upper Arlington, and

Westerville school officials of exploiting the threat of busing during their levy campaigns.

36. Robert Weiler interview, November 13, 1992.

37. Black voters were consistently the strongest supporters of school levies, while white voters on the district's northwest and southern fringes composed the staunchest opposition. A consultant's review of the spring 1978 defeat concluded that "a permanent and *complete* overruling of the Duncan Court . . . would be helpful to passage of a levy, and *might* provide the crucial margin" (emphases in original). Still, given the divisiveness engendered by desegregation, it is remarkable that two of Columbus's four additional levy attempts between the *Penick* trial and implementation failed by less than 2 percent. "Voter Attitudes Toward a School Levy," survey prepared by Hugh M. Clark, August 1978, Columbus Public School District files.

38. Until the late 1960s, Ohio school tax levies were "continuing"— they lasted a set number of years and had to be renewed by voters. A change in the law, however, made all tax increases permanent except emergency levies and bond issues. Voters were more reluctant to approve "additional" operating levies—in essence, permanent tax increases—than finite "continuing" levies; the legal change, however, enabled districts to make fewer appearances on the ballot.

39. Columbus was not the only urban system in Ohio having little success at the voting booth. Out of twenty-seven levies attempted by Ohio's eight biggest school districts between 1971 and 1979, twenty-five failed. By contrast, between 1945 and 1968, the Columbus Public Schools had passed all twenty-two of its ballot issues. Robert Sohovich, "Levy Defeat Is Not the End Davis," *CD*, March 28, 1979; Don Baird, "Funds for Alternative Schools to Be Included in 7.6 Mill Levy," *CJ*, August 18, 1981.

40. The rollback law was amended to the state constitution in 1980.

41. In 1977 and 1978, ninety-five thousand Ohio students in fifteen districts (including Toledo) missed classes due to closings caused by insufficient funds, earning the state the dubious distinction "America's School Closing Capital." "More Districts May Close Schools Near End of 1978," *CD*, April 9, 1978; Chris Eversole, "Levy Said to Ensure Open Schools," *CJ*, March 26, 1979.

42. Tom Sheehan, "Bonner, Prentice Back Levy in November," *CD*, June 24, 1981.

43. The percentage of Columbus Public School students receiving Aid to Families with Dependent Children grew from 11 percent in 1968 to

25.3 percent by the implementation of desegregation in 1979. Micki Seltzer, "Still Not Teaching Inner City Students, Dorothy Lenart Says," *CP*, August 11, 1973; "The Board in Columbus: Facing a Challenge," speech by Charles Hermann to the Columbus Kit Kat Club, April 16, 1985, Columbus Public School District files.

44. From the early 1970s to the early 1980s, the percentage of Columbus adults with children in the public schools dropped from 39 to 27. More adults with school-age children meant easier levy efforts, as voters with a direct connection to the district were more amenable to raising their own taxes than those with no personal stake in the schools.

45. Chris Eversole, "Where Have All the Pupils Gone?" *CJ*, April 11, 1979.

46. "Northwest Principals Report Enrollment Drop," *Northwest News*, August 30, 1978. Between the end of the 1976 school year and the start of the 1980 school year, Columbus's enrollment dropped from 96,571 to 73,698 (24 percent). Whites and blacks left in roughly equal yearly proportions (85 percent and 15 percent, respectively), though black enrollment in general remained relatively steady. From 1976–77 through 1980–81, overall black enrollment dropped from 30,991 to 28,778 (8 percent), while overall nonblack enrollment dropped from 65,580 to 44,920 (32 percent). Robert Sohovich, "Davis Expects Hike in Black Students," *CD*, January 2, 1978; Robert Sohovich, "Rate of Student Migration from City Not Easing Up," *CD*, March 20, 1979; enrollment figures from Columbus Public School District files.

47. Overall, Franklin County saw a 23 percent public school enrollment decline between 1973 and 1983, from 183,856 to 141,691. Columbus dropped 32.9 percent, Upper Arlington 36.3 percent. The only districts to grow were the outlying suburbs ringing the city's north and northwest sides: Westerville, 3 percent; Worthington, 3.5 percent; and Dublin, a phenomenal 79.4 percent. Page and Taylor, "Columbus Schools Facing 'Resegregation.'" See also Shuara Wilson, "Dublin Schools Grow Fastest," *CD*, November 5, 1984, for 1979–84 comparison.

48. Columbus real estate consultant Kenneth Danter posed this question in a 1990 article about the city's home-building market. He asked, "Traditionally, suburban schools have been perceived as being better, but to whom does that perception belong—developers or home buyers?" His conclusion was that there had not been enough development within the district to provide an answer. "Until enough lots are developed to give home buyers economic, geographical, and conceptual alternatives," he wrote, "we cannot make definitive conclusions." Kenneth Danter, "Co-

lumbus City Schools: A Case of Two Perceptions," *BIA Builder Update*, December 1990.

49. Don Epler interview, March 14, 1994.

50. Aggregate housing units in the city of Columbus grew 29.7 percent during the 1970s. Figures compiled by the City of Columbus Development Department, Planning Division Research Section, from United States Census Bureau data.

51. Robert Weiler interview, October 19, 1992. The Robert Weiler Company was a prominent local real estate brokerage firm founded by Weiler's father in 1938. Weiler, whose four children attended Columbus schools, had been actively involved with the district since the early 1970s. Weiler's denial of a race-risk nexus was echoed by other representatives of the real estate community during interviews and in newspapers. Developer Don Epler: "[Builders and developers] are driven not so much by the schools, but where the sales are." (Epler interview); Don Cary, vice president of Fritsche Homes: "If the market was there, the builders would build there. People aren't coming in asking for Columbus schools. The market drives itself." (Don Cary interview, winter 1992); Tom Simpson, M/I Homes vice president: "Evidently there's not [a Columbus Public Schools market] because no one is building there." (Cynthia Crane, "Northwest: Straddling School Systems," *Upper Arlington News*, April 17, 1985).

52. A phrase such as "significant black presence" is, of course, difficult to define precisely. However, studies have shown the residential "tipping point"—the racial ratio at which white residents of a neighborhood begin to flee as more black residents move in—to be as low as less than 10 percent black. For overviews of these studies, see Massey and Denton, *American Apartheid*, 88–96; Metcalf, *From Little Rock to Boston*, 221; Gerald David Jaynes and Robin M. Williams Jr., eds., *A Common Destiny: Blacks and American Society* (Washington, D.C.: National Academy Press, 1989), 140–44; and David Armor, *Forced Justice: School Desegregation and the Law*, 117–53.

53. See Jennifer L. Hochschild, *The New American Dilemma*; Derrick Bell Jr., ed., *Shades of Brown: New Perspectives on School Desegregation*; also, Bell, *And We are Not Saved: The Elusive Quest for Racial Justice*, and *Faces at the Bottom of the Well: The Permanence of Racism*.

54. Levitt quoted in Jackson, *Crabgrass Frontier*, 241. See Ira Katznelson and Margaret Weir, *Schooling for All: Class, Race, and the Decline of the Democratic Ideal*, 207–22.

55. A Franklin County Fair Housing Research Study compiled for county commissioners estimated that "within four or five years the majority

of students in Columbus schools will be black. In the minds of the public there will be one black school system—Columbus—and fourteen white (suburban) school systems" ("Race Relations Analyst Pictures Polarization," *CD*, March 30, 1980). Similarly, while noting that city schools "will continue to play a central role in the quality of life of Central Ohio," the Columbus Area Chamber of Commerce's January 1981 "Five Year Plan" predicted that "the Columbus Public School system's total population will continue to decline, while its black population will grow from 30 percent to 50 percent. [It] will continue to face increasing challenges in substantive areas."

56. In a 1981 report, Gary Orfield spotlighted the common areas as a unique and ominous feature of Columbus's desegregation-housing relationship. "Blacks in the metropolitan area are highly concentrated in certain Census tracts within Columbus," he wrote, "all of which were within the part of the city served by the Columbus public schools. This means that, although the metropolitan community has a relatively low black population (and very few Hispanics), the racial problem for the public schools is a rapidly growing one, posing a long-term threat to the city's school desegregation efforts. . . . The fundamental problem for Columbus is that demographic trends have undermined existing school desegregation plans." Gary Orfield, "Columbus Schools and Housing," 27, 40, Columbus Public School District files.

57. For Richmond, see John V. Moeser and Rutledge M. Dennis, *The Politics of Annexation: Oligarchic Power in a Southern City*.

58. Frank Lomax, "Proposed Future of the MCSC," May 1980, MCSC Records.

59. Ninety-five percent of Franklin County's African American population lived within the boundaries of the Columbus Public School District, according to 1980 U.S. Census Bureau figures. In 1983, the *Citizen-Journal* reported, the Columbus schools "educated 92 percent of the blacks in Franklin County's public schools and 82 percent of the students who qualified for subsidized lunches and milk." No school district in the county at the time had a black population of over 5 percent. Page and Taylor, "Columbus Schools Facing 'Resegregation.'"

60. "'Choices for the 80's': Superintendent's Status Report on the Columbus Public Schools," November 1, 1978, 11, Columbus Public School District files. Kettell quoted in "City's Plans for Schools Irk Suburb," *CD*, November 28, 1978. Davis quoted in Robert Sohovich, "Annexation Possibility Seen for City Schools," *CD*, September 19, 1979.

61. The district had closed forty-nine schools since 1972. Annexation discussions emerged as the board was considering shutting down another fifteen—several of which were situated on the district's periphery—even as suburban systems continued to build schools in the common areas nearby.

62. The fourth new board member was John T. Bonner Jr., who was selected by Probate Court judge Richard Metcalf to complete Steven Boley's unexpired term. Boley had been elected to city council that fall. Robert Sohovich, "Six School Board Candidates Urge Annexations," *CD*, October 21, 1979; "Board's 4-Seat Change Historic," *CD*, December 17, 1979.

63. Marilyn Greenwald, "Board Candidates View Teamwork as Necessity," *CJ*, October 25, 1979; Robert Sohovich, "Board OKs 15 School Closings, Eyes Annexation Idea," *CD*, April 30, 1980; Robert Sohovich, "Suburban Consent Needed for Schools to Annex," *CD*, June 20, 1979.

64. During the spring of 1980, the Supreme Court sent conflicting signals regarding the continued validity of already rare metropolitan remedies. In late April, the Court ordered an interdistrict remedy for Wilmington, Delaware; two weeks later, it affirmed without comment the rejection of a similar plan in Atlanta. For Wilmington, see Dimond, *Beyond Busing*, 283–339, 388–94; for Atlanta, see Gary Orfield and Carol Ashkinaze, *The Closing Door: Conservative Policy and Black Opportunity*, 103–48.

65. Moreover, argued board members, Columbus had a legal responsibility to explore the option of annexation. Failure to challenge the existence of the common areas, they contended, could be interpreted by the courts as a refusal to act affirmatively to eliminate illegal segregation. Robert Sohovich, "Metropolitan Busing Still in Talking Stage," *CD*, June 22, 1980.

66. The state board had been found co liable in both the Columbus and Cleveland desegregation cases. "Columbus Board Considers Annexation of Areas Served by Suburban Schools," *CJ*, May 1, 1980; Robert Sohovich, "Talk of School Annexation Could Stir Up The Suburbs," *CD*, May 1, 1980.

67. A 1979 report by the Mid-Ohio Regional Planning Commission (MORPC) found that the Columbus Schools could gain $14.1 million in tax revenue by annexing the entire common area, a revenue increase of 16.4 percent. In addition, more students would enable the district to claim more state aid. The report noted, however, that expenses would rise as well. Robert Sohovich, "Proposal Says Annexation Could Fatten School Fund," *CD*, June 26, 1979; Robert Sohovich, "Board OKs 15 Closings"; Marilyn Greenwald, "Closing of 15 Schools Gets Final Board OK," *CJ*, April 30, 1980.

68. Carole Williams interview, February 22, 1994.

69. Robert Sohovich, "School Annexation Issue Causes Debate," CD, May 15, 1980. The districts most active in the antiannexation movement were those with the most students and tax revenue to lose. For example: Dublin—39 percent of its students, 25 percent of its taxable property, 12 percent of its area; Scioto-Darby (Hilliard)—9 percent of its students, 25 percent of its taxable property, 25 percent of its area; Groveport-Madison—19 percent of its students, 29 percent of its taxable property. South-Western—5,000 students, $120 million in taxable property; Worthington—25 percent of its students, 35 percent of its tax revenue. Joseph Blundo, James Breiner, and Robert Albrecht, "Suburbs Opposing School Annexations," CD, May 2, 1980; James Breiner, "Housing Slowdown Aids District," CD, May 11, 1980; "Groveport-Madison Officials Vow to Fight Any Annexation," CD, May 13, 1980; "Over 400 Opposing Annexation Proposal," Columbus Messenger, May 26, 1980; Robert Ruth, "Democrats Block School Annexation Issue Vote," CD, June 26, 1980; Jay Wuebbold, "Democrats Block Senate Panel Vote on Annexation Bill," CJ, June 26, 1980.

70. James Breiner, "700 Rally Against School Annexation," CD, June 12, 1980.

71. The possibility of voters actually approving such a transfer was considered so far-fetched that it never even entered the debate.

72. Mary Pollman, "Suburbs, City Square Off," Northwest News, September 17, 1980.

73. Robert McMunn, "School Busing Cited in Home Price Rises," CD, December 2, 1980.

74. "Annexation Feasibility," CD editorial, May 22, 1980, emphasis added.

75. The legislation banned territory transfer to school districts with over 7,500 students without the approval of the affected district. It was approved 69–5 by the house and 27–1 by the senate. Governor Rhodes signed the moratorium into law on October 10, 1980. Jay Wuebbold, "Two-Year Ban on Annexation Is Enacted," CJ, September 19, 1980; Robert Ruth, "Annexation Delay Passed," CD, September 19, 1980; "Two Legislators Praise, Criticize Signing of Law Delaying School Annexations," CD, October 12, 1980.

76. More new development in the common areas made Columbus school board members even less likely to risk the uproar an annexation effort would invariably cause. Also, the more controversial the annexation request, the more unlikely the state board was to approve it.

77. Marilyn Greenwald, "Schools Superintendent Says Columbus Needs to Pass 3.88 to 12.32-Mill Levy," CJ, June 11, 1980.

78. Robert Sohovich, "Participation of Blacks Satisfies School Chiefs," *CD*, September 21, 1979.

79. C. Smith interview, January 7, 1991.

80. Asbury interview, January 7, 1991. For a thorough summary of Columbus's implementation year, see Julia Osborne, "Desegregation: The First Year," *CM*, September 1980, 86–108.

81. C. Smith interview, January 7, 1991; William Wayson interview, January 10, 1991.

82. Willis interview.

83. See the administration's status reports to the district court for the most comprehensive statistical picture of desegregation's impact.

84. *CJ*, June 29, 1979.

85. An added stress was Columbus's 1980 shift from junior high schools (grades 7–9) to middle schools (grades 6–8), a change that necessitated a second consecutive year of substantial student reassignment. The shift, intended to address a disturbing decline in the district's postelementary test scores, was a classic example of a common practice among desegregating school systems: the use of desegregation as a distraction to camouflage educational reforms that administrators and school board members might otherwise deem too disruptive to implement.

86. "See for Yourself," Columbus Public School District files; letter from Joe Davis to Joseph Imberman, executive director of the Columbus Foundation (which provided the district with $24,000 for "See for Yourself"), August 11, 1980, Columbus Public School District files; Robert Albrecht, "Realty Salesmen Get Sales Pitch from Principal," *CD*, March 4, 1980; Gene Maeroff, "Enrollment Drop Growing Threat to Public Schools," *New York Times*, September 7, 1982.

87. The levy's chamber-directed campaign turned the district's outdated textbooks into compelling symbols of fiscal need. East High teacher Gary Heffner noted that his 1969 senior psychology textbook promoted "so much stereotyping that I use it as an example of how roles change." Said administrator Norval Goss, "When a student is figuring problems and reads that hamburger costs 37 cents a pound, he's going to know something is wrong. . . . It's sort of a standing joke here. Do we fix leaking roofs and not buy books? Or do we buy books and have the rain leak through the roof on them?" Debra Phillips, "Stale Texts Hinder Teaching in Columbus," *CJ*, February 9, 1981.

88. The levy passed with 51.8 percent of the vote. For voter turnout breakdowns, see: "Levy Evaluation—1981," Columbus Public School

District files; Joe Dirck, "Espy, Levy Boosted by Black Voters," *CJ*, November 14, 1981; Michael Curtin, "Voters Shifted on Levy Support," *CD*, November 15, 1981.

89. Columbus Public School District Annual Report 1981–82, 3. Dietzel quoted in Debra Phillips, "School Levy Gets Voters' OK," *CJ*, November 4, 1981; Tom Sheehan, "Levy Won't Solve All of School Woes," *CD*, November 4, 1981. Moody quoted in Robert Sohovich, "Moody Says Schools Must Get Better," *CD*, March 25, 1983; "Moody Reflects on City, Life," *CD*, January 16, 1983.

90. Hyre interview.

91. Tom Sheehan, "Superintendent Rips Poor School Spirit," *CD*, October 7, 1982.

92. Tom Sheehan, "Hyre Invites Teacher Criticism," *CD*, March 8, 1983.

93. Tom Sheehan, "Back Us or Quit, Hyre Tells Staff," *CD*, January 24, 1983.

94. Willis interview; Debra Phillips, "Hyre's School Ministry: 'Get Involved,'" *CJ*, December 11, 1982.

95. Hyre interview.

96. Ibid.; Carole Williams interview, October 4, 1991.

97. Dan Page, "Teaching Students to Think Is Hyre's Goal," *CJ*, December 17, 1983; Karen Welzel, "Hyre Says Basics Are Not Enough," *CD*, December 17, 1983; Pat Hampton, "Hyre: City's Success Will Boost Challenge to Schools," *CD*, December.11, 1984.

98. By far the most influential of these studies was *A Nation at Risk: The Imperative for Educational Reform*, a 1983 report by the National Commission on Excellence in Education.

99. In 1984, the *Dispatch* called Hyre "one of a relatively new batch of Columbus leaders whose public image involves blatant, unapologetic positivism" (Julia Keller, "Hooray for Enthusiasm," *CD*, May 27, 1984). It was gung-ho Republican mayor Dana "Buck" Rinehart, however, who best embodied this new boosterism. Rinehart's guiding principle—"you can make a positive out of anything"—reached its comic apex in 1986 after Columbus garnered national attention when a huge sinkhole suddenly opened up in the middle of downtown, swallowing an unsuspecting (and unharmed) motorist. The city rescued the Mercedes and promptly began using it in its efforts to attract new conventions, transforming a near-tragic example of infrastructural deterioration into a bizarre civic emblem.

100. Not to mention, of course, the contribution of business to the tax rolls. Business generally provides around two-thirds of the city school district's local tax revenues.

101. SummerTech continued for the rest of the decade. As personal computers became more common and user-friendly, however, interest gradually waned, and the program eventually succumbed to budget cuts.

102. I Know I Can supplies Columbus students with both the informational and financial resources demanded by the college application process. It also provides "last dollar" tuition grants to needy graduates.

103. David Yost and Veronica Tyree, "Selection Hailed by Residents," *CJ*, August 25, 1982.

104. The original ten alternative schools (seven elementaries, two middle schools, and one high school) drew students chosen by lottery from a city-wide pool of applicants. The lottery was weighted to ensure racial balance.

105. Hyre quoted in Martha Crossen, "Quality Schools for Lucky Few," *Columbus Free Press*, March 1987. Tom Sheehan, "Long Waiting List Measures Success of City's Alternative School Project," *CD*, September 29, 1981; Sheehan, "Alternative School Pupils Above Average in Testing" and accompanying chart, *CD*, May 12, 1982; Sheehan, "Alternative Schools' Jury Is Undecided," *CD*, May 13, 1982.

106. Hyre interview.

107. Statistics from Charles Hermann, "The Board in Columbus: Facing a Challenge," speech to the Columbus Kit Kat Club by the director of OSU's Mershon Center for Research and Education, April 16, 1985, Columbus Public School District files.

108. Dan Page, "City Schools Buck Learning Barrier of Poverty," *CJ*, June 12, 1984.

109. All three were alternative schools: Berwick Elementary (17 percent), Linden Park Elementary (26 percent), and Monroe Middle (28 percent). "How Columbus Students Measure Up," *CD*, December 7, 1986.

110. Sharon Crook West, "Columbus Schools: The Critical Years," *CM*, December 1985, 53.

111. Robert Sohovich, "Hyre: Schools Have Image Problem," *CD*, April 29, 1983.

112. Beechwold/Clintonville, located north of the Ohio State campus, was one of the oldest and most stable neighborhoods in the Columbus Public School District. According to the 1980 census, whites outnumbered minorities in Clintonville 14–1, and other minorities outnumbered blacks 3–1. Patricia Mraczek, "Schools Head Praises Community, Seeks Support," *Booster*, June 6, 1983; Laurie Lascocco, "Hyre Speaks Positively of Columbus Public Schools," *Beechwold/Clintonville News*, June 8, 1983. Census figures from Jay Elhard, "Not Black or White: Growing Segment of Population Making an Impact," *Northland News*, August 28, 1985.

113. West, "Columbus Schools," 52–53. The race-class issue was further blurred, however, by the fact that for years, the city's black leadership had been abandoning the Columbus schools as well. As far back as Watson Walker, whose sons were two of the first three African Americans to attend the Columbus Academy, many black leaders had opted out of sending their children to schools in the city system. Though many influential blacks continued to live within the district's boundaries, often in comparatively integrated areas like Berwick and Olde Town East, they frequently chose private and parochial schools for their kids, a reality that has undoubtedly tempered black educational activism in Columbus. "They don't believe there's any hope," said the Urban League's Sam Gresham, whose three children attended Columbus schools, "so the most important asset in their lives, they're taking out of Columbus Public Schools and putting it somewhere else" (Gresham interview). Still, Hyre and other district leaders knew that recapturing the black leadership, while an urgent priority, was not alone enough to sustain the district's economic diversity; the black middle class by itself simply lacked the numbers, the resources, and the political clout to arrest the system's slow slide into poverty.

114. Hyre interview.

115. Ibid.

116. Gifford interview, October 4, 1991; letter from Jim Hyre to Beverly Robinson, an HER sales associate, December 4, 1984, Columbus Public School District files; "An Open Letter to Columbus Area Realtors" from Jim Hyre, published in *In Contract*, the Columbus Board of Realtors' newsletter, November 1985, Columbus Public School District files; letter from Hyre to Robinson, December 4, 1984, Columbus Public School District files.

117. Eibling was the son of former Columbus school superintendent Harold Eibling. Memo from Carole Williams to Stephen Eibling and Jim Hyre, January 15, 1985, Columbus Public School District files.

118. "Selling to Sellers" program description, Columbus Public School District files; memo from Laura Ecklar to Stephen Eibling, March 24, 1986, Columbus Public School District files.

119. District Court Order, *Penick et al. v. Columbus Board of Education et al.*, April 11, 1985, 3.

120. The order also echoed the sense of personal involvement that had characterized Duncan's handling of the case from the beginning. Wrapping up a decade of "terribly expensive, time-consuming, and agonizing" litigation, Duncan wrote, "I am well aware that the heavy burden of this case was and continues to be borne by the students. Their adjustment to the

difficulties of this case—none of which they caused—has commanded the Court's admiration, and the response from Columbus students sets a high mark for community citizenship. My thanks to all of you." Ibid., 14, 16.

121. Ibid, 15. The other race-related issue specifically cited by Duncan as an ongoing concern was the shrinking proportion of white students in the Columbus schools. Statistics from Kathy Gray Foster, "Violence Up Sharply in Schools," *CD*, October 2, 1985.

122. One factor that contributed to the discipline disparities was the persistent (relative) lack of black teachers in the Columbus Schools. In 1971, 12.9 percent of Columbus teachers were black; in 1986, 20.4 percent were black. During that time, the proportion of black students in the district grew from 28.2 percent to 43.9 percent. In their study of desegregation remedies, Meier, Stewart, and England concluded, "Without a doubt, the single best predictor of second generation discrimination is the percentage of black teachers [in a school district]." Kenneth J. Meier, Joseph Stewart Jr., and Robert E. England, *Race, Class and Education: The Politics of Second Generation Discrimination*, 106. Columbus black teacher statistics from "More Black Teachers Are Needed in Columbus Public Schools," *CP*, April 3, 1986; Holland quote from Paul Sussman and Michael Taylor, "Schools Still Aren't Color Blind," *CJ*, April 12, 1985.

123. District Court Order, April 11, 1985, 7–8. According to the district's 1978 "Choices for the 80's" report, 77.3 percent of the students expelled during the 1976–77 school year were black. Only 48.5 percent of the secondary school students suspended that year were black, but blacks made up only 32.1 percent of the district's enrollment at the time. Far more disturbing than the racial disproportionality of desegregation discipline statistics was their stunning rise in magnitude. Between 1976–77 and 1985–86, expulsions rose from 22 to 219, suspensions from 5,810 to 18,699, despite a drop in enrollment from 96,571 to 66,823. It must be noted, however, that the district's information-gathering capacity grew considerably during those years, so some of the disparity in numbers may be attributable to more complete data. "Choices for the 80's," 7–8; Foster, "Violence Up."

124. District Court Order, April 11, 1985, 8. Cunningham interview; "Results of the 1987 Student Opinion Survey," March 1987; "Columbus Public Schools Community Survey Results," 1985; memo from Dennis Benson to Laura Ecklar, December 17, 1985; letter from Laura Ecklar to Don Epler, April 19, 1987; all from Columbus Public School District files. Ecklar to Epler, April 19, 1987.

125. In 1979, the district projected that enrollment would drop to 59,846 by 1985 and 52,227 in 1989. Actual enrollment, however, stood at

66,823 in 1985–86 and 64,082 in 1989–90. Robert Sohovich, "Schools' Focus Shifts toward Higher Quality," *CD*, December 17, 1979.

126. District Court Order, April 11, 1985, 8–9. Cunningham interview. Composite SAT scores improved from 895 to 919 between 1980 and 1985. Composite ACT scores hovered between 17.0 and 17.4 during the same span. Summary of SAT and ACT results, 1980–87, Columbus Public School District files.

127. Memo to board members from Stephen Eibling, April 11, 1985, Columbus Public School District files.

128. Paul Sussman, "Order Lifted, but Buses Will Roll On," *CJ*, April 12, 1985.

129. "Planning in the Dark," *CJ* editorial, December 9, 1985. The plan returned the district's elementary schools to "K–5" centers, eliminating the K–3, 4–5 grade split left over from the original desegregation plan. In doing so, it reduced the number of students bused by eight thousand and reestablished parent-pleasing elementary school continuity. The plan also raised the number of alternative elementary schools from seven to fifteen and the number of alternative middle schools from two to six.

130. With a levy try expected the following spring, it also sent a carefully timed signal to Columbus voters.

131. Letter from Hyre to *CJ*, June 22, 1985; Gresham interview; "City Schools Get an A," *CD*, editorial, July 29, 1987, emphasis added.

132. Mark Ellis, "Hyre Exudes Confidence," *CD*, August 21, 1982; Debra Phillips, "School Hopeful Combines Candor with Humor," *CJ*, August 21, 1982; West, "Columbus Schools," 52; "Hyre's BIA Speech Challenges Columbus's Leadership," *Builder Update*, October 1984.

133. Hammond interview; McClary and Klein interview.

134. Kathy Gray Foster, "Schools Hire Help for Annexation," *CD*, February 7, 1986; "Can All Sides 'Win-Win' in Annexation Talks?" *Northland News*, February 12, 1986; Hammond interview.

135. Kathy Gray Foster, "Superintendents to Cooperate on Annexation Issue," *CD*, January 31, 1986; Rose Hume, "Open Mind Is Essential to Resolve Annexation," *CD*, February 5, 1986; Bob Barrow interview, October 10, 1991.

136. Kathy Gray Foster, "Negotiating Tactic a Winner," *CD*, January 12, 1986; Kathy Gray Foster, "Teachers Drop Plans to OK Pay Hike," *CD*, January 12, 1986; Kathy Gray Foster, "Superintendents to Cooperate"; "Annexation: A Lesson in Cooperation," *CD*, May 25, 1986; Debbie Briner, "Superintendents Review 'Win-Win' Proposal," *Northland News*, March 5,

1986; Kathy Gray Foster, "Schools Accord Is a Year Old," *CD*, May 16, 1987. Because of the number of parties involved, Goldaber extended win-win's standard thirty-day timetable to six weeks. The twelve school districts that took part in negotiations were: Canal Winchester, Columbus, Dublin, Gahanna-Jefferson, Groveport-Madison, Hamilton Local, Hilliard, Plain Local, Reynoldsburg, South-Western, Westerville, and Worthington.

137. Kathy Gray Foster, "Boundary Debate to Begin," *CD*, October 10, 1986; Gilbert Price, "Heard Facing Choices as New Year Unfolds," *CP*, January 9, 1986; Barrow interview; Radebaugh interview; Rose Hume and Dianne Keller, "Compromise May Solve Annexation Issue," *CD*, February 5, 1986.

138. See Adrienne Bosworth, "James Ebright: Rebel without a Cause?" *CM*, February 1985, 38–43.

139. Kathy Gray Foster, "Battle Lines Set in Busing Case," *CD*, December 7, 1984; Kathy Gray Foster, "Board Member Says Court Should Keep Busing Reins," *CD*, December 7, 1984; Paul Sussman, "School Annexation Pushed," *CJ*, December 8, 1984.

140. The Columbus Public School District's emblem was an apple.

141. The title of the debate was "The School Annexation Time Bomb: Ticking Toward 1986." Michael Taylor, "Ebright: School Annex Vote Similar to South African Policy," *CJ*, October 5, 1985.

142. Paul Sussman, "Ebright Rebuffed on School Annexation," *CJ*, February 20, 1985; Kathy Gray Foster, "Ebright Won't End Annex Try," *CD*, February 20, 1985. According to the notes of school district communications director Laura Ecklar, board members Williams, Heard, Holland, Eibling, and Charles Carlos all felt that annexation was not necessarily desirable. Eibling and Williams argued that Columbus did not need suburban students to become a great district, Holland believed that the costs of annexing these students would outweigh the benefits; Eibling considered nonannexation a pragmatic stance, a concession to political reality; and Williams and Heard contended that coterminous boundaries would just cause suburbanites to flee Columbus proper—instead, they maintained, quality programs must be developed to lure people back to the city schools. Ebright, however, argued that "'not unwinnable' is a weak argument" and said that board members lacked the data to support their cost-benefit claims. Columbus Public School District files.

143. Roger Viers interview, March 2, 1994; Young quoted in Robert Albrecht, "Board Explains Stand on School Annexation," *CD*, February 12, 1986; Robert Albrecht and Catherine Candinsky, "Board Upsets Superintendents,"

CD, February 12, 1986. Barr quoted in Christine Furr, Lynn Harbert, Richard Makkey, James O'Dell, and Jody Schultz, "The City of Columbus and Its Suburbs Try for 'Win-Win'" (graduate seminar paper for OSU Professor Dale Bertsch, May 22, 1990).

144. Toki Clark, "It's a Sellout—Moss on Annexation Agreement," *CP*, May 29, 1986; Kathy Gray Foster, "Superintendents to Cooperate on Annexation Issue," *CD*, January 31, 1986.

145. Two districts with particularly valuable industrial property at stake were South-Western, with its Fisher auto body plant, and Gahanna-Jefferson, with its AT&T plant and Limited warehouse.

146. Bob Wiedrich, "America Discovers Columbus: Ohio's Capital a 'Rustproof' Haven for Businesses," *Chicago Tribune*, November 30, 1986.

147. Columbus Development Department, "Growth Statement 1990," 58.

148. Dick Kimmins, "Local Business Growth Outpacing the Rest of Ohio," *Business First*, October 27, 1986.

149. "In Search of a City: A Special Section on Downtown Development," *CD* supplement, September 8, 1985, 4.

150. "Growth Statement 1990," 32.

151. Maintaining countywide peace was deemed essential for a more specific reason as well. In the spring of 1986, city leaders were waging an all-out campaign to pass a countywide 0.5 percent sales tax increase. The tax hike was proposed to fund construction of a domed stadium and convention center, a long-held goal of civic boosters. The $305,000 campaign, the most expensive in chamber of commerce history, was led by Columbus's most influential developers (Galbreath, Kessler, Schottenstein), business executives (especially Wexner), politicians (Mayor Rinehart), and many others. Though local leaders repeatedly called the proposed New World Center "the key to the future of the city," the tax hike was defeated, 53 percent to 47 percent.

152. The Columbus Foundation readily agreed to pay Irving Goldaber's fee, an indication of the business community's desire to see the controversy resolved.

153. Barrow interview; Hyre interview.

154. Jonas, "Local Interests," 224–25.

155. David Wagman, "Static Tax Base Spells Deficit for Schools," *Business First*, January 6, 1986; Kathy Gray Foster, "Board Expected to Support Citywide District," *CD*, February 5, 1986.

156. Lurie tracked the area's residential development patterns for the Building Industry Association. Kathy Gray Foster, "Home Builders Fear Annexation," *CD*, March 20, 1986.

157. Between 1980 and 1985, the Columbus school district's tax valuation grew at the third slowest rate of the sixteen school districts in Franklin County. The top four were all northwestern and northern suburbs: Dublin (61 percent), Hilliard (46 percent), Westerville (39 percent), and Worthington (34 percent). Wagman, "Static Tax Base."

158. Sean Horgan, "School Is Top Priority With Buyers," *CD*, February 23, 1986; Debbie Briner, "Realtors Reluctant to Comment on Annexation Effect," *Northwest News*, February 26, 1986.

159. Jonas, "Local Interests," 229–32.

160. Weiler interview.

161. Indeed, the builders PAC contributed more money in 1986 to the campaigns of representatives involved with annexation legislation than in 1984. The contributions of the Realtors PAC showed an even bigger increase, perhaps as a reward for resolving the issue. For example, real estate agents gave Representative Otto Beatty (D–Columbus), one of the sponsors of an annexation bill similar to the legislation finally approved, $1,000 in 1986, twenty times more than they had given him in 1984. David Wagman, "Developers Pushing for Passage of School Annexation," *Business First*, April 21, 1986; for political contribution figures, see Jonas, "Local Interests," 231.

162. Graff and Sutliff quoted in Kathy Gray Foster, "Home Builders Fear Annexation," *CD*, March 20, 1986.

163. Sutliff and Ruma quoted in Wagman, "Developers Pushing."

164. Kathy Gray Foster, "Home Builders Fear Annexation."

165. Robert Albrecht, "Schools Improving, Realtor Group Told," *CD*, April 23, 1986. The levy won with 55 percent of the vote. Kathy Gray Foster, "Columbus School Levy Passes Easily," *CD*, May 7, 1986; Beth Short, "'It Was a Vote of Confidence' Says School Board President," *Daily Reporter*, May 7, 1986; Bob Payne, "Team Effort Helps Issue 2 Make Grade," OSU *Lantern*, May 7, 1986.

166. Kathy Gray Foster, "Signs Plug City Schools," *CD*, May 15, 1986; Letter from Hyre to Pat Kearns-Davis, May 15, 1986, Columbus Public School District files.

167. This consolidation ironed out the multilateral complexity of the negotiations and enabled Columbus to bargain on equal terms with a single

adversary. It also inadvertently may have sealed off some of the city school district's negotiating leverage, however. Competing interests existed among suburban school systems that Columbus could well have taken advantage of. Some districts sought primarily to defend lucrative industrial property (Gahanna-Jefferson, for example); others wanted mainly to protect students and residential development (Dublin); still others hoped to preserve potentially valuable, but still undeveloped territory (Reynoldsburg); and a few were concerned about a combination of all three (Worthington, despite its existing boundary agreement with Columbus). Moreover, a couple of the districts with significant numbers of students at stake had internal conflicts that also possibly could have been exploited. Within the Dublin schools, for instance, bitter class divisions existed between students who lived west of the Scioto, in Dublin proper, and those who lived east of the Scioto in Columbus. By papering over these divisions, the Win-Win negotiating process may have prevented Columbus from following a divide-and-conquer strategy. In addition, it may have eased the suburbs' lingering, historical fear of Columbus by offering negotiators strength in numbers.

168. The superintendents also settled on a third major negotiating issue: the development of countywide educational programs. This branch of the bargaining grew into the Franklin County Education Program and School Services Council. While initially hailed as an innovative opportunity for interdistrict cooperation, the council was never enthusiastically embraced. It has since become a largely forgotten footnote to the more substantive aspects of Win-Win.

169. Thanks to OSU city and regional planning professor Dale Bertsch for providing me with several graduate student papers on the Win-Win process. Particularly helpful were Marcia Caton Campbell, Michael Todd Corwin, and Todd R. Limp, "The Columbus Area Public Schools' 1986 'Win-Win' Agreement: Conflict, Resolution and Future Prospects," no date given; and Furr et al., "The City of Columbus and Its Suburbs Try for 'Win-Win'" (cited n. 143 above).

170. From "School District Territory Transfers: A Columbus Perspective," Columbus Public Schools Win-Win summary, June 1986. Document provided by Bob Barrow during October 10, 1991 interview.

171. Some exceptions were written into the agreement. Eight districts chose to set aside certain lucrative or potentially valuable parcels of land so that, if annexed to Columbus, they would not be transferred to the Columbus schools.

172. Any revenue increase accrued by inflationary growth or periodic property value reappraisals did not fall under the revenue-sharing formula. For the first few years of Win-Win, the state footed the bill for the suburban districts. The hastily written tax formula became a source of controversy, however, when the state finally phased out its subsidies, forcing suburban systems to begin paying a portion of their tax revenues to the Columbus schools. Disagreement over the size of these annual payments almost shattered the Win-Win Agreement, but a compromise was reached, and the pact was renewed for another six years in 1992.

173. Viers interview; Craig Merz and Steve Stephens, "School Districts Feel Relief," *CD*, May 28, 1986; "Annexation Solution," *CD* editorial, May 22, 1986; Robert Sohovich, "Leaders Ponder Annexation Pact's Effect on Growth," *CD*, May 27, 1986.

174. Hyre interview. Also, Hyre noted, Columbus retained the option of initiating territory transfer requests with the state board if Win-Win broke down in the future.

175. Barrow interview; Weiler interview; Richard Fahey interview, February 1, 1994.

176. William Snider, "Unusual Settlement Ends Annexation Dispute in Ohio," *Education Week*, September 24, 1989; "Dr. Hyre's Remarks at Special Emergency Board Meeting," May 20, 1986, Columbus Public School District files.

177. Letter from Jim Hyre to Amos Lynch, June 10, 1986, Columbus Public School District files; Weiler interview.

178. Viers interview; Gary Holland interview, April 25, 1994.

179. Jay Elhard, "Crossen, Moss Blast Annexation Pact," *Northland News*, May 28, 1986; Gilbert Price, "Annexation a Million $$$$ 'Give-Away'," *CP*, May 26, 1986; Debbie Brincr, "Annexation Pact: Too Much Was Expected," *Northland News*, May 28, 1986; Gilbert Price, "It's a Sell-Out—Moss on Annexation Agreement," *CP*, May 29, 1986; " 'It Was Foul'," *CP* editorial, June 5, 1986.

180. Martha Crossen, Apple Alliance statement at the May 20, 1986 Columbus Board of Education meeting, Columbus Public School District files; Hammond interview; Price, "Million $$$$ 'Give-Away.'"

181. Kathy Gray Foster and Cliff Treyens, "Annexation Measure Easily Wins Passage," *CD*, May 22, 1986; Harrison Smith interview, November 16, 1992; Herb Cook Jr., "Win-Win Pact: Columbus Schools Lost-Lost," *Northland News*, May 28, 1986, and "Greenbrier Meeting Is No Win-Win Situation," *NewsEast*, February 25, 1987.

Chapter 4

1. Debbie Briner, "Under Hyre, Columbus Schools Became a Plus," *Northland News*, April 22, 1987; "Appeal to Hyre," *CD*, February 25, 1987; Kathy Gray Foster, "What Is Special about Jim Hyre," *CD* editorial, April 19, 1987.

2. Gilbert Price, "No Push for Black School Chief in Wake of Hyre's Resignation," *CP*, April 30, 1987; Rick Spencer, "Moss' Attempts to Thwart Reorganization Plan Fail," *CP*, May 7, 1987.

3. Rick Spencer, "Moss Calls for Audit of Columbus Schools," *CP*, April 23, 1986; Kathy Gray Foster, "Moss Wants Second Look at School Revamping," *CD*, April 19, 1987.

4. Kathy Gray Foster, "Hyre to Step Down in August," *CD*, April 14, 1987; Jay Elhard, "Hyre Resigns Top Columbus Schools Post," *Northland News*, April 15, 1987; Kathy Gray Foster, "Hang on to Hyre, Williams Tells Columbus School Board," *CD*, January 14, 1987; Carole Williams, "Looking Back on the Hyre Years," *Business First*, July 27, 1987.

5. Letter from Laura Ecklar to Don Epler, July 24, 1987, Columbus Public School District files; Rob Smith, "City Schools Get 415-Home Boost," *CD*, August 4, 1987; Gary Beckett, "School District Rejoices over Planned Subdivision," *Daily Reporter*, August 4, 1987; Jay Elhard and Scott Powers, "Developer's Plan Boon to Schools, Signal for Growth," *NewsEast*, August 5, 1987.

6. Letter from Bob Barrow to Ohio House Speaker Pro Tem Barney Quilter, May 22, 1987, Columbus Public School District files.

7. The M/I Homes developments were successful, according to several interviewees, but no similar subdivisions followed. McNeill Farms, meanwhile, faced several unexpected obstacles: obstruction from Jefferson Township residents; resistance from reluctant builders; complications from the development's proximity to Port Columbus Airport; and delays due to problems constructing and extending water and sewer lines. By 1994, said Don Epler, only a few dozen houses had been built. Epler interview; also, *Columbus Dispatch, Business First, Rocky Fork Enterprise,* and *Daily Reporter* articles.

8. Margaret Newkirk, "On with the Show," *CM*, February 1992.

9. Hammond interview; Pete Cass interview, October 29, 1992; Robert Sohovich, "Leaders Ponder Annexation Pact's Effect on Growth," *CD*, May 27, 1986.

10. The word *Wexley* was a play on Bexley, the affluent "inburb" where Wexner and many of the area's wealthiest businesspeople and professionals lived. Irritated by the nickname, the developers quickly christened their proposed community "The Villages at Rocky Fork." It remains, however, popularly referred to as Wexley. For a more complete description of the Wexley controversy, see Jonas, "Local Interests," 237–80.

11. More specifically, the city had canceled an unused contract with the Franklin County commissioners to provide services to Plain Township. The cancellation was part of a deal in which Columbus agreed to take control from Franklin County of several small, poorly functioning, environmentally hazardous water-sewer "package plants."

12. At the time, Columbus was also facing a movement in Washington Township (in northwest Franklin County) to merge with the city of Dublin. If this movement had succeeded, and Wexley had cut off growth toward the northeast as well, it would have virtually eliminated the city's ability to expand along its more developable northern perimeter.

13. Wexner interests versus Wolfe interests.

14. Progrowth New Albany officials versus antigrowth Plain Township trustees.

15. City councilman Jerry Hammond versus city councilman Ben Espy, school board member Bill Moss, and others.

16. Fahey interview.

17. Herb Cook Jr., Sally Helms, and Julia Osborne, "Rating the Suburban Schools," *CM*, April 1983; Tom Sheehan, "Schools' Growth Unclear," *CD*, May 8, 1983; Carol Hagelee, "Residents Welcome Wexley, but Want Control of Plain Schools," *Rocky Fork Enterprise*, April 27, 1988.

18. Weiler interview.

19. Columbus Public School District 1988–89 Annual Report.

20. James Kunde interview, January 22, 1994; Gresham interview.

21. Jay Elhard, "Board Blames Spats on Central, Newness," *NewsEast*, April 27, 1988; Smith interview.

22. Jay Elhard, "Underground Board Moves Surprising," *Northland News*, April 6, 1988.

23. Scott Powers, "Time to End Cross-Town Busing, Espy Says," *CD*, September 6, 1991; "Ben Espy Calls for an End to Cross-Town Busing," *Communicator News*, September 13, 1991.

24. Mike Curtin, "Boot Camp for Youths Is Proposed," *CD*, September 4, 1991.

25. See Robert Joiner, "Black Mayors Driving Away from Busing," *Emerge*, March 1994, 52–55.

26. Final Report, Citizens' Committee for Improved Student Assignment, December 10, 1991, 16, 31–32. The committee reported that 10,875 of the district's 64,000 students (17 percent) were bused "for racial balance purposes." The rest were bused for health, safety, or distance reasons, alternative schools, special education programs, or other nondesegregation purposes; 41.4 percent of the district's students walked to school.

27. "Proposed Student Reassignment Plan," Columbus Public Schools Office of the Superintendent, September 8, 1992. "Racially balanced" was defined as plus or minus 20 percent of the district's black-nonblack ratio, which, by 1992, was approximately 50–50.

28. Margaret Newkirk, "Dumping Deseg," *Other Paper*, September 10, 1992.

29. "Reassignment Plan: Board Split, but Careful Study Is Urged," *CD* editorial, November 8, 1992.

30. Statistics from "Growth Statement 1990," Columbus Development Department. Manufacturing as a percentage of employment dropped from 26.3 percent in 1970 to 14.9 percent in 1989 (56–57). The goods-producing sector of the economy consists of manufacturing and construction (59, 61).

31. Statistics prepared by the Planning Division Research Section of the Columbus Development Department from U.S. Census Bureau Data. In 1990, the city school district contained 94 percent of Columbus's African American residents and 88 percent of Franklin County's. The poverty rate figures were 16.5 percent and 6.1 percent, respectively, in 1980. The unemployment figures were 6.6 percent and 4.0 percent, respectively, in 1980.

32. "Growth Statement 1990," 43. "Central city" is generally considered the area inside Columbus's 1950 borders. These numbers are similar to rough figures the author compiled using composite state income tax records provided by the Ohio Department of Taxation. Using these records, the author found the average income for a family living within the Columbus school district in 1988 to be approximately $23,000, compared to over $39,000 for the rest of Franklin County. And, according to these estimates, the difference was growing, not shrinking: the average income of a city school district family in 1976 was approximately 20 percent lower than that of a family living in the area of Franklin County not served by the city schools; in 1990, the income disparity had grown to around 38 percent.

33. "Population, Health, Income, Crime," statistics compiled by the Columbus Urban League.

34. Massey and Denton, *American Apartheid*, 218.

35. "Greater Columbus Economic Development Strategy," 68. Portion of this unpublished Columbus Area chamber of commerce study provided to the author by chamber president Jonathan York.

36. The city school district's share of Franklin County's real property value shrank from 51.4 percent in 1980 to 43.5 percent in 1989. In the latter part of the decade, the annual growth rate of residential property value was 4.3 percent in the common areas, but only 0.3 percent in the city school district. In 1989, the common areas covered 79 of the city's 193 square miles. "Columbus City School District Revenue Growth Issues: Property Trends and Tax Abatement," Columbus Development Department Economic Development Division, August 1990, 1–4.

37. Ibid., 3; "Columbus Comprehensive Plan Development Factors Report," Columbus Development Department Planning Division, February 1991, 24.

38. Debbie Briner, "Hammond: Comprehensive Plan Key to City's Future," *Northwest News*, October 25, 1989.

39. Statistics taken from the minutes of the Citizens Committee for Improved Student Assignment; enrollment figure from Calvin Smith, April 10, 1991; territory area figure from Bob Barrow, April 24, 1991; all in Columbus Public School District files.

40. According to the Development Department report, "growth in the taxable value of personal property occurs through new investment in machinery and equipment, furniture and fixtures and other goods. It is an indicator of business investment." Personal property taxable value does not grow through appreciation, but depreciates over time. "Revenue Growth Issues," 6–7, 8.

41. The Wexley controversy in late 1987 initially exacerbated simmering tension between Wolfe and Wexner leadership factions. In doing so, however, it illustrated the paralysis that had resulted from the ongoing rivalry between Columbus's old and new guards. The two sides subsequently declared a truce and agreed to explore ways to begin cooperating on the big issues facing the city. The product of this cooperation was the Wausau conference, a December 1989 business leadership "retreat" at which the city's most influential executives identified education as one of their fundamental priorities.

42. Barbara Carmen and Mary Stephens, "Win-Win Schools Pact Now Appears Lose-Lose to Some," *CD*, April 28, 1991.

43. "Greater Columbus Economic Development Strategy," 108; Gerald Mayo, "To Compete, We Must First Teach the Children," *Chamber of Commerce Magazine*, April 17, 1990; "Greater Columbus Economic Development Strategy," 69, 108.

44. *Brown I*, 492.

45. Richard Weissbourd, *The Vulnerable Child: What Really Hurts America's Children and What We Can Do about It*, 224.

46. Tim Doulin, "Judge Behind Busing Order Hails Change," *CD*, February 9, 1996.

Bibliography

Primary Documents

"Annexation: Issues and Recommendations." Arthur D. Little, Inc., August 1970.

Annual Reports, Columbus Area Chamber of Commerce, 1948–89.

Annual Reports, Columbus Public Schools, 1958, 1978–92.

"Columbus City School District Revenue Growth Issues." Columbus Development Department, Economic Development Division, August 1990.

"Columbus Comprehensive Plan: Development Factors Report." Columbus Development Department, Planning Division, February 1991.

"Columbus Factpack." Columbus Development Department, Economic Development Division, 1990.

"Columbus: A Statistical Profile of the Columbus Metropolitan Area." Columbus Development Department and the Columbus Regional Information Service Department of the Columbus Area Chamber of Commerce, 1993.

"Draft—Columbus Public Schools: Goals and Strategies for Excellence." Columbus Area Chamber of Commerce, 1992.

"Draft—Kids Come First." Columbus Area Chamber of Commerce, 1991.

Eibling, Dr. Harold. "Dateline 2000." Paper presented at Columbus Area Chamber of Commerce "Columbus '76" symposium, October 19, 1966.

"Greater Columbus Economic Development Strategy." Report prepared for the Columbus Area Chamber of Commerce, 1993.

"Growth Statement 1990." Columbus Development Department, November 1990.

Orfield, Gary. "Columbus Schools and Housing" study. Columbus Public School District files, 1981.

"Proposed Student Reassignment Plan: School Board Priorities." Columbus Public Schools, September 8, 1992.

"Progress, Growth and Annexation." Columbus Department of Development, 1968.

"A Report to the Columbus Board of Education." OSU Advisory Commission on Problems Facing Columbus Public Schools, June 15, 1968.

"Strategic Communications Plan for the Columbus Public Schools." Columbus Public Schools, June 1990.

"Statement from Student Assignment Committee to the Board of Education." December 10, 1991.

"The State of Black Columbus 1990." Columbus Urban League, Inc., 1990.

Unpublished Files and Manuscript Collections

Columbus Public School District files.

Cunningham, Luvern. Papers. Ohio State University Archives. Columbus, Ohio.

Durham, Barbee William and Anna Mae. Private collection shown to author at the Durham home, Columbus, Ohio, with some materials given to the author.

Marshall, Thurgood. Papers. Manuscript Division, Library of Congress.

Metropolitan Columbus Schools Committee (Ohio) Records. MSS 747, Ohio Historical Society. Columbus.

Legal Decisions

Alexander v. Holmes County Board of Education, 396 U.S. 19 (1969).

Brown v. Board of Education, 347 U.S. 483 (1954) [cited as *Brown* I].

Brown v. Board of Education, 349 U.S. 294 (1955) [cited as *Brown* II].

Columbus Board of Education v. Penick, 443 U.S. 449 (1979).

Dayton Board of Education v. Brinkman, 433 U.S. 406 (1977) [cited as *Dayton* I].

Dayton Board of Education v. Brinkman, 443 U.S. 526 (1979) [cited as *Dayton* II].

Green v. County School Board, 391 U.S. 430 (1968).

Keyes v. Denver School District No. 1, 413 U.S. 189 (1973).

Milliken v. Bradley, 418 U.S. 717 (1974).

Penick v. Columbus Board of Education, 429 F. Supp. 229 (1977) [cited as *Penick* I].

Penick v. Columbus Board of Education, 583 F. 2d 787 (1978) [cited as *Penick* II].

Swann v. Charlotte-Mecklenburg Board of Education, 402 U.S. 1 (1971).

Newspaper and Magazine Articles

Most articles were taken from a complete review of the Columbus Public Schools' news clipping files, which include every article on the district printed in any available newspaper, magazine, or trade publication from 1972 to the present. The most commonly cited include *Columbus Call and Post* (cited as *CP*); *Columbus Citizen-Journal* (*CJ*); *Columbus Dispatch* (*CD*); and Suburban News Publications' various weekly neighborhood newspapers. Also frequently cited are articles from a complete review of both the *Columbus Business Forum* and *Columbus Monthly* (*CM*). Specific articles are cited in footnotes.

Interviews

Listed are the interviewees, their position(s) when associated with this story, and the dates of the interviews (CPS = Columbus Public Schools; CBE = Columbus Board of Education):

Anderson, Will, CPS principal and administrator. February 27, 1994.

Asbury, Damon, CPS administrator and superintendent. January 7, 1991; February 15, 1994.

Barrow, Bob, CPS lobbyist. October 10, 1991.

Brown, Rowland, MCSC executive director. January 6, 1991.

Cary, Don, real estate developer. Winter 1992.

Cass, Pete, Columbus City Council aide. October 29, 1992.

Castleman, Marie, CBE member. Fall 1991.

Cook, Kaye, NANS leader. February 15, 1994.

Cunningham, Luvern, *Penick* special master. January 9, 1991.

Danter, Ken, Columbus development trend observer. November 5, 1992.

Davis, Joe, CPS superintendent. January 3, 1991.

Days, Drew, III, assistant U.S. attorney general. December 6, 1990.

Dicello, Jewelyn, CPS principal and administrator. April 27, 1994.

Duncan, Robert, District Court judge. December 27, 1990; April 22, 1994.

Durham, Anna Mae, and Barbee William, Columbus civil rights activists. October 2, 1992.

Elam, John, MCSC Chamber of Commerce representative. February 4, 1994.

Ellis, John, CPS superintendent. January 26, 1994.

Epler, Don, developer. March 14, 1994.

Espy, Ben, Columbus City Council member. February 28, 1994.

Fahey, Richard, CBE member. February 1, 1994.

Gifford, Beverly, CPS administrator. October 4, 1991; Summer 1992.

Gresham, Sam, Columbus Urban League executive director. March 1, 1994.

Grossman, John, Columbus Education Association president. February 8, 1994.

Hall, Anne, CBE member. February 10, 1994.

Hamlar, David, CBE member. January 3, 1991; March 11, 1994.

Hammond, Jerry, Columbus City Council member. November 18, 1992.

Heard, Loretta, CBE member. April 15, 1994.

Henle, John, Columbus Chamber of Commerce official. March 3, 1994.

Holland, Gary, CBE member. April 25, 1994.

Hyre, Jim, CPS superintendent. October 30, 1991.

Klein, Carl, Columbus Development Department official. November 15, 1992.

Kunde, Jim, urban leadership consultant. January 22, 1994.

Lazarus, Cindy, Columbus City Council member. March 10, 1994.

Lomax, Frank, Columbus Urban League executive director. May 10, 1994.

Luck, Jim, Columbus Foundation official. March 9, 1994.

Luckey, Evelyn, CPS administrator. February 23, 1994.

Lynch, Amos, Columbus *Call and Post* general manager. October 17, 1991.

McClary, Steve, Columbus Development Department official. November 15, 1992.

McGory, John, Building Industry Association lobbyist. December 9, 1992.

Middleton, John, CPS superintendent. April 20, 1994.

Moody, Tom, Columbus mayor. January 9, 1991.

Moss, Bill, CBE member. May 5, 1994.

Moyer, Tom, CBE member. October 31, 1991.

NANS leaders (Sue Ferguson, Bettie Margeson, Joyce Popelar), antibusing activists. October 20, 1991.

Newman, Charles, CPS administrator March 2, 1994.

Pierce, Don, CEA, MCSC official. April 21, 1994.

Porter, Jack, Plain Local Schools superintendent. April 18, 1994.

Porter, Sam, CBE attorney. January 4, 1991.

Radebaugh, Pauline, CBE member. February 17, 1994.

Redden, Marilyn, CBE member. October 14, 1991.

Rinehart, Buck, Columbus mayor. April 5, 1994.

Seltzer, Marjorie, *Call and Post* reporter. October 20, 1991.

Smith, Calvin, CPS administrator. January 7, 1991; November 18, 1992.

Smith, Harrison, Columbus zoning and annexation attorney. November 16, 1992.

Smith, Robert, *Dispatch* editor. December 6, 1991.

Stein, Richard, NAACP attorney. January 2, 1991.

Vance, Bill, WBNS-TV news director. December 4, 1991.

Viers, Roger, Gahanna-Jefferson superintendent. February 15, 1994.

Wayson, William, Ohio State education professor. January 10, 1991.

Weiler, Robert, CBE member and developer. October 19, 1992; November 13, 1992.

Williams, Carole, CBE member. October 4, 1991; February 22, 1994.

Willis, Ed, CPS principal. October 4, 1991.

Wiser, Bert, CPS administrator. May 16, 1994.

York, Jonathan, Columbus Chamber of Commerce president. February 3, 1994.

Secondary Sources

Andrews, Adolphus. "Urban Redevelopment and the Structure of Power: The Impact of Private Interests on the Policy-Making Process in Columbus, Ohio." Ph.D. diss., Ohio State University, 1982.

Armor, David J. "After Busing: Education and Choice." *Public Interest*, no. 95 (Spring 1989): 24–37.

Armor, David J. *Forced Justice: School Desegregation and the Law.* New York: Oxford University Press, 1995.

Barber, Benjamin R. "America Skips School: Why We Talk So Much about Education and Do So Little." *Harper's* 287, no. 1722 (November 1993): 39–46.

Bates, Percy. "Desegregation: Can We Get There from Here?" *Phi Delta Kappan* 72, no. 1 (September 1990): 8–17.

Bell, Derrick, Jr. *And We Are Not Saved: The Elusive Quest for Racial Justice.* New York: Basic Books, 1987.

———. *Civil Rights: Leading Cases.* Boston: Little, Brown, and Company, 1980.

———. *Faces at the Bottom of the Well: The Permanence of Racism.* New York: Basic Books, 1992.

———. *Race, Racism and American Law.* Boston: Little, Brown, and Company, 1980.

———, ed. *Shades of Brown: New Perspectives on School Desegregation.* New York: Teachers College Press, 1980.

Bernard, Richard M., ed. *Snowbelt Cities: Metropolitan Politics in the Northeast and Midwest Since World War II.* Bloomington: Indiana University Press, 1990.

Bowles, Samuel, and Herbert Gintis. *Schooling in Capitalist America: Educational Reform and the Contradictions of Economic Life.* New York: Basic Books, 1976.

Bryant, Vinnie Vanessa. "Columbus, Ohio and the Great Migration." Master's thesis, Ohio State University, 1983.

Buncher, Judith, ed. *The School Busing Controversy, 1970–75.* New York: Facts on File, 1975.

Burgess, Patricia. *Planning for the Private Interest: Land Use Controls and Residential Patterns in Columbus, Ohio, 1900–1970.* Columbus: Ohio State University Press, 1994.

Carter, Harold Lloyd. "Domestic Colonialism and Problems of Black Education with Special Reference to Columbus, Ohio." Ph.D. diss., Ohio State University, 1976.

Chafe, William H. *Civilities and Civil Rights: Greensboro, North Carolina, and the Black Struggle for Freedom.* New York: Oxford University Press, 1981.

Chubb, John E., and Terry M. Moe. *Politics, Markets and America's Schools.* Washington, D.C.: Brookings Institution, 1990.

Citizen's Guide to Desegregation. Citizens' Council for Ohio Schools, 1976.

Coleman, James, Sara D. Kelly, and John A. Moore. *Trends in School Segregation, 1968–1973.* Urban Institute Paper 722–03–01, Washington, D.C., August 1975.

Cummings, Scott, ed. *Business Elites and Urban Development: Case Studies and Critical Perspectives.* Albany: State University of New York Press, 1988.

Curry, Constance. *Silver Rights: A True Story from the Front Lines of the*

Civil Rights Struggle. Chapel Hill, N.C.: Algonquin Books, 1995.

Danter, Kenneth. "Columbus City Schools: A Case of Two Perceptions." *BIA Builder Update,* December 1990.

Days, Drew. "School Desegregation Law in the 1980s: Why Isn't Anybody Laughing?" *Yale Law Journal* 95, no. 8 (July 1986): 1737–68.

Dimond, Paul. *Beyond Busing: Inside the Challenge to Urban Segregation.* Ann Arbor: University of Michigan Press, 1985.

Edsall, Thomas Byrne, and Mary D. Edsall. *Chain Reaction: The Impact of Race, Rights and Taxes on American Politics.* New York: W. W. Norton and Co., 1992.

Feagin, Joe R., and Robert Parker. *Building American Cities: The Urban Real Estate Game.* Englewood Cliffs, N.J.: Prentice Hall, 1990.

Fine, Doris. *When Leadership Fails: Desegregation and Demoralization in the San Francisco Schools.* New Brunswick, N.J.: Transaction Books, 1986.

Gerstner, Louis V., Jr., with Roger D. Semerad et al. *Reinventing Education: Entrepreneurship in America's Public Schools.* New York: Plume, 1995.

Ginzberg, Eli, ed. *Business Leadership and the Negro Crisis.* New York: McGraw-Hill, 1968.

Graglia, Lino. *Disaster By Decree.* Ithaca, N.Y.: Cornell University Press, 1976.

Gurwitt, Rob. "Getting Off the Bus." *Governing,* May 1992, 30–36.

Hacker, Andrew. *Two Nations: Black and White, Separate, Hostile, Unequal.* New York: Charles Scribner's Sons, 1992.

Harrison, Bennett, and Barry Bluestone. *The Great U-Turn: Corporate Restructuring and the Polarizing of America.* New York: Basic Books, 1988.

Hawley, Willis, et al. *Strategies for Effective Desegregation.* Lexington, Mass.: Lexington Books, 1983.

Hayes, Floyd W., III, ed. *A Turbulent Voyage: Readings in African-American Studies.* San Diego: Collegiate Press, 1992.

Herson, Lawrence J. R., and John M. Bolland. *The Urban Web: Politics, Policy, and Theory.* Chicago: Nelson-Hall, 1990.

Hill, Herbert, and James E. Jones Jr., eds. *Race in America: The Struggle for Equality.* Madison: University of Wisconsin Press, 1993.

Himes, J. S., Jr. "Forty Years of Negro Life in Columbus, Ohio." *Journal of Negro History* 27, no. 2 (April 1942): 133–54.

Hirsch, Arnold R., and Raymond A. Mohl, eds. *Urban Policy in Twentieth-Century America.* New Brunswick, N.J.: Rutgers University Press, 1993.

Hochschild, Jennifer L. *The New American Dilemma*. New Haven: Yale University Press, 1984.

Hodgson, Godfrey. *America in Our Time: From World War II to Nixon, What Happened and Why*. New York: Vintage Books, 1976.

Hunker, Henry L. *Industrial Evolution of Columbus, Ohio*. Columbus: Ohio State University Bureau of Business Research, 1958.

"Integration Turns 40." *Modern Maturity*, April-May 1994, 24–34.

Investing in Our Children: Business and the Public Schools. New York: Committee for Economic Development, 1985.

Jackson, Kenneth. *Crabgrass Frontier: The Suburbanization of the United States*. New York: Oxford Press, 1985.

Jacoway, Elizabeth, and David R. Colburn. *Southern Businessmen and Desegregation*. Baton Rouge: Louisiana State University Press, 1982.

James, Felix. "The American Addition: The History of a Black Community." Ph.D. diss., Ohio State University, 1972.

Johnson, William C. *The Politics of Urban Planning*. New York: Paragon House, 1989.

Jonas, Andrew. "Local Interests and State Territorial Structures: Integration and Fragmentation in Metropolitan Columbus in the Post-War Period." Ph.D. diss., Ohio State University, 1989.

Katznelson, Ira, and Margaret Weir. *Schooling for All: Class, Race, and the Decline of the Democratic Ideal*. New York: Basic Books, 1985.

Kearns, David T., and Dennis P. Doyle. *Winning the Brain Race: A Bold Plan to Make Our Schools Competitive*. San Francisco: Institute for Contemporary Studies, 1989.

Kirp, David. *Just Schools: The Idea of Racial Equality in American Education*. Berkeley: University of California Press, 1982.

Kluger, Richard. *Simple Justice*. New York: Vintage Books, 1975.

Kotlowitz, Alex. *There Are No Children Here: The Story of Two Boys Growing Up in the Other America*. New York: Anchor Books, 1991.

Kozol, Jonathan. *Savage Inequalities*. New York: Harper, 1991.

Lemann, Nicholas. *The Promised Land: The Great Black Migration and How It Changed America*. New York: Alfred A. Knopf, 1991.

Lukas, J. Anthony. *Common Ground: A Turbulent Decade in the Lives of Three American Families*. New York: Vintage Books, 1986.

Mair, Andrew. "Private Planning for Economic Development: Local Business Coalitions in Columbus, Ohio, 1858–1986." Ph.D. diss., Ohio State University, 1988.

Mark, Mary Louise. *Negroes in Columbus*. Columbus: Ohio State University Press, 1928.

Massey, Douglas S., and Nancy A. Denton. *American Apartheid: Segregation and the Making of the Underclass*. Cambridge: Harvard University Press, 1993.

Matusow, Allen J. *The Unraveling of America: A History of Liberalism in the 1960s*. New York: Harper Torchbooks, 1984.

Meier, Deborah. *The Power of Their Ideas: Lessons for America from a Small School in Harlem*. Boston: Beacon Press, 1995.

Meier, Kenneth J., Joseph Stewart Jr., and Robert E. England. *Race, Class, and Education: The Politics of Second Generation Discrimination*. Madison: University of Wisconsin Press, 1989.

Metcalf, George R. *From Little Rock to Boston: The History of School Desegregation*. Westport, Conn.: Greenwood Press, 1983.

———. *Fair Housing Comes of Age*. New York: Greenwood Press, 1988.

Minor, Richard Clyde. "The Negro in Columbus, Ohio." Ph.D. diss., Ohio State University, 1936.

Moberg, David. "Separate and Unequal." *The Neighborhood Works*, August–September 1995, pp. 9–11, 27.

Moeser, John V., and Rutledge M. Dennis. *The Politics of Annexation: Oligarchic Power in a Southern City*. Cambridge, Mass.: Shenkman Publishing Co., 1982.

Monti, Daniel J. *A Semblance of Justice: St. Louis Desegregation and Order in Urban America*. Columbia: University of Missouri Press, 1985.

Moreland, Curtina. "The Black Community of Columbus: A Study of the Structure and Pattern of Power in a Midwestern City." Ph.D. diss., University of Illinois (Urbana), 1977.

Moss, Bill. *School Desegregation: Enough Is Enough*. Columbus, Ohio: Danmo Publishing, 1992.

Murphy, Melvin L. "The Columbus Urban League: A History, 1917–1967." Ph.D. diss., The Ohio State University, 1970.

Nasaw, David. *Schooled to Order: A Social History of Public Schooling in the United States*. New York: Oxford University Press, 1979.

Nocera, Joseph. "How the Middle Class Has Helped Ruin the Public Schools." *Utne Reader*, September–October 1990, 66–83.

Ohio Civil Rights Commission. *Racial Imbalance in the Public Schools: A Survey of Legal Developments*. Columbus, Ohio: Ohio Civil Rights Commission, April 1965.

Ohio Department of Education. *Milestones: A History of the State Board of Education of Ohio, 1956–1989.* Columbus, Ohio: State Board of Education, 1989.

Oliver, Melvin L., and Thomas M. Shapiro. *Black Wealth/White Wealth: A New Perspective on Racial Inequality.* New York: Routledge, 1995.

Orfield, Gary. *Must We Bus?* Washington, D.C.: Brookings Institution, 1978.

———. *Toward a Strategy for Urban Integration: Lessons in School and Housing Policy from Twelve Cities.* New York: Ford Foundation, 1981.

Orfield, Gary, and Carole Ashkinaze. *The Closing Door: Conservative Policy and Black Opportunity.* Chicago: University of Chicago Press, 1991.

Orfield, Gary, Susan Eaton, and the Harvard Project on School Desegregation. *Dismantling Desegregation: The Quiet Reversal of Brown v. Board of Education.* New York: New Press, 1996.

Orum, Anthony. *City-Building in America.* Boulder, Colo.: Westview Press, 1995.

Phillips, Kevin. *Arrogant Capital: Washington, Wall Street, and the Frustration of American Politics.* Boston: Little, Brown and Co., 1994.

———. *The Politics of Rich and Poor: Wealth and the American Electorate in the Reagan Aftermath.* New York: Random House, 1990.

Pratt, Robert. *The Color of Their Skin: Education and Race in Richmond, Virginia 1954–89.* Charlottesville: University Press of Virginia, 1992.

Pride, Richard A., and J. David Woodward. *The Burden of Busing: The Politics of Desegregation in Nashville, Tennessee.* Knoxville: University of Tennessee Press, 1985.

Reichley, Joseph. *Conservatives in an Age of Change.* Washington, D.C.: Brookings Institution, 1981.

Rossell, Christine H. *The Carrot or the Stick for School Desegregation.* Philadelphia: Temple University Press, 1990.

Rusk, David. *Cities without Suburbs.* Washington, D.C.: Woodrow Wilson Center Press, 1993.

"School Desegregation: Making It Work." Proceedings of a conference on the successful implementation of school desegregation, sponsored by the College of Urban Development at Michigan State University and by the Rockefeller Foundation, East Lansing, Mich., July 7–9, 1976.

Squires, Gregory D. *Capital and Communities in Black and White: The Intersection of Race, Class, and Uneven Development.* Albany: State University of New York Press, 1994.

Stanback, Thomas M., Jr., and Thierry J. Noyelle. *Cities in Transition:*

Changing Job Structures in Atlanta, Denver, Buffalo, Phoenix, Columbus (Ohio), Nashville, Charlotte. Totowa, N. J.: Allanheld, Osmun, 1982.

Stanfield, John H., II. "American Businesspeople and the Ambivalent Transformation of Racially Segregated Public Schools." *Phi Delta Kappan* 72, no. 1 (September 1990): 63–68.

Stephan, Walter G., and Joe R. Feagin, eds. *School Desegregation: Past, Present, and Future.* New York: Plenum Press, 1980.

Taeuber, Karl. "Desegregation of Public School Districts: Persistence and Change." *Phi Delta Kappan.* 72, no. 1 (September 1990): 18–24.

United States Commission on Civil Rights. *Fulfilling the Letter and Spirit of the Law: Desegregation in the Nation's Public Schools.* Washington, D.C., 1976.

United States Commission on Civil Rights. *Twenty Years after Brown.* Washington, D.C., 1974.

United States Department of Education, Office of Educational Research and Improvement. *Synthesis of Existing Knowledge and Practice in the Field of Educational Partnerships.* Washington, D.C., 1993.

"Urban Education Today." *Journal of Planning Literature* 5, no. 1 (August 1990): 22–28.

Urofsky, Melvin I. *The Continuity of Change: The Supreme Court and Individual Liberties, 1953–1986.* Belmont, Calif.: Wadsworth Publishing, 1991.

Vander Weele, Meribeth. *Reclaiming Our Schools: The Struggle for Chicago School Reform.* Chicago: Loyola University Press, 1994.

Watras, Joseph. "What Caused the Retreat in Civil Rights? A Study of the Liberal Advances and Conservative Revolt in the Racial Desegregation of Dayton City Schools (1967–1977)." Paper presented at Midwest History of Education Society Conference, Chicago, Ill., 1993.

Weir, Margaret. "City-Suburban Conflict and the Politics of Defensive Localism." Paper presented at the Urban Poverty Workshop Series, University of Chicago, February 17, 1994.

Weissbourd, Richard. *The Vulnerable Child: What Really Hurts America's Children and What We Can Do About It.* Reading, Mass.: Addison-Wesley, 1996.

Wilkinson, J. Harvie. *From Brown to Bakke.* New York: Oxford University Press, 1979.

Williams, Juan. *Eyes on the Prize: America's Civil Rights Years 1954–1965.* New York: Penguin Books, 1988.

Willie, Charles Vert. *School Desegregation Plans That Work*. Westport, Conn.: Greenwood Press, 1984.

Willie, Charles Vert, and Susan C. Greenblatt. *Community Politics and Educational Change: 10 Systems under Court Order*. New York: Longman, 1981.

Wilson, William Julius. *The Truly Disadvantaged: The Inner City, the Underclass, and Public Policy*. Chicago: University of Chicago Press, 1987.

Wolf, Eleanor P. *Trial and Error: The Detroit School Segregation Case*. Detroit: Wayne State University, 1981.

Wolters, Raymond. *The Burden of Brown: Thirty Years of School Desegregation*. Knoxville: University of Tennessee Press, 1984.

Wong, Kenneth. *City Choices: Education and Housing*. Albany: State University of New York Press, 1990.

Woodward, Bob, and Scott Armstrong. *The Brethren: Inside the Supreme Court*. New York: Simon and Schuster, 1979.

Yarmolinsky, Adam, Lance Liebman, and Corinne S. Schelling. *Race and Schooling in the City*. Cambridge: Harvard University Press, 1981.

Index

Urban Life and Urban Landscape Series
Zane L. Miller and Henry D. Shapiro, General Editors

The series examines the history of urban life and the development of
the urban landscape through works that place social, economic, and political issues in the intellectual and cultural context of their times.